NORMAN STREET

NORMAN STREET

Poverty and Politics in an Urban Neighborhood

IDA SUSSER

Case Western Reserve University

New York   Oxford
OXFORD UNIVERSITY PRESS
1982

Library of Congress Cataloging in Publication Data

Susser, Ida.
   Norman Street, poverty and politics in an
urban neighborhood.

   Includes index.
   1. Brooklyn (New York, N.Y.)—Economic
conditions—Case studies.   2. Brooklyn (New
York, N.Y.)—Social conditions—Case studies.
3. Municipal services—New York (N.Y.)—
4. Finance, Public—New York (N.Y.)   I. Title.
HC108.N7S88   307.7′6   81–14129
ISBN 0–19–503048–6   AACR2
ISBN 0–19–503049–4 (pbk.)

Printing (last digit):   9 8 7

Printed in the United States of America

For Helene and Philip John

Preface

In the face of the deterioration of city services, budgetary cutbacks, and the 1975 fiscal crisis in New York City, this book documents the implications of broad political and economic changes for the lives of working-class people. It describes the struggles of a community confronting overwhelming incursions on its resources and economic stability. The combined disasters of industrial decline and fiscal policies leading to service reductions have assaulted this beleaguered population, as they now threaten to assault millions more of our nation's citizens. And far from being apathetic, these residents have responded to their plight with energy and anger, fighting political holding actions for the survival of their neighborhood in the face of almost certain defeat.

The study is set in a predominantly white working-class community—the Greenpoint-Williamsburg neighborhood of Brooklyn —during the 1975 fiscal crisis and its aftermath. It demonstrates that politics is an integral part of community life and examines forms of political expression as reactions to changing conditions. It is in this context that conflict over neighborhood resources can be seen as class conflict, for it represents the demands of working-class people as members of a class in the face of declining industrial employment and corresponding declining political influence.

When I chose Greenpoint-Williamsburg, I was looking for an industrial white working-class community. I suspected that many of the characteristics that have been attributed to blacks in community studies might also be found in white working-class areas suffering similar economic setbacks and constraints. For this reason I examined the expression of political consciousness of working and unemployed people who have been forced to rely on government subsidies. But it is also necessary to consider how race and ethnicity have interfered with the development of a sense of common purpose between groups. The book analyzes the daily experiences which divide blacks, whites, and Hispanics and the continuing impact of these divisions on political organizing.

Since neighborhood issues are often of primary concern to women, much of the book is devoted to social organization and friendship networks among women. Support networks similar to those described by Carol Stack (1974) for black women in a northeastern ghetto are found among both poor white and black women in this neighborhood. We can see clearly that sharing and support networks are essential to people living in poverty, and it is equally clear that economics stimulates the formation of these networks among all ethnic groups. The formation of local kinship and friendship ties is not only a strategy for economic survival but an essential element in effective political organization and mobilization in the neighborhood.

One of my main aims was to understand the way in which these local issues relate to national political and economic changes, and the way in which conditions described here are similar to conditions in declining cities throughout the country. I was particularly concerned with the impact of federal programs such as the military, public assistance, and Comprehensive Employment and Training Act programs as well as service reductions on the experiences of working and unemployed people. Working-class people around the nation have been subject to the same programs and cutbacks, and a detailed analysis of their influence in one community contributes to our understanding of the overall effects of changes in federal policies.

As an ethnography of an American urban neighborhood, this book develops a new approach in that it analyzes the daily life of working-class people within the constraints of a particular historical period. Although following in some ways the tradition of community studies such as William Foot Whyte's *Street Corner Society*,

Elliot Liebow's *Tally's Corner,* and William Kornblum's *Blue Collar Community,* it departs from that tradition in its emphasis on life-styles, values, and activities as they change in response to political and economic conditions within a clearly delineated national and local political context.

Community residents are shown to be confronting and actively responding to the political issues of their time. Nevertheless, their activities are shaped by neighborhood and family organizations and limited by economic dependency. This book analyzes the successes and failures of neighborhood protest. It also demonstrates the significance of such actions for the participants and the difficulties that must be surmounted before people can join together in collective action.

Many more people have contributed to this book than I am able to acknowledge here. I would, however, like to thank Conrad Arensberg, George Bond, Richard Cloward, and Leith Mullings for their comments on an earlier form of the manuscript. I am especially grateful to Joan Vincent for rereading numerous revisions and suggesting corrections. Marvin Harris and Bette Denich provided useful discussion in planning the research, and Roland Bonilla, John Paterson, and David Romes assisted me during the fieldwork. Gerald Oppenheimer and Carole Vance read parts of the manuscript and offered thoughtful criticism. Sally Conover, Beverly Silver and Ezra Susser proofread chapters, while Ruth Susser and Eliecer Valencia added helpful commentary. For encouragement and insightful comments, I am grateful to Celia Orgel, Bela Bianco, Lina Brock, Cheryl Benoit Mwaria, Tom Belmonte, and Michael Burawoy. Zena Stein and Mervyn Susser contributed both intellectual and emotional support toward the completion of the book. My husband, John Kreniske, gave invaluable assistance throughout and was a constant source of encouragement and ideas. Helene Kreniske provided both needed distractions and the incentive to finish.

I would like to thank Noelle Sterne for typing several drafts of the book. I would also like to acknowledge the assistance of a three-year Training Grant from the National Institute of Mental Health which enabled me to carry out the research. Finally, I am grateful to the people of Greenpoint-Williamsburg who made this study possible and whose friendliness and warmth helped me to continue. Although I would like to mention the names of several people in particular, this might violate their anonymity in the book. Some of the residents of Greenpoint-Williamsburg read a draft of the manuscript, and I am much indebted to them for their comments.

All of the errors in the book are, of course, my own.

New York   I.S.
November 1981

Contents

CHAPTER 1

Introduction

The apparent lack of political involvement and class consciousness of the American working class, relative to its European counterparts, has long puzzled social analysts. American workers have been accused of hedonism, exploitation, and the selfish pursuit of personal betterment through individual upward mobility. They have been regarded as a well-fed, complacent elite whose high standard of living derives from the exploitation of workers in the Third World. They have also been described as quintessentially immigrants as each influx of newcomers ritually enacts the riots and consumer-oriented demands said to have been associated with the emergence of capitalism in Europe.

Historians and theorists of the American labor movement have been especially concerned with the political motivation of American workers and the identification of critical events in union organizing. The defeat in the 1890s of the militant Knights of Labor and the strengthening of the less-challenging American Federation of Labor (AFL) was one such moment. Another decisive point was the destruction of the Industrial Workers of the World in the strikes of the early twentieth century. The Great Depression of the 1930s, which reduced American workers to destitution, was accompanied by an upsurge of socialism in the labor movement. This was particularly represented in the formation of the initially independent Congress of Industrial Organizations (CIO). The compromises of the labor movement with American business during World War II have been regarded as a further defeat and even betrayal of the collective interests of American workers. The merging of the AFL with the CIO in 1955 represented still another blow. Finally, of course, the open repression of the McCarthy era can be cited as yet one more explanation for the decline of socialism and a weakening of clear class interest in the labor movement.[1]

There is a long tradition of social scientists who have lived among the working class, interviewed people in detail, talked with them, and observed their attempts to improve their conditions of life.[2] Such studies have made a significant contribution to the discussion of the motives and moods of American labor. These ethnographies and sociological pastiches of working-class America do not confirm the impression of contentment and well-being attributed to workers in more abstract theoretical constructions. One shortcoming in such community studies, however, is that the people described appear timeless and are not placed fully within the historical circumstances to which they are responding (Castells, 1977; Hannerz, 1980). There is no attempt to analyze behavior or beliefs under changing political and economic circumstances. Nevertheless, important insights are offered in the Lynds' early work (1929); Whyte's *Street Corner Society* (1943); Hollingshead's early studies (1945); Gans's *Urban Villagers* (1962); Liebow's *Tally's Corner* (1967); and Rubin's *Worlds of Pain* (1976). In these studies American workers are portrayed as locked in their class position, struggling to survive the strain of scarcity and emotionally damaging lives.

The portrayal of the apolitical American worker developed through studies of the labor movement is also brought into question by recent research into behavior outside the formal channels

1. An extensive literature is concerned with the issues referred to in these two paragraphs. A few of the many sources which address these questions are: Perlman (1928); Pelling (1960); Chinoy (1965); Leggett (1968); Marcuse (1968); Goldthorpe et al. (1969); Thernstrom (1971); Aronowitz (1974); Laslett and Lipset (1974); Gutman (1976); Burawoy (1979); Edwards (1979); and Davis (1980).
2. See, for example, Lynd and Lynd (1929); Gans (1962); Komarovsky (1964); Liebow (1967); Gitlin and Hollander (1970); Howell (1973); Hannerz (1969); Kornblum (1974); Stack (1974); Rubin (1976); and Valentine (1978).

of the labor unions. Jeremy Brecher's documentation of the bloody and violent history of wildcat strikes (1974) throws a different light on the career of labor unions in America, as does Aronowitz's stress on employers' reinforcement of ethnic divisions (1974). Similarly, Piven and Cloward's analysis, *Poor People's Movements* (1977), describes a series of workers' struggles outside the purview of organized labor. These writings combined with the dismal picture conveyed through case studies of working-class life, suggest that while the American labor movement may in some senses appear apolitical, American workers have a long history of suffering, conflict, and politically motivated action.

The confusion generated by these opposing views of the American working class has been further complicated by the discussion of blacks, Hispanics, American Indians, and the early immigrants. When, as frequently occurs, such people are described as if they were the only poor in America, their problems can be characterized as temporary aberrations. White people who are poor and dependent on assistance tend to be assigned to particular ethnic classifications: Polish-American, Italian-American, and so forth. If they have lived in the United States for centuries, other terms are found to distinguish them from the mainstream of the American working class: hillbillies, Appalachian whites, "the other Americans." Thus to characterize these groups simply as ethnically conscious minorities obfuscates the actual composition and nature of the working class. The complicated issue of ethnic consciousness in America is an extremely important area for research, but it cannot be understood without a clear analysis of its relationship to the political consciousness and activism of the American working class.[3]

Rather than dispelling these confusions, Marxist theory has in some ways contributed to them by neglecting the daily ordeal of the American worker. The gradations between employment, under-employment, and unemployment have been characterized, and the

---

3. A recent fruitful effort in this direction has been Wilson's *The Declining Significance of Race* (1980). Other illuminating studies of this issue are Vincent (1974, 1979); Gutman (1976); and Mullings (1978). Kornblum (1974) discusses ethnic mobilization but without an analysis of class consciousness or conflict over political issues.

significance of the "reserve labor force" as a determinant to union organizing has been historically documented (Brody, 1970; Gordon, 1972). Yet the social meaning of these data and the importance of the political expressions of a working class divided and threatened have neither been adequately recognized nor sufficiently analyzed. This hiatus in the understanding of American class consciousness reflects a failure to come to terms with the American working class as it stands today. As Aronowitz (1974), Gutman (1976), and others have noted, analysts have chosen to regret the absence of a politically mobilized, class-conscious labor movement while neglecting other manifestations of political struggle among working-class people.[4]

With these issues in mind, I moved to a working-class district in New York City in October 1975. I lived here, among the people of Greenpoint-Williamsburg, Brooklyn for one year. For the next two years, I participated in neighborhood events and continued to carry on long discussions with the people of the area. I wanted to know how the neighborhood residents lived and worked, what they believed, and how they dealt with political issues. I sought to answer these questions by developing a detailed picture of the daily lives and difficulties of the people I came to know. To understand grass-roots political expression, it was essential to understand the ways in which individuals coped with the chafe and drag of economic constraints and the ways they struggled to develop collective action. Relying on community ties between neighbors and relatives, the working-class people I observed were constantly involved in local holding actions as they tried to influence political decisions that would affect their living standards. The formation of block associations, sit-ins to protest inadequate day care, and the occupation of buildings in reaction to the reduction of city services were frequent forms of political expression. These forms of collective action, built through the solidarity of neighborhood familiarity and shared experiences, are the subject of this study. In the context of Greenpoint-Williamsburg from 1975 to 1978,

4. Among exceptions to this statement are McCourt (1977), Burawoy (1979), and, of course, with respect to the English working class, Thompson (1966).

we shall investigate the conditions under which collective protest arises, the issues which become its focus, the reaction of established parties, and the consequences. On the basis of this analysis, we can assess the relative power of such neighborhood movements and the particular historical circumstances which lead to their success or failure in an advanced capitalist society.

In order to characterize collective action in Greenpoint-Williamsburg, we must examine historical trends and changes in the forms of political protest. In his pathbreaking and insightful analysis *Primitive Rebels* (1955), Hobsbawm singles out a comparable problem in a discussion of "pre-political" rebellious movements of the nineteenth and twentieth centuries. These movements conveyed political messages but were not organized around the control of labor power. Hobsbawm regards such collective action as "pre-political" because of the lack of revolutionary ideology in the language of the rebels. He restricts the term "political" to the organized labor movements of the industrial era. In his description of the "pre-industrial crowd," Rudé (1964) describes similar rebellious outbreaks. The assumption is that with the development of industry and the advance of capitalism, the characteristics of collective action changed, and labor movements became the prevailing form of political expression.

Hobsbawm's and Rudé's analyses are excellent, but the notion of the prepolitical implies that the movements they studied derived from a lack of political understanding rather than from restricted political opportunity. But were the members of the Neapolitan city "mob" unaware of their political reality, or were they mobilizing in the only way open to them? Hobsbawm assumes a greater differentiation between collective action in preindustrial society and under capitalism than may be the case. This may be due to the paucity of analysis of contemporary collective action. The correlations of preindustrial with prepolitical and industrial with political obscure significant characteristics that accompany the choice of particular forms of collective action in both preindustrial and industrial society.

The Tillys (1975) support Hobsbawm in the identification of trends and changes in the form of social movements, and both analyses ascribe these changes to the response of workers to emergent capitalism. The Tillys argue, however, that the "mob" was cognizant of its political situation and responded appropriately in the political milieu.

There is much history to suggest that as industrial manufacturing became the basis of the economy, precisely those workers whose jobs were losing their importance became the core of riots and mob actions (for example, Hobsbawm (1955); Hobsbawm and Rudé (1969); and Scott (1974).) These were people whose work was being made dispensable. With industrialization, traditional skills and activities that required sweat and muscle became superfluous. The skilled craftsman of the Neopolitan urban mob or the displaced English peasant had little choice but disruption and violence. When both job and workers are dispensable, there is little hope for organized strikes. If conditions such as these account for the nature of collective action and protest during the period of emergent capitalism, we can expect similar responses under comparable conditions in the present day.

Because shifts and changes in the need for workers are crucial to capitalist development, mass protest and disruptive collective action will constantly reappear in different sections of the economy as capital and industry move away to exploit new and cheaper labor markets, technology, and products. We must expect these forms of collective action to subside as new industries are successful and workers establish strong labor unions. From this point of view, both less-organized protest movements and strikes are inherent to capitalism. Poor people's movements are a rational response to changes in political control and economic allocations as industries require more or fewer skills or seek to reduce costs by shifting between regions, or even to other countries. The point is not that the individuals involved in riots or protest movements become disoriented by loss of work. Rather, the loss of labor as a bargaining resource forces people to use other modes of struggle for their political and economic survival. The unemployed cannot strike, and the underemployed cannot win strikes. Disruption and rioting are two methods for defending what is left to them.

If we are to understand the political consciousness of the

American working class, we must pay attention to the skirmishes in the background as well as to the actions of the vanguard. We must examine how groups act outside of the unions and outside the more dramatic events of the century. The history of commonplace, transitory collective actions can tell us something about the possibilities for more successful actions and the reasons for the failure of so many. The examination of the roots of small-scale collective action can therefore provide important insights into the constant struggles of working-class people engaged in the daily politics of survival. In turn, these insights bear on the functioning of the larger social system.

In these pages it will become evident that American working-class people depend on the state for many facets of their existence. If politics is defined in terms of activities directed toward maintaining or changing the state or the accepted structure of authority, there are many possible avenues for action. The cultural forms and social relations which people develop in response to their dependence contain the seeds for the formation of politically active groups and even social movements. Equally, the interconnections between landlords, public assistance, and local employment open channels for the intimidation and repression of the individuals who take such action. In an economy in which industry is declining, the state takes over many functions. It supplements wages and provides housing for workers; as a result, conflicts over the human costs of industrial change become directed at the state.[5] Poor people obtain food, medical care, and housing through persistent struggles with state regulations. It is the organization of collective protest to demand essential resources from the state that is one of the most striking features of political action among working-class people in Greenpoint-Williamsburg.

Local actions such as those described here are significant as a measure of political process. The frequency of collective actions attests to their import for the society at large. It signals both the ongoing transition being wrought by the owners of capital who plan urban development and economic change and the resistance

5. For a theoretical discussion of this issue in relation to housing, see Harvey (1976).

of workers unwilling to accept the conditions imposed upon them. Ultimately the appearance of cities and the geographic distribution of the national population reflects the outcome of these struggles.[6]

But the analysis of small conflicts and local collective organization also provides a key to the political consciousness of working-class America. The workers' view of the social system in which they live is expressed in these activities. It is in their fear of landlords, in frustration with the welfare system, and in cynicism toward local politicians that we can begin to trace factors which shape collective behavior and give it direction. When constant conflict around these issues is documented, it is difficult to maintain the concept of the apathy of the American working class.

If my observations are in any way typical, we can no longer regard the "passivity" of workers as a problem which needs explaining. They are not passive, and the questions we must ask delve beyond the psychological propensities of the American worker. To discover why conflict on the local level has not developed into wider movements more often, we must examine the minutiae of community life in the context of broader social and economic processes. This book demonstrates the frustrations and conflicts in a community which led to the development of a movement with a strong community base and the economic interests and political coalitions which strengthened the forces of repression. It is these interactions between the needs and fears of working-class people and pressures from the state and from middle-class people in the community that are brought to light.[7]

In 1975, when this study began, New York City was in the midst of an immense economic upheaval which has become known as the "fiscal crisis." In the summer of 1975, the political leadership of the city constantly threatened bankruptcy. As a result of this apparent financial disaster, municipal workers were laid off, public service unions were forced to accept lowered wage guidelines, city services were drastically cut, tuition was imposed at the

6. Mumford (1970) makes this point, and Castells (1977), Gordon (1978), Katznelson (1979), and others develop it.
7. Stanley Greer makes a similar argument about the significance of local repression in his excellent historical study of Gary, Indiana (1979). Bela Bianco discusses a like phenomenon in her description of capitalist development in São Paola, Brazil (1981).

City University of New York, and transportation fares were hiked 43 percent. The poor working class of Greenpoint-Williamsburg, particularly dependent on services such as municipal hospitals and public education, suffered the consequences of these changes. Their political activity and the anger which accompanied it has to be viewed in the context of this sudden, painful decrease in available services.

Since 1975 it has become clear that the "fiscal crisis" largely represented a speeding up of the transformation of New York from a city structured around light manufacturing and a poor working class to a city oriented toward middle-class people employed by major corporations (Gordon, 1978); Tabb (1978).[8] The same banks which withdrew their financial support in 1975 rapidly reinvested in real estate development in 1980. Manufacturing has left the city, and services for the poor are being reduced. At the same time, middle-class people are returning to the city, and the prices for cooperative apartments, along with rents, are spiraling. Major corporations are competing for air rights in order to construct high-rise office buildings in Manhattan. In Greenpoint-Williamsburg we can examine the social costs of this transformation and the response of poor working-class people caught in its grip.

The trends that have shaped the industry and social structure of the United States have also fashioned New York City and its neighborhoods. Chapter 2 traces the course of the city's economic and political development and the particular conditions which formed Greenpoint-Williamsburg. Greenpoint-Williamsburg does not have defining geographic characteristics, but certain population trends differentiate it clearly from surrounding areas. These same characteristics of the population affect political development and the composition of protest movements.

In the third chapter, we cross the boundary from statistical representation to the description of individual workers as they seek employment. Finding a job, working a short time, losing a job, and looking again form a part of the cycle of life in the neighborhood. This chapter describes the pervasive influence of

8. For an analysis of the effect of a slightly different economic restructuring on Boston's working class, see Sheehan (1981).

the state in terms of state-sponsored work programs and the other major work alternative: the military. Frequently the only work available in the neighborhood is in a government program where employment depends upon an individual's political usefulness. Through a consideration of the nature of work in Greenpoint-Williamsburg, we can understand the way employment precipitates far-reaching changes in the lives of individuals and the structure of the community.

When all else fails, working-class people fall into the domain of public assistance. The evidence collected in this study indicates that welfare clients are not a separate group of people cut off from the working population. They are working-class people temporarily without jobs. Welfare clients once worked; they live in households with other people who do work. They find jobs over a period of time and work when there is work. Sometimes they also work while receiving welfare assistance. Chapters 4 and 5 describe why this is so and examine the interactions between working-class people, welfare officials, and the intrusive, controlling, and even oppressive effects of welfare regulations.

Bureaucratic intransigency either cripples and confines recipients or provokes ingenious responses which distort relations between clients and welfare officials; the relationship then easily becomes one of adversaries. The unpredictable and hostile quality of welfare administration has immediate political implications: clients fearful of welfare inspection are less likely to draw attention to themselves through public political action. Because of the significance of public assistance as supplementary income in many poor working-class households, the vulnerability of welfare recipients to inspection and regulation has the potential to constrain their political involvement.

In a society in which economic resources and political power are all-important, poor people find themselves walled in by the very services which have supposedly been created to help them. Under close scrutiny, the regulations inherent in welfare assistance, along with other social services, appear as so many bonds to tie people to their social position. When welfare is viewed within the context of landlord-tenant relations and lack of employment opportunities, the ways in which these bonds strangle efforts to circumvent them become strikingly evident.

Chapter 6 identifies three types of landlords in Greenpoint-Williamsburg and relates each to different political and economic consequences for the neighborhood. Absentee landlords tend to be wealthier than resident landlords and have different reasons for their interest in property. The third landlord, the New York City Housing Authority, has yet other interests. Each form of landlord influences the distribution of the neighborhood population and the degree of deterioration of particular areas. This chapter also discusses the causes of the racial discrimination practiced by white working-class homeowners, which can be contrasted with the more open policies of absentee landlords. Such variations have important consequences for the growth of electoral constituencies and political power.

In spite of the austere social and economic environment, the people of Greenpoint-Williamsburg are not without hope. Chapters 7 through 9 examine the workings of a local block association and demonstrate how residents are able to muster their remaining resources to develop networks of households. Formed around child-rearing and domestic assistance, these networks serve as a base for local political action. The neighborhood cannot be considered in isolation, however, and due consideration must be given to the influence of federal funding of local programs. Briefly, block residents succeeded where programs were already established by the state; they failed when they sought services for which funds had not been previously allotted.

Chapter 10 analyzes the formation of a successful local movement and the way in which friendships and local cooperation facilitated its development. Here again, wider political changes created the conditions for the group to win its demands. Although racial hostility reduced the effectiveness of the campaign, rivalry in New York State politics, combined with the support of influential unions, generated widespread publicity and strengthened the movement. But such success is rare, and struggles seldom rise beyond the local level. Chapter 11 develops the significance of racial divisions and electoral politics as forces of political suppression. In the pervasive political machine and in the vituperance demonstrated by voluntary associations such as the American Legion, we see the dynamics which prevent local movements from growing beyond the community. It is here we find the forces that divide and cripple the community and turn one neighborhood against another.

I chose to study poor working-class people partly because they reflect basic issues in American society. Because they have the fewest defenses and stand at the end of the consumer line, they most obviously exhibit the problems passed on down that line. As Turner (1957) has pointed out, social relations are more easily observed at dramatic points of crisis when choices have to be made and dominant concerns emerge from the ideological haze which generally surrounds them. The period of "fiscal crisis" in New York City in fact reflects the crisis that accompanies economic transformation. The fiscal crisis exposes the machinery of city government, the economic processes on which it depends, and the powers that control its politics.

Individually, the poor are always in crisis. Since they subsist at an economic level with little to spare, daily life becomes a drama of survival. The daily round is to contend with, surmount, or succumb to perils that might be absorbed with little effect by the middle-class households. The forces which leave their scars on the poor are not isolated occurrences; they are fundamental features of our society.

In approaching these issues, my choice of method was determined by my desire to gain a clear insight into the lives of the neighborhood people. The data presented here, therefore, were gathered primarily through participant observation—a method that allows an intimate experience of the daily existence and conditions of the people studied. I initially selected Greenpoint-Williamsburg as the site for fieldwork because it was one of the two most heavily industrialized areas in Brooklyn, which, according to the New York City Planning Commission (1969), was the most industrialized borough in the city. Having ascertained this information in the library of the Long Island Historical Society, I took the subway to the Greenpoint Avenue stop to see what the neighborhood looked like. The next week I walked the streets and scrutinzed local papers in search of an apartment. This gave me a more thorough introduction to the area, during which I discovered the Polish-American Community Center and met there one of the women who was to introduce me to many of the residents described in this book.[9]

As one fieldworker among a population of nearly two hundred thousand, I was unable to work with large numbers of residents, and I cannot claim this account in any way typifies all the people who have made their homes there. Since I was interested in protest and neighborhood organization, I chose to follow a few events as they occurred in order to present a complete picture of the people involved and the processes leading to particular episodes. Some of the events I describe took place in Greenpoint, others in the Polish and Italian sections of Williamsburg.

I became involved in the activities and households of one low-income block on Norman Street so that I could obtain a view of domestic economy, cooperation and conflict between neighbors and kin, and political organization. I observed residents in interaction with social service agencies, at welfare hearings, in dealings with landlords and with the local hospital and clinics, and in search of employment. As part of the fieldwork, I also attended social gatherings, baby showers, funerals, weddings, and holiday festivities.

By noting interaction between welfare officers and clients, between landlords and tenants, between kin and neighbors, I worked out an outline of neighborhood social organization. The analysis of particular situations and events (Gluckman, 1940; Van Velson, 1969), in combination with the tracing of support networks, provided the basis for an understanding of the social context from which protest actions, party politics, and constraints on political activities emerged.

During the first six months of research, I attended most com-

9. The names of community centers and other local agencies have been changed, as have the names of local residents throughout the book. "Norman Street" itself is a fictitious address, and other street names have also been changed.

munity meetings which were listed in local newspapers or to which participants invited me. As protest actions occurred, I oriented my fieldwork around them. I took part in events and interviewed other people involved. The same people did not participate in each event, and residents of Norman Street were sometimes, but not always, present at protest actions in other sections of Greenpoint-Williamsburg.

A major protest action was the occupation of a firehouse which was scheduled to be closed down. Protesters occupied the firehouse for a year and a half, and after another year and a half of neighborhood protest, full protection was finally restored in June 1978. Over the first two years, I spent many hours in the large engine hall, which served as a social gathering place. There I talked with people from the neighborhood, with the firemen who remained, and with numerous politicians and community workers. I also obtained copies of the firehouse log written by demonstration participants, letters to and from city officials, and official Fire Department analyses and attended public meetings.

In the case of the school board elections, I employed similar methods. I attended board meetings, recorded disputes, and also observed the election campaign. Since the elections occurred near the end of the second year of the fieldwork, I was already familiar with many of the people concerned and had been observing meetings for some time. The campaign for the "parents' slate" was of particular interest to me, and I spent a large amount of time canvassing the neighborhood, interviewing residents about their preferences. I attended campaign meetings, spoke with many of the candidates, interviewed three of the four members of the parents' slate, and talked at length with all four. I was present at several polling centers on election day and was at the ballot-counting a few days later. To complement participant observation, I studied newspaper reports, campaign propaganda, and other documents.

In the dispute over the senior citizens' center, I interviewed neighborhood residents and senior citizens informally. I attended meetings and read newspaper articles, leaflets, and other community publications. The information about local political campaigns was gathered over a two-year period of observing meetings and political officials, following local news reports, and listening to issues discussed by politicians, local residents, and community workers.

As a fieldworker then, I followed events and participated in activities in the neighborhood. In this role I was unable to avoid taking sides on social issues. For example, although I talked to welfare officials separately from clients on several occasions, I observed *the process of welfare application* by accompanying clients and trying to help them through it. This limited my understanding of the constraints which clearly bound officials but provided insight into the barriers confronted by clients. Similarly, I was more familiar with the firehouse protest movement than with the decision-making processes of the mayor and fire commissioner, who had ordered the engine company closed. Through my involvement I came to know many of the protestors and the problems of fighting city hall. While this method is limited both by my partisanship and by the lack of data for all sections of the community, the use of event analysis and participant observation provided detailed, complex, and significant information about the way people live within the constraints of a changing political economy.

CHAPTER 2

A Changing Neighborhood

New York City was the first of the northeastern American cities to threaten bankruptcy. At the time commentators looked for reasons peculiar to New York. Since then numerous other cities have followed suit, and it has become clear that we are witnessing a general industrial decline in the Northeast and Midwest. In this sense a description of residents of Greenpoint-Williamsburg from 1975 to 1978 can be viewed as an early case study of the plight of working-class people in the face of the economic restructuring occurring throughout the United States. Although the experiences of the people described are in some ways unique, cuts in public services, high levels of unemployment, and deterioration of neighborhoods are phenomena to be found in all the northeastern and midwestern states in the 1980s.

Greenpoint-Williamsburg is first of all a product of changing conditions in New York City, but it is also the result of its own particular history. Greenpoint-Williamsburg has also been affected by its relations with those areas which form its boundaries. Each of these influences helped to shape and limit the political expression of the residents of the area. This chapter examines the trends in the composition of the populations of New York City and Greenpoint-Williamsburg. The significance of these characteristics, and the reason for their detailed presentation, will emerge later in the analysis. We will begin to understand the ways in which factors such as employment opportunities, racial distribution, and electoral and municipal boundaries generate the conditions for specific forms of political protest.

New York City

In 1970 New York City had a population of 7,802,046 (U.S. Bureau of the Census, 1972).[1] Of those who lived on incomes below the poverty level, 24.0 percent were "Negro" and 26.8 percent were "persons of Spanish language."[2] Although blacks and Hispanics were disproportionately represented among poor New Yorkers, approximately 49.2 percent of the people living below the poverty level in New York City were non-Hispanic whites.[3]

Between 1960 and 1970, there had been changes in the ethnic composition of New York City. Blacks continued to migrate from the South, and Puerto Ricans and other Latin Americans increased in numbers while whites moved out to the suburbs. The greatest decline in the white population of New York City between 1960 and 1970 was recorded in Brooklyn. There was a gain of

1. Although U.S. Census figures have been used throughout this chapter, in the absence of other data, it should be noted that the validity of such counts has been seriously challenged, particularly with relation to low-income populations, and the figures must be regarded as questionable approximations.
2. Poverty-level income was an index adjusted for metropolitan areas, family size, and other factors (U.S. Department of Commerce, 1974).
3. It is difficult to evaluate the census figures on this point, since Hispanics are often classified as white, and sometimes as "nonwhite." The U.S. Census policy states:

Data are shown separately in each table for two racial categories, white and Negro. The category "white" includes persons who indicated their race as white, as well as persons who did not classify themselves in one of the specific race categories on the questionnaire but entered Mexican, Puerto Rican or a response suggesting Indo-European stock. The category "Negro" includes persons who indicated their race as Negro or black, as well as persons who had such entries as Jamaican, Trinidadian, West Indian, Haitian and Ethiopian. The classification of families and households by race refers to the race of the family or household head. Other races . . . are American Indian, Japanese, Chinese and Filipino.

For persons of Spanish language, the 1970 U.S. Census states:

Persons of Spanish language comprise persons who reported Spanish as their mother tongue (i.e., the language usually spoken in the home when these persons were children) and also include all other persons in families in which the head or wife reported Spanish as his or her mother tongue. Persons of Spanish language may be of any race, although the large majority are white. (U.S. Department of Commerce, 1974, p. xiii)

285,000 blacks to a 1970 total of 656,000. The Puerto Rican population increased by an estimated 220,000, bringing the total for 1970 to 399,600. The non-Hispanic white population was reduced by 750,000 to a 1970 total of 1,506,000, which constituted 58 percent of the total population of the borough of Brooklyn. Despite the reduction in absolute numbers, the major land area remained more than 90 percent white. Of 780 census tracts in the borough, 100 reported no black residents at all (New York City Bureau of Health Statistics and Analysis, 1972). In other words, blacks and Hispanics were confined to specific sections of the borough.

The population of New York City rose from 1960 to 1970. By 1980, however, it had dropped 10 percent below the 1970 figures to 7,071,000 (U.S. Bureau of the Census, 1980). At the time of this fieldwork, both the population and economic conditions in New York City were suffering a marked decline.

In 1960, 140 of the largest corporations in the United States had their headquarters in New York City. By 1975, 44 of these corporations had left, and there was over thirty million square feet of unrented office space in Manhattan (Epstein, 1977). In that year the total number of jobs had shrunk to 90.1 percent of the employment available in 1970 (U.S. Congressional Budget Office, 1977, p. 290). Between 1969 and 1974, there was an absolute decline of sixty-eight thousand jobs. More than forty-three thousand manufacturing jobs were lost annually during those five years. Twelve thousand were lost from the apparel industry, one of the major industries in New York City and the largest employer in Greenpoint-Williamsburg in 1969. Federal government employment and wholesale and retail trade jobs were also decreasing. The only area, besides a small increase in services, in which there was an increase in absolute average annual employment from 1969 to 1974 was in local government. On the average nine thousand additional state and local employees were hired each year. No new industries or forms of employment had been developed in order to offset the large decrease in employment in the main industries of New York City (Sternlieb and Hughes, 1977, pp. 159–61). In 1970 the unemployment rate in New York

City was 4.8 percent, but by August 1975 it had risen to 11 percent. (U.S. Congressional Budget Office, 1977, p. 288).

These changes were not sudden but were rather the result of long-term trends. Between 1950 and 1970, the proportion of families in New York City with incomes below the nation's median income level rose from 36 percent to 49 percent (Epstein, 1977). The city also became "older" as that fraction of the population over sixty-five years of age rose from 8 percent to 12.1 percent (U.S. Congressional Budget Office, 1977, p. 298). Young people were leaving the inner city in search of work elsewhere.

New York City was not alone in this predicament. Census figures indicate that other large metropolitan areas were suffering from similar changes. In 1960 Standard Metropolitan Statistical Area (SMSA) populations were almost equally divided between central city and suburban residence. By 1970, 54 percent of the population lived in suburban areas, and by 1974, 57 percent had moved to the suburbs (Sternlieb and Hughes, 1977, p. 148). To add to the problems of inner cities, the aggregate family income in 1973 of families and unrelated individuals leaving the city between 1970 and 1974 was approximately $55.3 billion. Aggregate income for families moving into the cities was only $25.7 billion, which represented a loss of almost $30 billion through migration (ibid.). Such trends were partially the result of widespread highway construction and the availability of financing for suburban homes since World War II (Caro, 1974; Ashton, 1978; Orgel, 1981).

In addition to these changes, metropolitan areas in the northeastern United States have been subject to the largest loss in employment possibilities. Between 1967 and 1972, the growth rate in employment was more than five times faster in the South Atlantic states than in the Middle Atlantic states, which include the Northeast. Manufacturing employment in the Middle Atlantic states declined by 12 percent, while in the South Atlantic states it increased by 7 percent (Sternlieb and Hughes, 1977, p. 149). Georgia's rate of total employment growth between 1967 and 1972 was nine times that of New York State (ibid., p. 150).

Besides the loss in employment opportunities, financial difficulties in New York were exacerbated by the small share of federal tax money allotted to the city. From 1965 to 1967, New York City paid $3.2 billion more each year to the federal government than it received back in federal payments. By 1973 the city's net annual outflow in excess of federal input was $7.5 billion (Melman, 1977, p. 182). This deficit in federal expenditures in "civilian" states has been related to the increase in military expenditures in the southern states (Sale, 1977, p. 166). The trend in federal expenditures clearly accompanies the trend of population and employment increases in the South and Southwest and the long-term decline in northeastern and midwestern metropolitan areas.

Greenpoint-Williamsburg

To understand the depth of human social dislocation produced by these trends, we must examine the history of Greenpoint-Williamsburg and the people who made their lives there. Greenpoint-Williamsburg is built on the eastern bank of the East River. At night many people can see from their windows the arc of lights of the Queensboro Bridge or the colored spotlights at the top of the Empire State Building. And if one walks past the empty lots, the immense warehouses, and the whirring factories along the edge of the river, one comes to the thick logs of the old wooden piers and the rippling brown expanse of the water, across which one can clearly discern the cars driving up and down the East Side of Manhattan. Although it is so close to Manhattan, and its fate is determined by its position in New York City, Greenpoint-Williamsburg often appears like another world.

Early in the morning, when few people are on the streets, the pastels of the wood-frame houses, pink and green and light blue, contrast picturesquely with the gray stone of the church steeples. Later in the day, as the sun heats up and the streets become crowded with people and cars and buses, the long scar across the neighborhood, the Brooklyn-Queens Expressway, looms as a gloomy impassable barrier, and abandoned stores and vacant lots become more evident.

In the cool of a summer evening, the neighborhood once again assumes an exotic quality as women dressed in black bring their chairs out to sit on the street corners of the Italian section and form groups, conversing with their neighbors in Neapolitan dialect. Groups of young teen-agers wander by and may address a few words in English to the people seated on the sidewalks. Throughout other sections of Greenpoint-Williamsburg, people are also out on the streets, enjoying the long balmy evenings with their friends.

In many ways working-class residents of Greenpoint-Williamsburg seem to form an enclave, sheltered from the rush of city life. Some might even call it a backwater where the trends which have transformed New York City over the past fifty years have scarcely touched communal working-class traditions. One finds scenes reminiscent of films of pre–World War II New York, before the "white flight" to the suburbs and the havoc and destruction which urban renewal wrought on residential neighborhoods. As this book demonstrates, however, such fantasies are far from true. Greenpoint-Williamsburg is a product of New York's expanding industrial development in the late nineteenth century, and the forces affecting inhabitants there today are closely tied to the city's industrial decline.

In the second half of the nineteenth century, factories began to move out to Greenpoint-Williamsburg from the congested areas of Lower Manhattan. During the same period, numerous tenement buildings and frame houses were constructed for the expanding population of factory workers (Pratt, 1911; Merchants' Association, 1921; New York City Planning Commission, 1974). In 1903 the Williamsburg Bridge was built, connecting Greenpoint-Williamsburg with the Lower East Side of Manhattan. This facilitated the movement of workers and industry to Greenpoint-Williamsburg and other parts of Brooklyn.

Industry in the area continued to expand through the early 1900s. It was aided by the possibilities for development of Newtown Creek, a tributary of the East River, for easy transport; by a convenient railroad; by expanses of available land; and by city and federal assistance (Merchants' Association, 1921, p. 31).

From the late nineteenth century, Greenpoint-Williamsburg was destined to house a working-class population. Members of many different ethnic groups, attracted by the availability of employment and housing, moved across the river from Manhattan. People from a variety of nations and backgrounds chose not to settle in the crowded ethnic enclaves of Manhattan but to search for better opportunities in other areas. As Edward Pratt's 1911 study demonstrates:

> Determining factors in the distribution of workers were the hours of work and wages. Nationality or race, on the other hand, did not play an important part. So far as could be determined, the Italians and Jews live as near their work as they can. Little Italy and the Ghetto, in most congested Manhattan, seem to have little effect on the workers employed in the other boroughs. (P. 191)

Pratt claims, more specifically:

> The analysis of the data returned by the workers in Williamsburg, furnishes additional evidence for questioning the theories which assert that nationality is one of the chief causes of congestion. They also throw doubt upon the theory that nationality is one of the fundamental factors in determining the distribution of factory workers. These data affirm the conclusion that workers, no matter what their nationality, desire to avoid the crowded and congested sections of Manhattan, and do so when the location of the factory permits it. (P. 169)

The trend described by Pratt did not obstruct the formation of new ethnic enclaves as factory workers began to leave Manhattan. German and Irish immigrants settled in Greenpoint-Williamsburg in the late nineteenth century, and the Irish remained the largest ethnic group in the area through the 1920s (Pratt, 1911; Merchants' Association, 1921). In the early 1900's, an influx of Italian immigrants established themselves in one section of Williamsburg. (Cordasco and Bucchioni, 1974). Polish immigrants also started to arrive in Greenpoint around the 1900s, their numbers increasing after World War II. Orthodox Jews had lived in Williamsburg since the 1800s. In the 1940s large numbers of Hassidim and other religious Jewish sects, fleeing persecution in Europe, followed influential rabbis to establish a strong community in Williamsburg (Kranzler, 1961; Poll, 1969).

Since the 1950s the Hispanic population has been growing as migrants from both Puerto Rico and the Dominican Republic, along with second-generation Hispanic-Americans, have settled in Greenpoint-Williamsburg (Rosenberg, 1974, p. 49). Since the 1950s American blacks have been moving into city-owned housing in Greenpoint and Williamsburg.

In 1975 a variety of ethnic groups were still represented in different sections of Greenpoint-Williamsburg, both new migrants and second- and third-generation Americans. Many people regarded themselves as "Americans" without particular ethnic origins. Although the proportions of different ethnic groups have changed over time, in 1976 several of the groups, such as the Italians and the Slavs, were still predominant in the same neighborhoods where they had formed a majority in 1921. According to the 1970 census, the three largest ethnic categories in Greenpoint-Williamsburg were Italian (49,540), Polish (15,802), and Russian (15,809) (U.S. Department of Commerce, 1973).[4]

Every few blocks of Greenpoint-Williamsburg can be identified with a particular ethnic group. Distinctive food shops—the Polish bakeries, Italian cheese and sausage shops, Hispanic bodegas, and Jewish delicatessens—are squeezed between the regular stores and scattered through the residential streets. Despite the obvious ethnic segmentation, however, most neighborhoods are quite heterogeneous: in Hassidic Williamsburg, men with long sideburns and women with covered heads and dark stockings can be seen on the streets, but so can Hispanic and other people walking through or living in the area. Polish and Italian sections can be easily identified, but many others from a variety of backgrounds actually live in these neighborhoods. Rather than examining ethnic distinctions, this book seeks to describe some of the commonalities that existed between groups which found themselves in a similar economic position in New York City at a particular moment in American history.

Greenpoint-Williamsburg is a New York City health district

4. The census excluded Hispanics and included both "foreign-born" and "native of foreign or mixed parentage."

and was one of sixty-two community planning districts adopted by the City Planning Commission in 1968 (New York City Planning Commission, 1969). In many senses the area does not have "defining" characteristics: until 1968 it was not encompassed by any overriding municipal boundaries. It does not reflect exclusively any particular ethnic group, type of housing, industry, or other employment. However, in relation to the surrounding neighborhoods, definite trends can be distinguished that serve to describe the district.

According to the 1960 census, the population of Greenpoint-Williamsburg was 193,000.[5] In 1970 the U.S. Census counted only 176,000 people. Evidently, as in New York City as a whole, the population of Greenpoint-Williamsburg has been decreasing (New York City Bureau of Health Statistics and Analysis, 1972).[6]

The ethnic composition of Greenpoint-Williamsburg also shifted. Between 1950 and 1969, the Puerto Rican population rose from 10,984 to 41,563 (New York City Bureau of Health Statistics and Analysis, 1962). In 1970 there were 65,179 "persons of Spanish language," 153,814 "whites," 18,173 "Negroes," and 3,714 "members of other races" in Greenpoint-Williamsburg (New York City Department of Research and Planning Information, 1974).[7] Young Hispanic families were moving in while young white families moved out, leaving a large proportion of elderly whites behind. This corresponds to a pattern throughout north and central Brooklyn where black and Hispanic people were replacing an earlier non-Hispanic white population (ibid.). Although this trend is evident in Greenpoint-Williamsburg, a significant number of non-Hispanic white families and young white

5. These figures were abstracted from records of the New York City Bureau of Health Statistics and Analysis (1961). The figures are used here because the Department of Health has compiled statistics from U.S. Census data for "Williamsburg-Greenpoint," which corresponds to the community planning district of "Greenpoint-Williamsburg." Data abstracted directly from the U.S. Census are divided into 53 census tracts between tracts 453 and 593.
6. By 1980 the population had dropped to 135,000 (U.S. Bureau of the Census, 1980).
7. These figures add up to more than the total population of Greenpoint-Williamsburg since, as mentioned above, "Persons of Spanish language" are generally also counted as "white."

people remain, and a major determining characteristic of the neighborhood is that the influx of Hispanic people has not so far led to a mass exodus of non-Hispanic white families.

In 1970 the rate of unemployment in Greenpoint-Williamsburg was 5.8 percent (U.S. Department of Commerce, 1973).[8] In March 1978, when labor market information on community planning district boards became available, the unemployment rate in Greenpoint-Williamsburg was 12.1 percent (New York City Department of Labor Market Information, 1978). Although these figures are not directly comparable with the 1970 figures, they provide evidence for deteriorating conditions in the intervening eight years.

The population of Greenpoint-Williamsburg in 1970 was not evenly distributed. Several blocks were over 97 percent white with between 5 and 15 percent "persons of Spanish language." The border between Williamsburg and the neighboring district had a white population of less than 70 percent and a black population of almost 30 percent. The Hispanic population was over 50 percent, which suggests that the non-Hispanic white population made up only 15 percent of the inhabitants (New York City Bureau of Health Statistics and Analysis, 1974, pp. 53, 54).

Parts of Williamsburg and Greenpoint were classified as low-income areas by the 1970 U.S. Census (U.S. Department of Commerce, 1974, p. xxi). These figures were compiled in 1970, and by 1975 larger portions of Williamsburg and Greenpoint could have been considered low-income areas. Data also indicate that in terms of the essentials for a healthy environment, the income which classifies a family as poor should be raised above the level calculated on a national scale. The nonfarm income for a household of four was considered poverty level if it fell below $3,748 a year (U.S. Department of Commerce, 1974, p. xii). Expenses in New York City were significantly higher than in many other places, and the evaluation of the cost of living in the federal statistics did not take this sufficiently into account. To pay for

8. This was the unemployment rate for the 14th Congressional District, which in 1970 encompassed an area slightly larger than Greenpoint-Williamsburg.

essentials such as rent, gas, electricity, public transportation, and food and clothing, a family of four in Greenpoint-Williamsburg in 1975 required at least $5,000 a year.[9]

In the higher-income areas of Greenpoint-Williamsburg, families with members under eighteen years constituted approximately 50 percent of the population. In the other areas, the proportion of families with young children was higher, reaching 71 percent in the poorest section (New York City Bureau of Health Statistics and Analysis, 1974, pp. 32–33). The number of families with female heads and young children was also greater in the blocks with a lower median income (ibid., 1974, p. 32). The proportion of persons over sixty-five years of age was greatest—approximately 11 percent—in the blocks of Greenpoint with higher family income. In other parts of Greenpoint-Williamsburg, the proportion of senior citizens dropped as low as 5 percent (ibid., p. 31).

The southern border of Williamsburg adjoins a large section of Brooklyn known as Bedford-Stuyvesant. In this area more than 20 percent of the population had incomes below the poverty level (U.S. Department of Commerce, 1974). The poor maintenance, pervasive consequences of absentee landlords, and abandoned buildings here constituted a constant and visible threat to the residents of Greenpoint-Williamsburg and had some significance for political developments.

In terms of several distinct measures such as housing and health, Greenpoint-Williamsburg could be distinguished from neighboring poorer districts. Ethnicity, income, unemployment rates, family structure, and age differences established a clear gradient. There was a higher proportion of whites, a slightly higher although relatively inadequate median family income, slightly lower unemployment levels, fewer female-headed families, and a lower proportion of youths in Greenpoint-Williamsburg than in Bedford-Stuyvesant.

In comparison with middle-income neighborhoods such as

9. Based on a calculation of $110 a month rent, $30 a month for gas and electricity, $160 a month for food, and $150 a month for clothing and public transportation (with 50¢ fares), a household of four would require an income of $5,400 a year. This does not provide for medical or other exceptional costs.

Brooklyn Heights (with a median income in 1969 of $10,368),[10] Greenpoint-Williamsburg could be considered a poor neighborhood. The median income for Greenpoint-Williamsburg in 1969 was approximately $6,959 (U.S. Department of Commerce, 1973).[11] Although an income of over $6,000 may not appear to cause hardship and deprivation, living expenses in a metropolis are often greater for lesser rewards than in other geographic locations. At the same time, Greenpoint-Williamsburg differed in degree from deteriorating neighborhoods surrounding it. As we will see, the similarities and differences between Greenpoint-Williamsburg and the neighboring poorer districts structured the forms of political action and types of demands and issues which arose between 1975 and 1977.

There was also a gradient between Greenpoint and Williamsburg. Residents of Greenpoint had higher incomes, represented an older group, had fewer female-headed families, and were less likely to be Hispanic than residents of Williamsburg. These differences both reflected and influenced political activities and the provision of services as they varied between the two sections.

Industry and Employment

One quarter of the industrial jobs in New York City were in Brooklyn in 1969 (New York City Planning Commission, 1969). There were 225,000 manufacturing or wholesaling jobs, of which 90 percent were classified as blue collar. The largest concentration of manufacturing jobs was in Greenpoint-Williamsburg and Newtown Creek, which together accounted for one half of the jobs in the borough. Over half the employees in Brooklyn worked in five industries. Fourteen percent of the workers were in apparel manufacture and, following that, in food, metal, machinery, and electrical industries. The median annual wage for workers in Brooklyn was almost $6,000 in 1969. Nearly 40 percent earned

10. This figure is the 1969 income recorded for the 13th Congressional District.
11. The 14th Congressional District (which encompassed Greenpoint-Williamsburg) had a median income of $6,959 (U.S. Department of Commerce, 1973).

under $5,000, and 30 percent earned more than $7,000. Nearly one half of the work force was Puerto Rican or black (ibid.).

In Greenpoint in 1969, there were 5,600 jobs. The largest employer was an electrical parts factory, Leviton Manufacturing Company, which employed one third of the workers (New York City Planning Commission, 1969). In Williamsburg there were 90,000 jobs in 1969, and the largest employers were the American Sugar Company, E. and M. Schaeffer Brewing Company, and the Lumber Exchange Terminal, which was situated along the East River (ibid.). Around Newtown Creek there were a number of wholesaling and distributing firms. Gallo Wine Company and several meat-packing concerns were also significant employers, and the presence of a number of warehouses made trucking a common occupation.

In 1976 the Schaeffer Brewing Company transferred its factory out of Brooklyn, leaving a skeletal administrative staff. The Rheingold Brewing Company also left during the same period. These were instances of the industrial emigration which contributed to the high local unemployment levels. Since 1970 several of the other large employers in the area, such as Leviton Manufacturing Company in Greenpoint and the S&S Corrugated Paper Machinery Company in Williamsburg, have also threatened to leave and have only remained in Brooklyn with the incentive of subsidies from the city.

Figures from a low-income area in Williamsburg indicate that the largest number of people were employed as unskilled workers in factories, especially (among the women) as sewers and stitchers (U.S. Department of Commerce, 1974). A large number of women also were clerical workers, and many men were employed as service workers or craftsmen. More Hispanics were employed as machine operators, while few were skilled craftsmen (ibid.). The concentration of women and Hispanics in such unskilled work as machine operators coincides with views of the American work force presented in theories of the dual economy and underemployment (Gordon, 1972).[12]

12. Such theories suggest that there are two sectors within the American working class, those with permanent, well-paid, unionized jobs and those who are confined to temporary, insecure, low-paying work. White working-

The black population was small but, unlike the Hispanic population, appeared to have a slightly higher proportion of craftsmen than operatives. Of 1,732 male service workers, a large proportion were Hispanic (959) and black (383), compared to only 363 whites (U.S. Department of Commerce, 1974). Among the employed women, the pattern was somewhat different. The white non-Hispanic women were employed disproportionately in clerical jobs, while the highest proportion of black and Hispanic women were employed as operatives, (ibid.).

It is difficult to determine wages for each kind of job, since census data are collected in terms of family income. Some of the data, however, give an approximate indication of wage levels. In 1970 the mean family income for all races where there was one earner in the family was $5,791 (U.S. Department of Commerce, 1974). This amount may actually be greater than the average wage, as it may have included supplementary income from welfare or Social Security, but the average wages for one person could not have been greater. An indication that they were in fact lower comes from the mean earnings of unrelated individuals, which were $4,775. Although this figure may have been skewed by the large number of old people and by young people not yet established in the job market, it suggests that the wage of a single person averaged $5,000 a year at most.

Housing

The median rent in Greenpoint-Williamsburg was $90 a month in 1969 (U.S. Department of Commerce, 1973),[13] and my data suggest that it was between $100 and $200 in 1976. Some residents, especially senior citizens who had occupied the same apartments for many years and whose rents had been restricted by rent-control laws, were still paying $90 in 1976. Cases were reported

---

class males tend to find work in the better-paid sector while minorities, women, and youth are thought to be restricted to the low-paying employment opportunities. The fact that members of the same household are often found in different sectors of the labor market brings into question theories of differential socialization and education between the two sectors.

13. Housing figures apply to the 14th Congressional District in 1970, not to Greenpoint-Williamsburg alone.

in which rent was only $50, but apartments with such low rentals were often extremely dilapidated.

While much housing in Greenpoint-Williamsburg was built prior to 1939 (U.S. Department of Commerce, 1973), a great many buildings date back to the turn of the century when tenements were built to accommodate European immigrants who came to work in local factories (New York City Planning Commission, 1974). The median number of rooms in a household unit was four, and the typical shape of the apartments resembled a long passage with alcoves serving as rooms (U.S. Department of Commerce, 1973). In 1970, 12 percent of the housing units in the 14th Congressional District did not have bathrooms, and 4 percent lacked some or all plumbing facilities (ibid.). In the relatively better-off 15th District (which is made up of Brooklyn Heights and surrounding areas), by contrast, only 6 percent of the housing units lacked bathrooms and only 1.8 percent lacked some or all plumbing facilities (ibid.).

In 1970 the median value for owner-occupied units in the 14th District was $17,349, while in the 15th District it was $26,434 (U.S. Department of Commerce, 1973). Even though some people might own the building in which they lived in Greenpoint-Williamsburg, they were not necessarily well-off. In fact, homeowners were in a distinct minority, with only 13 percent of the units in the 14th District owner-occupied, compared to 25.3 percent in the 15th District (ibid.). In Greenpoint there were a large number of owner-occupied apartment buildings. In certain sections of Williamsburg, similar patterns were to be found. In its poorer sections, however, absentee landlords were common, and some of the worst landlords in New York City owned buildings in Williamsburg. The process of deterioration that resulted from the devastating practices of absentee landlords will be described in chapter 6, and analysis of the connections between absentee landlords, neglect, arson, inadequate fire protection, and the increasing poverty of the city government and residents of working-class neighborhoods is a major concern of this work. A third type of landlord was the New York City Housing Authority, which was responsible for the maintenance of public housing in the area.

Municipal Boundaries and Services

Greenpoint-Williamsburg, like many other neighborhoods in American cities, lies within the jurisdiction of seemingly innumerable government agencies. This is a matter of some concern, for the lack of one coherent unit whose bounds are known to residents subtly influences their sense of community and, in consequence, the development of local political action.

Although the City Planning Commission reports of 1969 recognized Greenpoint-Williamsburg as a district, Community Planning District 1, other commission reports (1974) and city services tended to divide the area into two neighborhoods, Greenpoint and Williamsburg. Electoral districts included other parts of Brooklyn and sometimes even sections of Manhattan within their boundaries. The mental health areas, police districts, health districts, planning districts, and community school districts in Brooklyn were all defined by different boundaries.[14]

Greenpoint-Williamsburg was served by three police precincts. Williamsburg, from the Brooklyn-Queens Expressway to Metropolitan Avenue, and the whole of Greenpoint were served by the 94th Precinct. The rest of Williamsburg was divided between the 90th and 93rd precincts, which also included parts of other low-income areas.

From Newtown Creek to Metropolitan Avenue, Greenpoint-Williamsburg was served by Battalion 36 of the New York Fire Department. Two firehouses, whose services were much disputed (see chapter 10), were responsible for this area. A large section of the rest of Williamsburg was covered by the 35th Battalion, and a further section was divided between the 34th and the 29th battalions. As with the population, the data on fires form a gradient. A larger number of fires occurred in the lower-income areas (Wallace, 1976). The incidence of fires was partly an indication of the deterioration of neighborhood buildings and also contributed to the speed with which they decayed. As will be seen

14. Such confusion has in some cases aided officials, both elected and appointed, in amassing enormous political power. For an example, see Caro's portrait of Robert Moses in *The Power Broker* (1974).

later, the occurrence of one fire on a block raised the risk of future fires on the same block and led to an escalation in the number of burned-out buildings in a wide area around. For this reason the distribution of fire battalions and the provision of fire protection by the city constituted a significant factor in area maintenance and the composition of the population of the neighborhood.

School District 14 included all of Greenpoint-Williamsburg and a small neighboring section. The district was supervised by the District 14 school board, which was elected by citizen residents in the district as well as by noncitizen parents with children in its schools. A school board election will be discussed in more detail in chapter 11. In 1975 District 14 included four high schools, five junior high schools, and seventeen primary schools.

Of eighteen day care centers in Greenpoint-Williamsburg in 1975, only one was in Greenpoint. Many women who lived in Greenpoint regarded Williamsburg as foreign territory and, despite the lower proportion of young children in Greenpoint, the shortage of day care centers there inconvenienced Greenpoint families. Along with the problems already mentioned, this contributed to the political attitudes and behavior of residents in the two neighborhoods by fostering resentment among Greenpoint mothers.

The difference between the two areas is also brought out by their transportation links to Manhattan. Williamsburg is served by subway lines which connect directly with the Lower East Side of Manhattan and do not go through Greenpoint. Another line goes from Queens through Greenpoint to Williamsburg and then to Brooklyn's commercial center. This is the only line that passes through Greenpoint. People from Greenpoint generally travel the circuitous route through Queens to reach Manhattan (often an hour's journey), although many can look out on the Empire State Building, the World Trade Center, and a length of the East River Drive in Manhattan from their kitchen windows. Greenpoint is close to Manhattan, but the subway journey into the city is tedious; in contrast, Williamsburg is only a couple of stops by bus or subway from Manhattan.

The Williamsburg and Queensboro bridges, the Brooklyn-Queens Expressway, the Long Island Expressway, and the Queens Midtown Tunnel make Greenpoint-Williamsburg easily accessible by car. Except for traffic jams, the area is conveniently located for travel by car out to Long Island or into Manhattan. It is partly this useful location that has led the community planning board and the city commissioners to consider the area for the development of future middle-income housing.

There was one hospital in the area, Greenpoint Hospital, which was declared obsolete in 1969. In 1976 a new hospital was almost completed in the Hispanic and black neighborhood closer to Bedford-Stuyvesant. There was much controversy over the closing of Greenpoint Hospital, however, and neighborhood agencies demanded that an emergency service be maintained there. Although local residents criticized conditions and service at the hospital (as did the city evaluators), they valued its proximity. The hospital was used by many of the neighborhood people despite its poor reputation and their own distrust of the medical services.

Clinics in the area provided free services for babies such as weighing and immunization and also supplied quantities of free baby food for newborn infants. Some poor people eligible for Medicaid took their children and themselves to private doctors in the neighborhood.[15] When they went to the doctor's at all, those not eligible for Medicaid saw private doctors and were billed or else attended the less costly ambulatory clinic at Greenpoint Hospital. Families of men in military service could obtain free medical treatment if they went to the doctors at the army base. For most of these families, however, the difficulties of transportation precluded this, and they used local medical services for which they were eventually (though only partially) reimbursed by the army insurance system.

Religion

There were numerous churches in Greenpoint-Williamsburg, but most with large congregations were Catholic. One church in Greenpoint held most of its services in Polish. This church and

15. Persons are eligible for Medicaid if they receive welfare assistance, Supplementary Security Income, or if annual income is less than $2,900. A family of four with an annual income of less than $5,000 is eligible for Medicaid (New York State Department of Social Services, 1977).

three others which exercised much influence in Greenpoint and parts of Williamsburg were attended predominantly by whites. In one section of Williamsburg, there was also a large Hassidic population and a number of synagogues.

There were thirty-five parochial schools in Greenpoint-Williamsburg in 1975. Catholic schools were connected to particular churches. Just below the Williamsburg Bridge were a cluster of yeshivas (Hebrew-English day schools) organized by the Hassidic population.

Community Agencies

Social services in Greenpoint and Williamsburg, such as assistance with welfare enrollment, family difficulties, drug abuse, child abuse, and other community problems, were supplied by a variety of different agencies funded from many sources. A few agencies hired qualified social workers, but others were largely staffed by untrained community workers. One of the oldest such agencies was a settlement house of the kind founded in the early 1900s. Other agencies were closer to ethnic self-help organizations, funded by both private contributions and whatever public funds might be available.

The availability of funds from the Office of Economic Opportunity in the mid-1960s had led to the founding of one umbrella organization in the Williamsburg area. This organization assisted with unemployment and housing problems and distributed summer jobs among unemployed youth. A second umbrella organization was formed with the use of CETA (Comprehensive Employment Training Act) funds in 1975 and will be described in more detail in chapter 3. Both of these organizations and the combination of community agencies connected with them had significant political influence in the area.

Community agencies functioned as mediators between public services and the poor. They obtained federal, state, and municipal funds and services and supervised their distribution in the neighborhood, in this way building up considerable clout. Many of these agencies were nominally connected with local political officials and, as will be seen, were important in both formal and informal political processes.

Services provided by community agencies were vague and not always effective. Sometimes assistance in dealing with economic or family problems was provided, but often it was not available. Such agencies served to some extent as information disseminators through the neighborhood, and also, of course, as an important source of employment.

Political Districts

The electorate of New York City votes for federal, state, and city political representatives. The federal representatives are congressmen and senators. Senators are elected by voters all over New York State, while congressmen are elected only by their congressional districts. State representatives are senators and assemblymen. State senators are elected by state Senate districts, assemblymen by Assembly districts, and city councilmen are elected from councilmanic districts to serve on borough councils. District divisions are not stable and several, including the congressional and councilmanic districts, have been altered since 1972.

The congressional districts cut Greenpoint right down the middle. They also divide sections of Williamsburg. Each of these districts was hotly contested by different political interest groups with access to influence over planning. Before 1972 the areas with large non-Hispanic white populations, including Greenpoint-Williamsburg, formed one district, and the neighboring predominantly black, low-income area of Bedford-Stuyvesant was divided into two. In the latest divisions, Greenpoint-Williamsburg was divided between the 12th and the 14th districts. This split threatened the political influence of groups which relied on blocks of votes from Greenpoint.[16]

The most recent state Senate redistricting divides Greenpoint-Williamsburg between districts 18, 23, and 25. The bulk of the area is included in District 18, along with a large section from

16. Earlier figures, from 1969, all refer to the original 14th Congressional District, which included all of Greenpoint-Williamsburg.

Bedford-Stuyvesant. Greenpoint-Williamsburg is more or less encompassed by the 58th Assembly District, though parts of the area are in the 57th. The councilmanic districts which incorporate parts of Greenpoint-Williamsburg are 27 and 29.

The implications of these divisions for political organization are discussed in chapter 11. The very evident efforts at gerrymandering contributed to a cynical attitude toward formal politics among many poor voters. The changing boundaries also detracted from any grass-roots effort to develop a sense of territorial political identity, leaving the field open for established party politicians and editors of the local papers to shape blocs of voters to suit their interests.

Since the 1960s conditions for residents of New York City have declined. The number of available jobs has decreased, rents have risen, and the levels of unemployment and people receiving welfare assistance have increased.

The situation in Greenpoint-Williamsburg has followed a similar pattern. The residents are becoming poorer, and the area is deteriorating as storefronts, factories, and other buildings are gradually abandoned. Fires are becoming a more common problem. In comparison to middle-class residential areas of Brooklyn such as Brooklyn Heights, Greenpoint-Williamsburg is a poor neighborhood.

In relation to Bedford-Stuyvesant, the population of Greenpoint-Williamsburg has a higher median income, tends to own more housing, has a larger proportion of older people, fewer female-headed families, a much larger proportion of non-Hispanic white people, and fewer burned out houses. Between Greenpoint and Williamsburg a similar relationship is evident. Greenpoint has a higher median income, an older population, more homeowners, a majority of non-Hispanic white residents, few female-headed families, and fewer, although an increasing number, of burned-out houses than Williamsburg.

There is a second trend in Greenpoint. Real estate speculators are attempting to interest young couples from Manhattan in the low-cost brownstone houses that are still available, and there have been attempts to expand some of the pleasant residential aspects of Greenpoint. Certain blocks have been particularly well kept up and are inhabited by doctors, lawyers, politicians, and businessmen with a vested interest in the maintenance of the area. Williamsburg lacks the renovated brownstones and the professional class which has contributed to their upkeep, although artists have begun to move into lofts in abandoned warehouses.

Greenpoint-Williamsburg, then, has representatives from the middle class and the poor within its boundaries. Notwithstanding the minority of professional and business families, the overwhelming character of the neighborhood is working class. Within this category a gradient can be detected from Greenpoint through Williamsburg to Bedford-Stuyvesant, from the better-paid craftsmen through the poorer families dependent on temporary employment and welfare. The number of poorer families increases toward Bedford-Stuyvesant, and ethnicity changes from predominantly non-Hispanic white through Hispanic toward predominantly black neighborhoods.

The different methods of sectioning Greenpoint-Williamsburg for various services such as the Fire Department, Police Department, community school districts, and electoral districts affect activities within the area. Not only is each service the responsibility of a different agency or accountable to a different politician, but residents within blocks of each other, or sometimes on opposite sides of the same street, have to consult separate offices and attempt to influence different politicians in order to effect any changes at all. On the one hand, this serves to differentiate the inhabitants and to break down units that might possibly cooperate to improve the neighborhood. On the other hand, the variety of agency divisions and political districts allows residents to call on several different politicians for any particular issue, and this in some ways may increase rather than decrease their political influence.

CHAPTER 3

A Changing Workplace
and Its Consequences

There were several alternating sources of income among poor working-class people in Greenpoint-Williamsburg.[1] Forms of employment included factories, construction work, maintenance work, working as a shop assistant, community programs, and secretarial work. A second alternative open to both men and women was military enlistment, which required that an individual leave the area although his family would receive benefits in addition to salary. Public assistance was a third source of income. Crime, including both drug-trading and burglary, provided a supplemental income for a few individuals, and examples of such cases are mentioned later. Each of the three expedients—local employment, military enlistment, and reliance on public assistance—had implications for household structure, for social organization, and for political action in the area.

By and large jobs were temporary and insecure, and public assistance was a common recourse. Among the prized jobs in the neighborhood were those created by CETA in 1975. Next to work in a factory with a strong union, employment through CETA was most desirable. This was despite the constant threat that funds might be terminated and the program abolished by the federal government.

1. For an illuminating description of similar alternating work patterns among poor American black ghetto dwellers, see Harrison (1972) and Valentine (1978).

Local Industry and Commercial Employment

As described in chapter 2, wages in local factories were low and conditions poor. A wage of $2.50 an hour was considered good, and $2.10 an hour or $90 a week was a more usual wage. Strongly unionized trades such as construction work or work in the meat factories paid higher wages. Firms with less active unions, such as the local electrical parts company, paid the same low or minimum wages as those in the packing and dyeing industries.

In order to illustrate the effect of employment factors upon social and political activity in the neighborhood, documentation will be provided from ten households studied intensively, persons connected with them, and those who participated in local protest actions.

Among the twenty-three men studied, six worked on and off in construction trades but were unemployed during the period of field research; two were truck drivers with intermittent employment; two worked in an electrical parts factory; two worked in other factories; one was a hotel dishwasher; one loaded trucks; four were employed by CETA; one was in the United States Armed Forces and two had just returned (they were subsequently employed temporarily in construction work); and two were unemployed and intermittently in prison. Out of the forty women, three had worked as cleaners in assorted factories; two as shop assistants; six in the local electrical parts factory; one as a meat packer; four as secretaries; two as unskilled accountants; ten as CETA employees; and two as domestic help. However, not all of the women were employed in 1975–1976. Ten were receiving public assistance, and five of the men lived in households receiving public assistance during this time.

Few of the positions in local industry or commerce offered security. This was illustrated by the experiences of several people. In 1976 workers who had been employed in the electrical parts factory for two or three years were laid off when business became slack. They could, however, expect to be notified when demand increased. One of the men who drove trucks had worked for the same company for sixteen years. He was a member of the International Brotherhood of Teamsters but still did not have a permanent position. He appeared at work every morning at 7 A.M. and waited in line for his assigned number to be called. If there was not enough work, he went home without earning a day's pay. If he did not appear one morning, he forfeited his assigned place in the line. The next day he would have to wait until all the assigned numbers had been called. After sixteen years of work in the same place, he had no security and received no sick pay. One day a supervisor caught him taking ten minutes extra for his lunch hour. The next morning he was fired. A year later he still had not found a new job and was receiving unemployment benefits. A man who worked in a machine-repair factory and a maintenance worker were both laid off during 1976–1977. Three women who worked as secretaries were laid off during 1976. However, all three found new jobs within six months. They were in a better position than the majority of women in the study, who were not qualified for such jobs. A woman who worked in a meat-packing factory was laid off and rehired by another firm in 1974. The data collected on employment suggest that it was easier for women to find work as secretaries or low-paid factory workers than for men.

Besides layoffs and firings, another common source of job loss was a consequence of factories moving out of New York City to new plants, inaccessible to the former work force. Four women who had been working in factories had been unemployed and dependent on public assistance for various lengths of time due to industry moving out of the neighborhood. Three women had been working for two years in a local dye factory. When the factory moved to Yonkers, it did so without officially firing its workers. Workers were offered severance pay if they left but were told that they could commute to Yonkers if they chose. The firm organized a bus service from Greenpoint to Yonkers in order that former workers might help instruct unskilled employees at the new site. After three weeks two of the women stopped working, unwilling to spend several hours in transportation. The third chose to remain on the job although the bus service was cancelled. She found herself commuting by subway and bus for six hours every day. After two weeks of this experience, she was forced to give up. The fourth woman worked for Schaeffer Brewing Company in Williamsburg as an accountant. When the company moved out of

Brooklyn she lost her job, although some of the administrative staff were retained and moved to Queens.

Stable, well-paying union jobs were difficult to obtain and often required personal contacts. One young man had found a well-paying job in a meat-packing factory through his wife's contacts. Her friend's husband's father was working as a foreman at the time and arranged the hiring.

The significance of such occupational opportunities for the social organization of low-income working-class families in Greenpoint-Williamsburg lay in the temporary and insecure nature of available employment. The women had worked for two or three years and then found themselves unemployed for months or years at a time. The men also changed their place of employment frequently, although they were employed for longer periods.

When the subject came up, people tended to disparage work in the local factories, although they themselves might have worked there. They regarded such work as their last choice of employment. In addition to the lack of security, working conditions contributed to the undesirability of the jobs.

The conditions in a Williamsburg cheap purse factory where I worked as a packer were unsavory. The factory consisted of a single warehouse with different machines in different sections. The machines never stopped, and the noise level was painfully high. Cats roamed around between the machines, presumably to reduce the number of rats. The only separate room was the manager's office, containing two large tables covered with papers and layers of dust and two wooden chairs. When I appeared to start work, the factory manager informed me that he did not think it would suit me. He said that the wages were too low for a woman to live alone on. He explained that most of his workers lived with their families and that their incomes were supplementary to the household, not sufficient to support them. There were fifty people, men and women, working in the warehouse, which was situated in a desolate, factory-dominated area along Flushing Avenue. When work stopped for the lunch break, which was the only break of the day and lasted for one hour, the workers sat in little groups between the machines and ate the food that they had brought. Some women took their food to eat in the bathrooms. The toilet facili-

ties were completely stopped up. The floor was uneven and had
an earth rather than a cement covering. The sink was filthy, and
water constantly trickled out of the cold water faucet. The women
stood in line waiting for a drink of water and gossiping, apparently
happy to have free time away from the machines. Women stayed
in this bathroom through the lunch hour, joking and eating their
food. Such conditions were not an incentive to people in Greenpoint to accept jobs in local factories if there were any possible
alternatives.

In the face of the low pay, insecurity, and poor working conditions of local factory employment, the importance of other aspects
of the job market and forms of financial support becomes clearer.

Enlistment in the United States Armed Forces

Men from at least three of the ten households studied had recently
been stationed at army bases in the southern United States while
their wives stayed in Brooklyn. One man returned in January
1975, the second in June 1976, and the third was still a serviceman in June 1978. Two of these men claimed they had signed up
because no other employment was available. The same two men
married while they were in the army. One remained in military
service for a year after he was married. After their first baby was
born, he returned home at his wife's insistence to look for work
but did not find full-time employment for two years. The second
man enlisted when his girlfriend became pregnant. She lived on
public assistance with the child, and he sent her money from his
military wages. When she became pregnant for a second time,
with twins, they married so that she would receive the family
stipend provided by the military. Other benefits for military families included refunds for medical expenses and discounts at the commissary. However, since the commissary was situated at the army
base at Fort Hamilton, access was difficult, and few Greenpoint-
Williamsburg women managed to find a car to drive to the store.

The three men in the army were only allotted short leave
periods, sometimes a few days at a time, and their lives were
closely monitored. When the twins were born, their father was not
allowed to leave until a social worker from the hospital inter-

vened and telephoned the Red Cross.[2] Only after the Red Cross contacted the military authorities was the father finally allowed a week's leave. One of the twins had remained in an incubator at the hospital, and the mother was under heavy strain. She was caring for two children at home and visiting a third, newborn child in a hospital that was a forty-five-minute bus journey away. The wife did not know until the day her husband arrived whether or not he would be permitted to visit. Similar events occurred at other periods of crisis in the household. The appearance of the father could never be relied on but was dependent on decisions of military authorities, communicated through the Red Cross.

The insecure position of the wife of a serviceman led these women to move in with their own mothers or their husbands' relatives. In this way they secured assistance with the daily crises of child-rearing and reduced their expenses. Thus a man's enlistment in the military was liable to precipitate major changes in household composition. Adjustments occurred both in his own household and in other households on which he and his wife or girlfriend might rely for support.

Military regulations reinforced certain attitudes which were common among low-income people in Greenpoint-Williamsburg. The imposition of external decisions, combined with lack of recourse and the threat of punitary measures, represented an intensification of the form of bureaucracy to which people had become accustomed in their dealings with public assistance and other public programs. Wives could not telephone their husbands directly. They had difficulty ascertaining the conditions under which leave was permitted, and policy in this matter did not appear consistent or predictable. Wives were afraid to create difficulties by insisting on the cooperation of the military authorities. They were also afraid that at some point they or their husbands might do something contrary to regulations and that financial support would be withdrawn.

The military controlled the domestic lives of both the man who enlisted and his wife or girlfriend. A stipend was sent to the wife, and it was raised with the birth of each child. Army regulations

2. The Red Cross served as an intermediary between the families of servicemen and the military authorities.

determined when and for how long a husband visited his family. Travel fare home was supplied.

In two cases in this study, the army was a precipitating factor in marriage. Parents who had previously been living together unmarried married when the father joined the army so that the family might receive a military stipend and other benefits. In both cases marriage had been deferred in order to facilitate the mother's enrollment for public assistance. If the mother claimed that the father was unavailable, his earnings would not be considered in the evaluation of her allowance for welfare assistance.[3] Thus in contrasting ways, military enlistment and public assistance affected relations within the household. Even the decision to marry was influenced by the consideration of regulations in these two national bureaucratic systems. In these ways military enlistment had more far-reaching implications for neighborhood social organization than those of other forms of employment. The implications were as extensive as, although different from, the influences of the public assistance programs described in later chapters.

The CETA Program: Employment and Political Connections

Job opportunities associated with the CETA program were the result of a series of decisions by the federal government following the Emergency Employment Act of 1971. In 1973 the Comprehensive Employment and Training Act was passed, and in 1974 the Emergency Jobs and Unemployment Assistance Act. In May 1975, with national unemployment levels at 8.9 percent, the Emergency Employment Appropriations Act passed the House and the Senate. Although the original bill was vetoed by President Ford, the employment measures it contained were finally approved in 1975. In 1978, amid continuing debate, the CETA program was still in operation, although employment was still dependent on uncertain federal legislation.[4] In 1981 the Reagan administration discontinued a large proportion of the remaining CETA jobs.

3. For a more detailed discussion of the welfare budget, see chapter 5.
4. For a discussion of the history of the public employment programs of the 1970s and the national debates surrounding them, see Hallman (1977).

Federal regulations required that a public service employee be laid off for thirty days before rehiring on the CETA program. Other workers had to have been unemployed for only seven days. Each program also had residency requirements. Workers had to live in the areas where they were hired, but these requirements were not strictly implemented (Hallman, 1977). The program was not aimed at particularly disadvantaged workers and, in comparison to their proportion among the unemployed, older, male, educated workers were more likely to be hired for CETA positions than younger, less educated, and female workers. The CETA positions were advantageous jobs for poor working-class people. In relation to the Emergency Employment Act as it operated from 1971 to 1973, Hallman remarks: "Wages were up for clerical, sales, service, bench work, farming, and forestry occupations, and down for professional, technical, managerial, processing, machine trades, and structural work" (ibid., p. 142). Of the employment program ratified on December 31, 1974, and implemented in the first six months of 1975, he states: "There was no shortage of applicants, and in a few places there were near riots as hundreds crowded in to apply for the few jobs available" (ibid., p. 180). Thus CETA positions were highly prized jobs in many areas of the country.

Public employment programs had been in operation in New York City since the provisions were first approved in August 1971. The Human Resources Administration (HRA) had assigned CETA employees to the Board of Education, Health and Hospitals Administration, and the Police Department. In response to union pressure, particularly from the United Federation of Teachers, a fourth of these emergency jobs were directed to rehiring laid-off employees. Other jobs were restricted to entry-level positions which would not interfere with the opportunities for promotion of current employees (Hallman, 1977, p. 118). These restrictions resulted in a divided pay scale: rehired workers were paid salaries of $10,000 to $12,000 a year, while those veterans and disadvantaged poor who were hired in the entry-level positions were earning only $5,000 to $7,000 (ibid., p. 77). Similar divisions in pay scale were still in operation in 1975 when CETA funds were distributed in Greenpoint-Williamsburg.

The low pay and entry-level jobs available to disadvantaged workers provoked hostility and controversy toward the CETA program among many segments of the population. Community organizers on the Lower East Side of Manhattan, where a large population of politically active, poor working-class people was to be found, refused to apply for CETA funding. They feared the adverse reaction of local residents toward positions that were regarded both as union-breaking and exploitative of poor workers. Trained community organizers were accustomed to twice the pay allotted to community organizers employed by the CETA program. However, none of these objections to the CETA program were raised by Greenpoint or Williamsburg residents. Perhaps they were less politically informed than residents of other parts of the city, or else the advantages of employment outweighed these considerations.

In 1975, following the authorization of CETA Title VI on December 31, 1974, several thousand jobs with pay scales ranging from $7,000 to $12,000 were introduced throughout New York City. The program was greatly expanded, and jobs were distributed in numerous public service departments as well as in all branches of the City University of New York. A local city councilman informed an active community organizer, Pat Newton, that funds would be available from the Human Resources Administration in New York City. She contacted fourteen community agencies and organized the Greenpoint-Williamsburg Council to apply for funds from the New York City Board of Estimate. Pat Newton was an astute politician with much experience in the neighborhood, and the coalition included influential individuals from many different groups in the area. The council included the Northside Neighborhood Committee, the Italian-American Committee, the Polish-American Community Center, Greenpoint Educational Center (which was directed by the co-district leader of the Democratic party in Greenpoint-Williamsburg), the Greenpoint-Williamsburg Improvement Council (which was conected to the local state senator and directed by a candidate for the school board elections), the Women's Center (organized by Pat Newton), Williamsburg Neighborhood Services (directed by an influential woman who was also a member of several other neighborhood boards), a Neighborhood Housing Council (with affiliations with the Pratt Center for Community and Environmental Development), and Woodlawn Housing Community Services. Since officials from the Democratic party also knew people on the Board of Estimate, their influence may have helped the Greenpoint-Williamsburg Council obtain approval for its application.

Each of the fourteen agencies received a portion of the allocated money sufficient for salaries of about ten employees at $7,000 to $9,000 a year. Operating expenses were not included, and each agency had to raise contributions from local banks, businesses, residents, and other sources. The term of the original contract was from May 12, 1975, to February 9, 1976, but the coalition had received a verbal commitment for contract renewal through June 30, 1976, and the CETA positions were still receiving funds in May 1978.

The council formed a board composed of representatives from each of the different agencies. Grievances among CETA employees in each agency were submitted first to the agency directors and next were to be brought before the council board. Finally, CETA employees could appeal to the Department of Employment of the HRA. Each agency had its "liaison" officer whose official position was to mediate between the board and the agency. In practice, the liaison officer seemed to mediate between the director of Williamsburg Neighborhood Services and the agencies, since board meetings were held infrequently. Although each agency was responsible for its own hiring, much political maneuvering was connected with the hiring and firing of CETA employees, involving both the members of the board and Williamsburg Neighborhood Services. Agencies had problems maintaining independent hiring and firing practices and also conforming with the requirements of board members. Constructed on a political coalition, the Greenpoint-Williamsburg Council was subject to pressures associated with different political interests, and employees were often threatened with the loss of their jobs if they voiced contrary views in public. In several instances CETA employees were fired and rehired by different agencies in the coalition.

Since CETA jobs were advertised only for a week and had to

be filled quickly (as one of the conditions for their allotment), the people hired generally had some connection with local organizations. A person had to know when and where hiring was taking place and to realize that he or she might qualify. The jobs were a new phenomenon in the area, and many people were not aware of the eligibility requirements. It was mainly those people who were informed by a friend connected to the employers or who knew the organizers themselves who managed to obtain positions. Although Greenpoint and Williamsburg residents were hired under the CETA program, each agency also hired college-educated unemployed workers from outside the area. The opinions of these employees and their interests had some impact on the projects and orientations of the various agencies. The Women's Center employed women with feminist orientations, which they expressed more forcefully and in different ways from Greenpoint-Williamsburg women. The Neighborhood Housing Council employed architecture students with considerable ability in writing proposals and planning projects for the area. The hiring of such educated workers conformed with the national pattern of the CETA program, in which, as mentioned above, proportionally larger numbers of unemployed but not disadvantaged workers were served.

The position of CETA employees and their ability to obtain and retain jobs depended partly on the political interests of the agency directors and partly on pressures and alliances which developed within the board of the Greenpoint-Williamsburg Council. Thus the CETA funds and the employees hired affected the development of events in the neighborhood, and, as will become evident, the involvement of employees in local organizations.

Since many of the appointments were originally political, CETA became the focus of much attention. Factions developed within the council and among the employees. Retaining a CETA position came to require attendance at evening meetings, for example, those of the school board or civic council, allegiance to certain directors, and participation outside regular work hours in events organized by the agencies.

Most of the community agencies were involved in services such as assistance with welfare applications; action projects, including the attempt to keep Greenpoint Hospital facilities available or the effort to maintain the local firehouse; adult education; concern with child and wife abuse; and the improvement of facilities for young children and senior citizens. Local events, such as the Bicentennial Barge, and fund-raising activities such as dances and an annual fair were also organized.

Employment in the CETA program affected not only political action in the neighborhood but also household structure. Many women who had previously been active in local voluntary organizations obtained positions with the program. The immediate demand for the jobs was an indication that such women, while unemployed at the time, were ready to take full-time work. Lack of opportunity rather than the absence of financial need or the responsibility for domestic chores had prevented them from working earlier.[5]

Despite salaries lower than those received by qualified social workers, an individual's employment in the CETA program often considerably raised a household's standard of living. This change affected household composition in a variety of ways. At least two people whom I encountered, a man and a woman in their twenties, moved out of their parents' households after becoming CETA employees. Prior to obtaining CETA jobs, they could not have paid their own rents. At least three wives separated from their husbands after CETA employment provided them with independent incomes. In two households where husbands and wives stayed together, the extra money generated from the wives' CETA salaries made it possible for each family to invest in a house although in one case the husband was intermittently unemployed.

The involvement in community activities required by CETA employment placed heavy demands on households. A wife or husband might be employed ten hours every day, including attendance at neighborhood meetings after work hours almost daily. If children were placed in day care centers, arrangements had to be made for the husband or another relative to collect the child. Often the wife's absence precipitated major conflicts in the home, sometimes resulting in partial marital separations. The active participation of the Women's Center and feminist women from Man-

5. For a discussion of this issue in relation to women in the labor market, see Oppenheimer (1970).

hattan in neighborhood activities also engendered doubts among Greenpoint-Williamsburg women employed at the center about their own marriage and child-rearing roles and their relationships with their husbands.

The influence of the CETA program on the politics of Greenpoint and Williamsburg has to be seen as a consequence of the financial advantages of the jobs, in relation to the high level of unemployment in the area and the unappealing alternatives of factory work, military enlistment, and public assistance (to be considered in the next two chapters). Despite accusations that the CETA program was replacing well-paid union jobs with dead-end positions at half the salary, Greenpoint and Williamsburg residents welcomed the employment. In the face of local alternatives, a poorly paid position with no promise of permanence, even if it was dependent on political favors, stood out as a privileged opportunity.

Each form of employment open to poor working-class residents of Greenpoint and Williamsburg, in local industry, the CETA program, or the United States Armed Forces, carried with it implications for household structure and political organization in the neighborhood. The form of employment affected household composition, the situation of women, and arrangements for child supervision. The insecurity of employment in local industry may have put pressure on workers to remain unmarried and to rely partially on public assistance. The poor working conditions and lack of employment opportunity sometimes discouraged women from looking for jobs and reduced the earning capacity of the household. Among the people I observed, military enlistment altered household composition and precipitated marriages but tended to weaken bonds between husband and wife by placing distance and institutional barriers to communication between them. Employment in the CETA program also influenced household composition when improved finances allowed members of a household to move to their own apartments. However, CETA employment also placed strains on the household because of the levels of participation in community activities required.

Low wages, poor working conditions, and high levels of unemployment created a situation in which political jobs were highly valued and protest feared. The dependency of workers set the scene for patronage. It created the possibility for CETA employees to be persuaded to support factions which seemed to ensure their jobs. At the same time, in situations where they were encouraged by directors of community agencies, CETA workers employed as community organizers stimulated participation in local organizations and, as will become evident later, initiated and provided support for protest actions in the area. However, each of these actions sparked controversy among members of the board of the Greenpoint-Williamsburg Council and precipitated opposition tactics such as those discussed in chapter 11.

Household composition and political organization among poor working-class residents of Greenpoint and Williamsburg were in part a consequence of the structure of occupational opportunity. The behavior of residents in the area and their activities can only be understood when viewed in relation to employment possibilities and their constraining and structuring effects on household organization and political involvement.

CHAPTER 4

The Welfare System: Interaction Between Officials and Clients

Welfare assistance reflects a crucial aspect of low-income life: interaction with government institutions. Attitudes and roles fostered by the public assistance program indicate the constraining influence of state bureaucracies, upon which low-income people are commonly dependent. The description presented here of relations between clients and officials and of pressures on each side also stands as a general picture of experiences of low-income people in the United States. As the discussion of the neighborhood in the previous chapter makes evident, Greenpoint-Williamsburg economic life reflected that of the nation from 1975 to 1977. Just as high unemployment, military enlistment, and the CETA program were nationwide phenomena, so was the welfare program. Since reliance on welfare assistance was a more constant factor in the structuring of most low-income households than any particular job situation, it is important to discuss the process and its influences in some detail.

This chapter outlines the procedures which an applicant had to follow in order to enroll for public assistance. The focus is primarily on interaction between client and welfare officer, and the officers' perceptions of their role in the welfare bureaucracy are analyzed. The next chapter examines problems and attitudes which welfare regulations generated among clients.

Aid to Dependent Children, later to become Aid to Families

with Dependent Children (AFDC), was created by Title IV of the Social Security Act of 1935. This was a federal program, administered under regulations which differed with each state. In 1977 each state contributed from 17 percent to 50 percent of assistance costs, depending on its relative per capita income, as well as 50 percent of administrative costs. In fiscal year 1977, federal expenditure was estimated at $5,718 million, and each month, on the average, over ten million recipients in over three million families received financial aid (Lawrence and Leeds, 1978). Aid to Families with Dependent Children–Unemployed Father (AFDC-U) is a similar program, administered under the same regulations as AFDC. In fiscal year 1977, $400 million of federal money was spent on AFDC-U to supply, on the average, 700,000 recipients in 150,000 families with monthly financial assistance.

AFDC was designed to help cover the minimum cost of food, shelter, clothing, and other items of daily living to needy dependent children living in broken homes. AFDC-U supplies similar assistance to families where both parents were present but the father was unemployed.

Home Relief and Veterans' Assistance were given to needy individuals and to families who did not meet the requirements of the federally aided AFDC program and were not eligible for Supplemental Security Income (SSI), the federal program for the aged, blind, and disabled.[1] Aside from the eligibility requirements, the regulations applying to each program were the same.[2]

Public assistance in New York City was supervised by the New York State Department of Social Services and administered by the New York City Department of Social Services. At the time of this study, there were thirty-six income maintenance centers in New York City from which welfare assistance could be obtained by eligible applicants. Fourteen of these centers were in Brooklyn.

1. SSI was a program administered by the United States Social Security Administration for those who were sixty-five or over, blind or disabled, and were in need as determined by the regulations of the administration.
2. Regulations discussed in this book were taken from *Income Maintenance: Sourcebook for Regulations* (New York State Department of Social Services, n.d.). This was the book of regulations used by welfare officials at the income maintenance center for Williamsburg residents.

Recipients were assigned to centers according to the zip code of their residential address.

In order to apply for welfare assistance, clients had to complete application forms several pages long. The forms were distributed to community service agencies where assistance in filling them out was available. Income maintenance centers were not organized to assist recipients; the orientation of welfare officials was not always in the client's favor. In fact, we shall see that regulations involved in public assistance were often so complicated as to require an intermediary between welfare officials and clients. Workers from community service agencies frequently filled this role. They assisted clients in negotiating complicated regulations, applying for welfare assistance, and requesting a fair hearing if the application was not accepted.

Welfare allocations were not easy to obtain and required expenditures of energy that most people would avoid if possible. Many eligible clients gave up in the face of bureaucratic delay and seemingly insurmountable obstacles. If a person made his way through the maze once, he was often reluctant to jeopardize his position by attempting to alter his status in any way.

The Welfare Process

The income maintenance center for Greenpoint-Williamsburg lies in downtown Brooklyn. Relief applicants must take either a bus or two subways to reach the office which serves them. (A welfare office in Williamsburg provides only Social Security checks for senior citizens.) There are several offices of the New York City Department of Social Services in downtown Brooklyn. The events described here occurred at the Williamsburg center in connection with applications for welfare assistance based on regulations for families on AFDC and Home Relief as they were in 1976.

In order to apply for welfare, an individual had to appear at the correct office for his district by 10 A.M. If he arrived after that time, he was liable to be refused service and told to return the next day. Many people arrived by 8 A.M. or earlier in order to be near the front of the line at 9 A.M. when the offices opened. Often the lines were long. Several guards in uniform supervised the people waiting. At 9 A.M. the receptionist at the information desk began to hand out numbers. Each person on line received a number and was then sent to sit on wooden benches in the main hall until his number was called.

Lunches and thermoses of coffee were in evidence. The period of waiting was unpredictable but often extended. Although the system allowed welfare officers to take staggered lunch breaks, the applicant could not leave in case his number was called. No numbers were assigned after 10 A.M., and none were called after 2 P.M. If a recipient had a problem which had not been solved by 2 or 3 P.M., it was common for him to be left waiting until 5 P.M., when he was instructed to return the following morning.

On the benches in the waiting section were numerous young women with their children scrambling around them. Many were foreigners sitting with neighbors and relatives, interpreters who came to help them through the system. A few couples sat together, the men often staring bleakly ahead of them. Older women could be seen, sometimes with their sons or daughters, sometimes alone. Many of the people looked pale and bewildered. Others looked angry and upset. On the second floor, where the applications were filed, the level of noise was considerably heightened, but downstairs on the wooden benches people waited quietly. Only the children caused their mothers to raise their voices or hit them from time to time. Groups of Hispanic people, Hassidic men, Italians who spoke no English, black people, and Americans without ethnic affiliations were to be found waiting at the Williamsburg income maintenance center.

When a number was called, the individuals concerned were directed to the line for "groups" by one of the many guards who patrolled the center. Welfare workers at the counter assigned clients to one of the officers responsible for that group of applicants. On any day there might be from one to two hundred people waiting on the line. Often a mother, her son and daughter, and a friendly neighbor would walk over and begin their passage down the line. The neighbor and children came to help with translation and assist with bureaucratic difficulties. The "group" receptionists checked forms to certify that the client had brought the correct information and identification. If something was missing, such as the appointment forms, the applicant was told to return the next day with the right material. If the papers met the clerk's approval, the client was sent upstairs to wait for an interview with a welfare officer.

Upstairs, people sat on chairs arranged along the sides of two walls. In the center of the large hall were long rows of desks, each supplied with a telephone and covered with papers. At approximately ten of the more than twenty-five desks, welfare officers were seated. About five of these officials were generally busy interviewing clients.

As a client made his way to the second floor, an officer was informed by telephone. Any available officer was chosen since it was welfare policy not to assign any one official to a particular client. In the past each client was the responsibility of a single official, but the policy was recently changed. Welfare administrators claimed that this was to increase efficiency. It also reduced the influence of a client over the official and prevented any form of special help or interest from developing on the part of the welfare representative.

The client climbed the stairs and again took a seat. He was usually unaware of which officer he was waiting for, but was accustomed to waiting until called. A client might sit and watch unoccupied officials for several hours before his name was called; sometimes he was called over immediately. This interview with the officer was the initial step of a long process. The welfare worker sat with his papers in front of him while the client stood opposite. The worker usually began by asking for identification. If it was the client's first visit, he handed him an application form, DSS-1994, Application of Need for Public Assistance, and told him to return the next day with the form filled out. He would also hand the applicant a list of identification forms and letters which were required in order that the application be considered.

If the client had already filled out the application, possibly at a community service agency, he handed it over to the officer along with the assortment of other forms which had been requested. A new applicant was generally required to furnish the welfare officer with a rent stub and information and evidence about previous jobs and forms of maintenance. Other letters might be requested, depending on the nature of the case, the attitude of the particular worker, and current departmental policy. The New York State regulations read:

> *Establishing the Facts:* The basic document for establishing facts concerning eligibility is the DSS-1994, Application of Need for Public Assistance. The primary source for all information is the A/R [applicant/recipient] himself, members of his household and public records. Information from the above individuals shall be verified when necessary, either by documentation or by confirming information from others, such as employers, relatives, banks, insurance companies, landlords, schools and social agencies. Any persons likely to be able to throw light on events or conditions claimed are considered valid sources for verifying A/R statements. (New York State Department of Social Services, n.d., item B-a-01)

It was not a legal requirement that letters be notarized. A department supervisor had circulated directives informing officers that this was not expected. Nevertheless, I observed that each officer required that letters about previous maintenance and other information be notarized.

After his application was accepted, the client was sent for a medical examination, which required different waiting lines in another part of the building. This was followed by an interview about possible employment and further waiting. Next the client was often sent for several compulsory and usually fruitless job interviews. Registration for welfare assistance generally necessitated three or four return visits to the center, and each visit could require a full day of waiting. The visits could be spread out over a period of weeks, depending upon how busy the center was and when the client chose to return.

The periods of waiting and the frequent return visits required by officials were not a necessary direct result of regulations of the New York State Department of Social Services. The regulations did not require particular material evidence, but they did call for "personal evaluation" of evidence on the part of the official, thus permitting more stringent requirements to be enforced at his discretion. It was this stipulation that contributed to delays experienced by welfare applicants.

On each of the four occasions I witnessed, when the client presented his rent stub, information about previous employment, and present medical disability or need for support, he was delayed by the official. After up to an hour or more of discussion, wrangling, or simply waiting quietly while the officer made inquiries in other parts of the building, the client was told that he had presented insufficient information and instructed to return in a few days or the next morning with the necessary documents. Often such documents were unobtainable, and the official's request prevented the client from applying for assistance.

A sick twenty-two-year-old man, for example, was required to return to a migrant labor camp in New Jersey in order to collect evidence that he had been employed there two years previously and that the firm he worked for had paid his fare from Puerto Rico. The man presented to the official the contract for the work, which he still possessed. On the contract, which he had signed, it was clearly stated that he had to work at the camp for two years in order to repay the company for his fare from Puerto Rico. The officer would not accept the client's documentation, even though he had the contract before him as evidence of previous employment. He appeared to be creating difficulties because of a personal evaluation that the applicant was not eligible for welfare despite his fulfilling the formal requirements.

Such idiosyncratic action on the part of welfare officers was common. They considered it legitimate and an essential requirement of their jobs. Officers felt justified in disbelieving clients who presented formal evidence of their situations. They manifested this disbelief and mistrust of most applicants by making their own personal requirements stiffer than the rudimentary format which was outlined in department policy.

From the point of view of the welfare department, the officers were right. Clients were not providing them with completely accurate information, and in challenging formal proofs, officials were carrying out their assigned tasks. It was difficult for any recipient to conform to the requirements for obtaining welfare. As we shall see later, the regulations could not be uniformly imposed on the day-to-day contingencies of people's lives. However, people who went through the welfare process were generally in legitimate and often desperate need of the money. They were also legally entitled to public assistance, which was officially provided as a "last resort" for all people without adequate means of support. They had difficulty molding their lives to fit the stringent regulations under which the bureaucracy distributed its funds. When the correct evidence and information was presented, welfare officers were required to register the client. Many of them delayed the process because they felt the evidence was faulty. They seemed unaware that it was the regulations of the bureaucracy itself that created conditions under which people had to present false evidence to obtain money to which they were legally entitled.

Much of the blame for high taxes and government expenditure has long been attributed to welfare costs. A major concern of both national and municipal administrations has been to reduce enrollment for public assistance. For the past eight years, because of the financial straits of New York City, the pressure on the Department of Social Services has been to cut down on expenses. Saving money can be translated into restricting welfare rolls as much as possible. As we have seen, this may be carried out largely through exposing clients to excessive delays and difficulties. Only when the pressure of clients protesting in welfare offices balanced the pressure on officials not to provide assistance were significant gains in access to benefits made by the poor (Piven and Cloward, 1971). Welfare officers were not encouraged by the directors of income maintenance centers to enroll large numbers of clients. On the contrary, as the extensive regulations and complicated requirements attest, the major concern was to prevent an individual with resources or any possibility of alternative income from receiving assistance.

In light of these policies, the difficulties which welfare clients underwent were not simply a result of the inefficiencies of a mushrooming bureaucracy or a problem of implementation of policy which could be ironed out with correct planning. The problems certainly cannot be attributed to the personalities of the welfare officials, themselves under severe bureaucratic constraints. They were a direct or indirect result of planning.

CHAPTER 5

The Welfare System: Regulations and the Life of a Welfare Recipient

Bureaucratic delay, combined with stringent regulations, shaped the behavior of clients. Such influences were not always in the direction intended by the regulations. The conjunction of regulations for welfare assistance with the varied and complicated lives of recipients led to a system which did not correspond either to the explicit requirements of the New York State Department of Social Services or to the needs of poor people. This lack of correspondence contributed to the sense of fear and insecurity among low-income working-class people which was fostered both by the uncertain employment situation already described and, as we shall see, by landlord-tenant relations. Each of these situations affected the development and effectiveness of efforts toward political articulation.

Clients were required to inform the department of any change of address. If they moved to a new apartment, an officer had to inspect it before rent would be paid. I witnessed several situations where a delay in the housing division at a welfare center led to or accentuated crises in the home.

In one case a woman had a large hole in her kitchen floor. She claimed to have seen rats climbing through it. The Department of Social Services had sent someone to inspect her apartment, and her description was corroborated. Although the woman had located a new apartment, no one arrived to inspect it. Her family had been living with the rat hazard for over a week, delayed only by the lack of departmental approval for her move. Finally, in response to pressure from me and several representatives from community agencies, she managed to obtain an emergency approval to move. Rigid regulations applied to changing lives constantly placed recipients in the wrong or, as in this case, forced them to live under intolerable conditions.

As stated by *Income Maintenance: Sourcebook for Regulations,* "Eligibility for a grant is determined to exist when there is a deficit between the amount required as specified in the regulations establishing the Standards of Assistance and the available resources of the A/R" (New York State Department of Social Services, n.d., item B-a-01). In 1976 the "Statewide Monthly Standard of Need," exclusive of shelter and fuel for heating, was calculated as follows:

Number of Persons						
1	2	3	4	5	6	Each Additional Person
$94	$150	$200	$248	$318	$368	$50

The household of a pregnant woman was considered increased by one person from the fourth month of pregnancy (for basic allowance only), when the condition had been medically verified (New York State Department of Social Services, n.d., item B-f-03). The amount for each household's check was computed through calculation of all income from relatives, employment, assets, or other sources which the household received.[4] If the total outside income was less than the statewide monthly standard of need for the number of household members, a household was

4. Transportation and eating expenses at work were calculated and subtracted from the total household income:

Monthly Standard of Need:
Restaurant Allowance Schedule

Dinner in a restaurant	$29
Lunch and dinner in a restaurant	$47
All meals in a restaurant	$64

(New York State Department of Social Services, n.d., item B-f-03) entitled to assistance to make up the difference. Checks were mailed every two weeks for one half of the sum of money necessary to make up the total allowance for each household size listed above.

Three examples of welfare budgets are given below.

1. Mary Sanchez's household, January 1976:

Mrs. Sanchez, Jeannie, Anthony, Sharon, and her three-year-old son lived in Mrs. Sanchez's apartment. Jeannie, Anthony, and Sharon were Mary Sanchez's children. Sharon was married to Roberto, who was away in the army. When he came home, he also lived in the apartment. When Jeannie's fiancé came home from the army, he lived there too. Only Mary Sanchez and her dependent Jeannie were registered in Mrs. Sanchez's file at the welfare department.

Mary Sanchez paid $104 a month in rent, which she received in biweekly checks of $52 from the welfare department. The checks had to be signed by both herself and the landlord before they could be cashed. She also received $54 every two weeks for living expenses. Nineteen dollars had been substracted because she owed back rent. She had previously taken part of her rent allowance for household expenses, and the welfare department now took the money out of her biweekly allotment to pay back the landlord. Out of the $54 for living expenses, Mrs. Sanchez was entitled to spend $22 for $46 worth of food stamps. These subtractions left her $32 to live on for two weeks. With this money she had to pay the gas and electric bills and buy clothing, soap, and necessities other than food. She also paid for transportation, for cigarettes, and for her major form of entertainment, evenings at bingo. Anthony had no other source of support, and Mrs. Sanchez paid for his expenses as well as Jeannie's with her allowance. Sharon received $216 a month from the army for herself and her son. She contributed most of this money toward household expenses.

On the day that Sharon's check arrived, Sharon and her mother generally went directly to the supermarket. They cashed the check and bought the numerous groceries that they had had to do without the week before. Sharon also paid off the debts that Mrs. Sanchez had incurred during the previous month when neither of them had had any money. Some bills, however, such as the gas and electric, mounted up until even Sharon's check was not sufficient. Sharon was lucky if her check lasted until the second week of the month.

2. Jenny Ferguson's budget, September 1975:

Mrs. Ferguson's husband, John, had just left the army. They had one two-week-old son. Mr. Ferguson received $57 a week unemployment. They received $33 every two weeks as a supplement from the welfare department. The Ferguson's were able to buy $44 worth of food stamps for $25 every two weeks. They received a welfare allowance only for food, gas, electricity, and other purchases, as the welfare department maintained that the unemployment payments should cover their rent of $140 a month. When outlining her budget for me, Jenny Ferguson remarked, "Now you can see why we were starving."

3. Eugenia Romanes's budget, March 1976:

The Romanes welfare budget was supplementary to Juan Romanes's earnings. Mr. Romanes earned $240 every two weeks. A husband's wages are calculated by the welfare department with work expenses such as transportation subtracted. Mrs. Romanes received $64 from unemployment compensation. Over a two-week period, their total income was $304, and their rent was $80. This left them with a total of $224 to spend. Welfare allowed $184 for a family of six. Twenty-five dollars was added to the $184 for every additional person. Since the Romanes household had *nine* people, their welfare allowance should have totaled $259. Therefore the Romaneses should have received an extra $35 in addition to their biweekly income of $224.

In fact, Mrs. Romanes did not receive anything from the welfare department for six months. After her first visit to complain, they assigned her a check for $10.80 every two weeks. After her second visit, when she still had received nothing, she was allotted a supplement of $12.80 every two weeks.

Welfare recipients were often penalized by inflexible regulations in connection with the calculation of their budgets. The amount of assistance for each household was decided according to the number of residents. This number was not constant, and clients were required to inform the department of any change in their situations. If recipients failed to report reductions in household composition, they were likely to be charged with fraud or lose some portion of their supplement.[1] Instances of such charges will be described later in the chapter. The difficulties involved in complying with these apparently simple regulations about reporting dependents and the problems which the requirements created in the lives of welfare recipients are amply illustrated in several of the following examples.

Jeannie Sanchez (age seventeen and registered for welfare assistance in her mother's household) was leaving her mother Mary's apartment to marry a man who lived on an army base in the South. Mary Sanchez informed the welfare department of her daughter's scheduled departure. Jeannie had had her engagement shower and arranged to leave in May. Mary Sanchez's welfare allotment for Jeannie was cancelled.

Just at this time, however, Jeannie's fiancé ran into legal problems with the army. He deserted to escape arrest for drug-trafficking, and was soon back in New York City. Jeannie did not leave her mother's household until late August. Mary Sanchez did not inform the welfare department of this change. In the intervening three months, she was supporting herself, her daughter Jeannie, and her nineteen-year-old son Anthony on the basis of a welfare

1. According to the New York State Department of Social Services:

In case of suspected fraud which was or should have been referred by a local social services department to a district attorney or other prosecuting official pursuant to the provisions of this department, and in which case there is evidence in the judgment of the social services official of such local department, which clearly establishes that the applicant or recipient of public assistance and care willfully withheld from such local social services department at the time of his application for public assistance and care, or any time thereafter, information about his income or resources, and as a result of withholding such information from the local social services department, the applicant or recipient has received grants, or public assistance, or care at public expense to which he was not entitled in whole or part, the social services official shall recover the amount of public assistance granted or the cost of care provided to the applicant or recipient to which he was not entitled as follows:

Recoupment is made irrespective of income or resources at any time (there is no 12 month limit), only where the applicant or recipient is well aware of and understands his responsibility to report changes in circumstances which might affect his eligibilty or grant. . . . So as not to create a hardship, recoupment is limited to 10% of the household needs. When there are 2 or more recoupments being made for different reasons, the limit is 15%. (New York State Department of Social Services, n.d., item B-i-04)

allotment for one person. Her rent was paid, and at this time she received $47 every two weeks for food and other expenses. Some of that money went to pay for food stamps. Jeannie found a part-time job before she left but was not able to retain it for long. Anthony had been unemployed as a construction worker for over a year, and his unemployment compensation had expired three months earlier. He had been unable to register for welfare due to previous irregularities.

When Anthony first found a job in construction, in his father's union, Mrs. Sanchez claimed that he had left for California. In this way she was able to continue to receive welfare although her son, then sixteen years old, was earning an income. Her husband had left her with four young children ten years earlier. Since she claimed that his whereabouts were unknown, his earnings did not come under review at that time.[2] When Anthony became unemployed for an extended period, he was justifiably afraid to request welfare assistance for fear that his mother's previous arrangements would be questioned. At his application for assistance, he would have been required to list his history of employment and his prior forms of maintenance. Answers to such requests might have caused Mrs. Sanchez to be charged with fraud.

In a similar situation, to be described later, a woman was charged with a $28,000 debt to the welfare department when officials suspected that she was living with her husband without informing them. Such a debt would have been subtracted in small portions from her biweekly allowance.

2. *Income Maintenance: Sourcebook for Regulations* requires that relatives contribute to the maintenance of the household:

> There shall be reviewed with the applicant the whereabouts of close relatives and their ability and willingness to assist him financially. The nature and extent of past assistance shall be explored, together with the appropriateness and possibility of continuing or initiating assistance at this time. The ability of legally responsible relatives [which include Spouse responsible for Spouse, Parent for Minor—whether or not parents are married, Stepparent for Step-minor] shall be evaluated and their obligations explained. (New York State Department of Social Services, n.d., item B-3-01)

If a father was not supplying financial support for the child, the mother or responsible individual was usually required to bring her case to Family Court to establish that the father was unavailable and that she was entitled to welfare assistance.

It is clear that Anthony's refusal to apply for welfare and his subsequent dependence on his mother's allotment were based on a real danger of jeopardizing the financial position of the household, which was already precarious.

The reporting of dependents was not a simple matter. It involved evaluation of all members of the household, their opportunities for employment, and future problems which they might encounter. Although Mary Sanchez was aware of the complications, often, as in Anthony's case, the decision to evade regulations in one period caused later problems. In Jeannie's case the opposite problem occurred. In complying to the letter of the regulations, Mary Sanchez forfeited benefits to which she would have been entitled.

A second situation, unknown to Anthony, provides further justification for his failure to apply for welfare. A welfare recipient's son moved back into her household. He was unemployed, and she was supporting him on her allotment, which already included four daughters, two of whom had their own children. The welfare department refused to accept the son's application, citing insufficient evidence of prior maintenance. When the case was taken before a "fair hearing" (an appeal process within the state Department of Social Services which will be described later), the hearing officer accused the young man of dealing in drugs and refused to grant him welfare. In so ruling he was sending the applicant back to continue living from drug-trafficking. His history was held against him, preventing any change in his life-style.

These examples show that reporting extra dependents did not automatically lead to an increase in a welfare recipient's budget. On three occasions when I witnessed young men applying for welfare, their applications were turned down.[3] In two of the cases previous maintenance was the problem. Neither man had proof that he had been working steadily at any time before applying. The welfare officers held this against the applicants although both had statements from relatives saying they had previously supported

3. A man or woman over age twenty-one but without children of his or her own, living in the household of a recipient of AFDC and without other forms of support, would register for Home Relief. Such a person would register at the same center as the AFDC recipient, and his forms would be included with the recipient's. The budget would be calculated for the entire household.

them and no longer wished to do so. Whether or not these statements were authentic, it appeared that young men were presented with greater difficulties when they tried to register than were young women. The latter tended to have children and when they did not, as in the case of Jeannie Sanchez, it still appeared relatively easier for them to register as household dependents.

The question of prior maintenance was a major problem for young men. If a man could not prove to a welfare official's satisfaction that his resources no longer existed, he would be refused assistance. To prove this he had to produce evidence of previous legitimate finances. The term "last resort" was used by a director of a welfare center in his explanation of this aspect of policy to a meeting of representatives from community agencies in March 1976. It refers to the requirement that

> the value of an asset that is convertible to cash shall be utilized as a resource so as to eliminate the need for public assistance. To this end all applicants and recipients shall pursue the possibility of converting all potentially availabe resources as a condition of eligibility. . . .

> Resources include individual or family financial assets, income from employment, eligibility for or the receipt of benefits, and the social resources available through the family or community.

> Each financial asset or resource available or potentially available should be identified. These would include contributions from friends and relatives, income from employment, stocks, bonds, bank accounts, work related benefits, etc. (New York State Department of Social Services, n.d., item B-c-01)

This requirement sometimes functioned as a Catch-22. A person with resources was refused welfare assistance. However, if he claimed to have no resources, he must have been lying. How could he have survived long enough to apply? (Several welfare officers were heard to ask this question with impatience.) Thus complying with the letter of the law in requests for assistance for dependents did not always guarantee adequate funding and often created further difficulties (such as accusations of drug-dealing) for those who attempted to initiate the process.

Problems with Social Service Regulations
Caused by Job Insecurity

A welfare recipient was supposed to report to the department when
he or a listed dependent found a job. The temporary nature and
insecurity of most available jobs made this a risky proposition. On
three occasions women I knew told the welfare department that
they or their husbands had found jobs, and within a few weeks the
job fell through. They had to go through much red tape and
trouble to reopen their cases.

For example, Jenny Ferguson closed her case when her husband
found a job in construction. Two weeks later he lost the job. Mrs.
Ferguson described the situation this way:

> Me and John and Christopher [her son] lived with my aunt until
> John got a job. But he was fired, for being late a couple of times.
> We were up all night with Chris being sick, and he was late and
> then he was fired. Then he got a job window-cleaning. They fired
> him because there was a slowdown at work, and they had to keep
> the guys in the union working there longer. Then he didn't have
> a job for one year, except for jobs on the side, that you couldn't
> count on. So I went down to welfare. I had to lie that he wasn't
> there.

A year later, when her husband had been employed driving a
truck for six months, she still had not reported his employment
to the welfare department. Her rent was partially paid by the
assistance. Although Mrs. Ferguson was afraid that she might have
to pay the money back if she was discovered, she was not sure
that her husband would continue working, and the money was
needed.

Jenny Ferguson had also moved to a new apartment without
informing the welfare department. She had requested permission
to move from an apartment which had no heat and where water
dripped through the roof onto the children's bed and the closet.
Welfare had refused to grant her the extra rent. She had moved
anyway and expressed her position as follows:

> My kids—if I have to go on the corner and sell myself they're
> going to have everything I didn't. I would steal. I'm already

doing something illegal—with the welfare. They didn't want me to move. They're only paying rent from the other apartment [$104 a month]. They don't know I moved. [Her new rent was $200 a month.]

Jenny Ferguson could have moved to a cheaper apartment and in this way would have received the full rent in public assistance. But she and her husband chose to move to the more expensive and better-maintained apartment without informing the welfare office.

Gloria Johnson's case provides a second illustration of the effects of job insecurity on the client's compliance with welfare regulations. She and her household were living on welfare when she was unexpectedly hired as a secretary for one of the CETA positions. She did not inform the welfare department, and welfare continued to pay her rent and send her a biweekly check.

Gloria Johnson lived in Woodlawn Housing and paid rent to the New York City Housing Authority. When someone in the local housing office discovered that she was working, Mrs. Johnson cancelled her welfare assistance. A month later she was laid off, and she again applied for relief. Three months later she was rehired for the same job while she was still receiving welfare subsidies. Six months later she was again laid off. Two months after this, she was rehired. After she had been working for three months more, the Housing Authority again forced Mrs. Johnson to cancel her welfare checks.

The obvious insecurity of Gloria Johnson's job and her husband's inconstant employment contributed to her illegal acceptance of welfare. Mr. Johnson worked as a maintenance man. He earned comparatively good wages while he was working but was often out of work. He had previously been a drug addict and still drank excessively. Mrs. Johnson remarked:

I never budget with my husband in mind. I can't rely on him. Sometimes he gives me $5 or $10, sometimes $150. When he's working he gets $213 per week. But he even gives money to his mother—he buys her expensive appliances and things. He bought her a washing machine.

On another occasion she explained:

> I always calculate for the rent and the phone bill out of my check.
> Anything he gives me is just extra money. He says he doesn't give
> me money because I won't depend on him.

Gloria Johnson earned $286 every two weeks from CETA,
which came to $8,000 per year. Her rent was $127 per month,
calculated by the Housing Authority as a subsidized rent for a
welfare recipient and paid by the welfare department. She also
received a stipend from welfare and intermittent support from her
husband, who sometimes lived in another apartment. She paid
$44 for $82 worth of food stamps. Gloria Johnson's household
consisted of her children, aged seven and two, her two brothers,
and, irregularly, her husband. One of her brothers was an unemployed alcoholic with no form of support other than his sister.
The second brother was attending college and received welfare
support as Mrs. Johnson's dependent. She received $134 from the
welfare department every two weeks.

Although Mrs. Johnson did not inform the welfare department
of her own employment or her husband's, she was not misleading
officials when she claimed her right to welfare as a "last resort."
She was always in debt, although she spent her money on little
besides the necessities of survival, and she was responsible for the
support of five people. She was acting illegally in relation to
welfare regulations, but not in the context of her right to financial
aid. She had no other resort.

Mrs. Johnson was careful to state that there had been times
when her husband had supported the whole family. She was simply
unable to count on his continuous employment, or on receiving
the money that he did earn. It was the level of job insecurity and
general financial uncertainty as well as the reality of being in
constant debt which led her to ignore social service regulations.

Gloria Johnson's alcoholic brother was probably legally eligible
for welfare assistance but was not listed as her dependent. As an
alcoholic he would have had to have been checked out by the
doctors at the welfare center and shunted between different departments. Sometimes alcoholics are classified as permanently

disabled and sent to the Social Security department.[4] Sometimes they are placed on the welfare rolls. Often they are dropped, or themselves give up, somewhere between the two departments.

When Mrs. Johnson acted to change her own welfare status, she always had to calculate how her college brother's dependency allowance would be altered. She also had to consider the likely duration of her own job and those of her frequently unreliable husband. She had to assess the influence these shifts would have on the New York City Housing Authority and the direction in which her rent would be changed. It was numerous outside factors such as these which clashed with the inflexibility of the welfare regulations. Both black women like Gloria Johnson and low-income white women like Jenny Ferguson risked lawbreaking in order to obtain the financial assistance which was essential for the provision of their households.

The "Face-to-Face"

One method employed by the welfare center to keep its records accurate and to trace irregularities such as those described above was the "face-to-face" interview. Welfare recipients were officially required to appear for a "face-to-face" (as they called them) every six months. Sometimes a year elapsed between the actual scheduling of these appointments.[5]

4. The regulations state:
   Some individuals who habitually drink and to excess may not be found to be sufficiently disabled because of it to qualify for Social Security Insurance. However, such individuals because of their drinking problem are unable to hold a job or otherwise support themselves. The social service official in these instances can require participation in an alcoholism rehabilitative program as a condition of eligibility. (New York State Department of Social Services, n.d., item B-m-01)

5. The regulations state:
   Policy: A redetermination of eligibility, including a face-to-face interview, based on a reconsideration and re-evaluation of all factors of eligibility that are variables shall be made periodically.
   Interpretation: Redetermination must be undertaken when new information is received or there are significant changes in the case situation, provided that all factors of eligibility are subject to review, analysis and re-checking. In all other cases, the requirement for periodic redetermination prevails. . . .
   All evidence in hand should be re-evaluated as to completeness and consistency, and particularly as to current relevancy. Information, such as medical or relevant resources, should be followed up for currency. New

When my informants were required to appear for a face-to-face, they went into a state of panic. There was always some regulation with which they had not fully complied. Even when they were not aware of any noncompliance, they were afraid that some unpredictable difficulty might surface.

Mary Sanchez did not appear for her scheduled interview because she was so worried about the changes that might be made in her budget. Gloria Johnson did not appear the first time because she could not show her rent bill, which had been raised. She was afraid of damaging her college brother's welfare status if she closed her own case. In each case, when the person finally appeared at a rescheduled face-to-face, the interrogation was not overwhelming, and they appeared relieved.

Mary Sanchez's budget was not lowered because of her immense unpaid gas and electric bills, as she had feared. She managed to avoid showing the bills. If the debts had been paid by the welfare department, they would have reduced Mrs. Sanchez's biweekly check in order to take back the money over time. She did not know how her household would survive if her welfare check was reduced in any way. Often they went without food, and they did not have money for cigarettes or the utility bills. Mary Sanchez preferred to live by candlelight and buy take-out food than to have her allowance further reduced to pay gas and electricity bills. She was understandably afraid of the face-to-face and put off the interview for over a month.

Gloria Johnson calculated that if she closed her welfare case, she would profit more from her reduced rent (graded by the Housing Authority according to income) than she would if she received her brother's dependency allowance. She simply went to her rescheduled face-to-face and closed her case without any problem.

---

information should be gathered where required from the recipient and collateral sources contacted for reliable data on which to base a decision as to current eligibility and the specifications of changes that have transpired. . . .

Following the initial determination of need and eligibility, the first redetermination must be made in three months of that date. Subsequent redeterminations, at a minimum, must be made every six months thereafter. (New York State Department of Social Services, n.d., item B-b-05)

Often the face-to-face was perfunctory. However, the fear remained that at some point a more thorough investigation might take place. This anxiety did not keep welfare recipients from manipulating the system, in accordance with necessity. It did contribute toward preventing protest or the reporting of irregularities that were directed against them.

Gloria Johnson's case illustrates how anxiety prevented the reporting of irregularities directed against a client. When an official of the branch of the New York City Housing Authority responsible for Mrs. Johnson's building discovered that she was working as well as receiving welfare assistance, he called her into his office. Instead of informing the welfare center that she was receiving aid illegally, the official simply raised her rent to correspond to his reevaluation of her income. She was also charged a back rent of over $200 to correspond to this new evaluation. Although she was paying a higher rent ($148 a month), Mrs. Johnson's rent bills continued to list her original rent of $127.

Gloria Johnson suspected fraud in the local housing office. People who lived in Woodlawn Housing were convinced that some rent was not reaching the correct authority. But she did not lodge a complaint because of her precarious position with the Department of Social Services. The second time that a local office of the New York City Housing Authority was informed, possibly by her employers, that she had started work again, Mrs. Johnson's rent, then down to $110, was raised to $191. The staff member at the local housing office promised her that her rent would be lowered to $94 if she were not receiving welfare assistance. This was a strong incentive since she owed $330 in back rent.

Mrs. Johnson calculated her expenses, including the assistance that her college brother received and that he would lose if she closed her welfare case. She concluded that it was cheaper not to receive welfare and to have the rent lowered. She suspected that the housing office might be charging her an excessive unlisted rent raise, but, she was not prepared to inquire about it because of the money she owed them and because of her own problems with the welfare center.

The cases described above illustrate two important aspects of the relationship between welfare recipients and the process of being on welfare. First, they show that the fluidity and complexity of daily life could not be accommodated by welfare regulations. Thus at one time Gloria Johnson was supporting her husband, her two brothers, her two children, and herself and had no income from employment. Within a week the situation might have changed. She might have found a job, or her husband might have moved out. Her alcoholic brother might have disappeared, or she might have left her children with one of her relatives. A week later her husband might have returned, her children might have been sent home, or she might be out of a job. Similar changes might as easily have occurred in Jenny Ferguson's or Mary Sanchez's households. The numerous permutations of daily life among poor people of Greenpoint-Williamsburg could never have been reflected and processed adequately or quickly enough through the welfare bureaucracy. There would have been no need for these changes to be considered at all if the regulations had not been unrealistic.

Second, the rigidity of welfare requirements generated an atmosphere of fear around many of the activities of everyday life. For example, Joannie Gonzalez and Mary Sanchez both remarked to me that they were afraid to open their mail from the welfare department. They feared an announcement that their subsidies would be reduced. All informants were afraid of the face-to-face and most, including Joannie Gonzalez, Mary Sanchez, Jenny Ferguson, and Gloria Johnson, were afraid to telephone the welfare department. As described in the previous chapter, welfare clients often went down to the office accompanied by relatives or neighbors. This may have been a consequence of their fear of the visit and their need for company, whether or not they needed help with translation from Spanish, Italian, or Polish into English.

As illustrated above, in instances where an outsider might suggest that the welfare client demand certain rights or question the legitimacy of official measures, recipients remained silent. They were afraid to jeopardize other aspects of their support. Often outspoken individual protest resulted in the loss or delay of a client's application. A welfare official might use his control of resources to punish a client who caused him any trouble. Recourse, as will be outlined below, was a long and uncertain process.

Each action had to be calculated in a number of different ways and its consequences evaluated before complaints would be lodged. The numerous financial dependencies and the precariousness of the household budget tended to dampen enthusiasm to stand up for rights that the client often felt had been forfeited by previous illegitimate manipulations with regard to welfare regulations. Not least in such considerations was the low chance of success of formal protest.

Recourse for a Welfare Recipient

If a client was turned down for aid or felt he had been subject to illegal treatment, he could file for a fair hearing. People who had scheduled a fair hearing must already have overcome many of the problems and fears outlined above. They also had to have filed the correct forms and followed through on the process to request the hearing itself. Generally welfare clients did not initiate such cases themselves but were encouraged by community organizers or social workers in local agencies to file suit against restrictive practices in the welfare department. Piven and Cloward (1971) discuss the importance of such outside agency workers in the access of eligible people to the welfare rolls. They document a significant rise in the welfare rolls during the 1960s and attribute it to an increase in community organizing funded by the large-scale poverty programs set in motion by the Office of Economic Opportunity. They point out that it was community workers who began to encourage the use of the fair hearing as a recourse for applicants. The number of fair hearings increased nationally over the 1960s along with the number of welfare recipients (ibid., p. 335). Although numerous poor immigrants and urban dwellers had been eligible for assistance, it was not until community organizers urged them to overcome the hurdles of the welfare bureaucracy that they were able to obtain the financial aid to which they were entitled (ibid., chapters 9 and 10).

The New York State Department of Social Services regulations list acceptable grounds for the fair hearing:

a. denial of assistance
b. failure to determine applicant's eligibility and, if eligible to

issue a cash grant or authorize medical assistance within 30
days of date of original request

c. inadequacy in amount or manner of payment of assistance
d. discontinuance in whole or in part
e. objection to policy as it affects applicant/recipient's situation
f. any other grants affecting entitlement, or the amount or the
   time of payment. These also include, but are not limited to,
   determinations of employability, even though grant remains
   unaffected. . . .

A request for a fair hearing shall not be denied or dismissed
except where it has been withdrawn by the applicant/recipient in
writing, or has been abandoned. (New York State Department of
Social Services, n.d., item B-6-09)

The hearing was held in a New York City court building, and the
verdict could be appealed until it eventually reached the New York
State Supreme Court.

Probably with assistance and encouragement from a community
agency worker, a client would fill out an application, outlining his
grievance. If the application was approved by the New York State
Department of Social Services, the client received notification of
approval within a month of the date for which the hearing would
be scheduled. Out of four applications for a fair hearing which I
observed, none were refused.

On the appointed date, the client had to appear at an office in
Lower Manhattan, an approximately forty-five-minute subway
journey from home. The client and accompanying relatives were
repaid for the subway fare in both directions ($1 for each in-
dividual). The recipient might also appear with a community
agency representative. No clients whom I observed had filed for
fair hearings without outside help. However, although an agency
worker might have assisted the client in applying for a fair hearing,
he might not appear at the actual interview. On two occasions
when I accompanied a client to a fair hearing, an agency worker
had asked me to substitute for him.

At the courts, despite several lines of waiting people, hearings
tended to take place within an hour of the time scheduled. Clients
were entitled to legal aid, and there was an office at the courts
where legal aid personnel, mostly law students, might be consulted.

If it was arranged beforehand, legal aid counselors might accompany a welfare applicant to the fair hearing.

When I consulted them, legal aid counselors were not able to help me work out the budget to which the client with me was entitled. For instance, an applicant had a problem concerning an educational stipend. Most stipends did not exclude a person from receiving welfare, but some did. Neither the legal aid lawyers, the welfare officer in charge of the case, nor the state representative who presided over the fair hearing were able to determine whether the stipend, for a training program in which the Hispanic client learned English, disqualified him from receiving welfare.

Present at this hearing were the client and a special prosecuting officer who worked full-time as the welfare representative in fair hearing cases. A representative from the state welfare office in Albany presided over the case. He was required to tape the procedure unless the client requested that the hearing be held off the record. If a hearing was not taped, a client could not claim a mistrial, as evidence would not be available. Some social workers, experienced with fair hearings, claimed that untaped, off-the-record hearings might turn out more favorably, as they were preferred by prosecuting officers. Such unofficial hearings were supposed to reduce antagonism of the prosecuting officers toward the welfare clients, making compromise easier. Others maintained that once the client had found it necessary to request a fair hearing, the point at which the charity of the prosecuting officer could be relied upon had passed, and legal procedure was his strongest ally. A fair hearing was not, however, an infallible asset for a client. The state officer from Albany was not a neutral observer but a representative of the New York State Department of Social Services. The client and his representative might find themselves pitted against two departmental representatives, one of whom, barring further appeal, had final decision.

The interests of the state representative may be gauged by one illustration of a conversation with a welfare client and a prosecuting officer before the tape was turned on for the hearing to begin officially. Present at this hearing were the client, a young Hispanic man of nineteen; his sister, whom he had brought along as translator; the official translator, a woman whom the state representative insisted on appointing; the prosecutor for the welfare center; the state representative; and myself, present at the request of an outside agency worker who could not herself appear. The state representative listened to the welfare prosecutor and turned to the client to suggest that he had been delinquent in not coming back to the welfare center, thus making clear his prejudice in the case.

During the taped hearing, the prosecutor concentrated on showing that the client had not returned often or regularly enough to the center and had been denied welfare because he had not presented the full information requested. The records showed that he had returned twice to the center with a letter from his mother stating that she had maintained him previously and could no longer do so. The prosecutor maintained, probably correctly, that on each occasion when the client had returned, further information had been requested and that the client had finally ceased to come. The client maintained that he had heard nothing from the welfare office, and that each time he had come down to the center he was forced to miss a day of English classes for which he was penalized at his school.

Since the necessary information and letters were in the files, it would have been possible for the state representative to rule that the client be admitted to the welfare rolls. Nevertheless, the officer from the state proceeded to interrogate the client once again about prior maintenance and to confuse and intimidate him. He eventually asked the client if, when he lived with the friend whom he claimed had supported him, they had earned money from the sale of drugs. The applicant admitted that dealing had been a source of income. However, his previous form of maintenance, as his social worker had informed the applicant and as I pointed out to the interrogator, was not at issue. It was no grounds on which to reject the present application. The legitimacy of the application should legally have rested on whether or not welfare was the client's last resort. As evident from his history, his only other resources were illegal and thus further evidence of his lack of outside support.

Each statement of the applicant was translated by the official translator, but only those questions addressed directly to him were translated for him, so that he could not grasp the complete proceedings and was disoriented. At the end of fifteen minutes, the state's representative concluded the hearing and said that the results would be mailed to the social worker's office within ninety days.

About two months later, the client was informed that his application had been refused, not on the grounds that he had other support through an educational stipend but because there had been inadequate information presented as to his previous maintenance. This, as remarked before, appears to be an obstacle often placed in the way of young men applying for welfare, especially since it is up to the personal discretion of each officer to determine what "adequate" information of previous maintenance entails.

It would have been possible to reschedule a new fair hearing or to appeal the case, or for the client to have returned to the welfare center to file a new application, following the involved procedures outlined earlier. But the applicant by this time had lost hope of receiving welfare and did not wish to pursue the case further. He preferred to support himself with the temporary educational stipend and to continue to live with his mother, who paid the rent and provided food for her whole household from the welfare checks that she had been able to obtain. The response of the welfare department that the applicant had supplied inadequate information of prior maintenance was in fact an admission that there was no official reason why he should not have received welfare. Besides procedural irregularities, his application was legally acceptable.

A second fair hearing that I observed was the case of Joannie Gonzalez. Mrs. Gonzalez's mother and father were Italian-American. She grew up in Williamsburg with five brothers and sisters and married a Puerto Rican man when she was nineteen. Her brothers and sisters and her mother still lived in the neighborhood. Joannie Gonzalez and her husband Ricardo had three daughters. After seven years of marriage, he left the family and became an alcoholic and a drug addict. He returned periodically, drunk, and beat up his wife. On several occasions she called the police. She tried locking her husband out altogether, and he climbed in through a neighbor's window. From then on, afraid that the police might not respond in time, Mrs. Gonzalez let her husband in when he came. In this way she averted the more humiliating scenes.

When her husband left her, Mrs. Gonzalez applied for welfare assistance. At the time of the fair hearing, she had been on welfare for sixteen years. In 1972 her landlord tried to have her evicted from the apartment where she and her children had been living for twenty years. He had harassed all the other tenants into leaving, and hers was the only remaining rent-controlled apartment. The case went to court, and Joannie Gonzalez won.[6] Having lost the case in the courts, the landlord tried to create problems for Mrs. Gonzalez with the welfare department, for if she lost her assistance, she would not be able to afford the rent and would be forced to move.

For these reasons the superintendent of her apartment building informed the welfare department on April 6, 1972, that "Ricardo Gonzalez lives in the apartment with a friend and they sell dope. Mrs. Gonzalez is not there." On April 11, 1972, the department found this information "unverifiable" and continued to send the welfare checks to Mrs. Gonzalez.

A month later the department received a new complaint. The superintendent stated that he had seen Ricardo Gonzalez leaving for work every morning and that he received mail at his wife's address. A welfare officer made a visit to the apartment and recommended that Mrs. Gonzalez continue to receive assistance.

On February 13, 1973, the landlord submitted a complaint that Mrs. Gonzalez was not eligible for assistance because he had observed her "inter-relating, moving back and forth within apartments" in his building. The implication was that she had a relationship with another man who should take financial responsibility for the family. The case was considered, and the inspector general "failed to find any evidence of ineligibility."

Although the welfare department had ruled in her favor each

6. Mrs. Gonzalez kept detailed records both of her court cases with the landlord and her notifications from welfare. I was able to examine these official documents in order to verify the dates and sequence of her account. It was this same systematic record-keeping which allowed her to win the cases as she did.

time she had been accused, the issue was not closed. On March 29, 1977, Mrs. Gonzalez received a notice of intent to reduce her welfare assistance from April 8, 1977. The letter stated that she owed the welfare department $27,641. It claimed that her husband had been living in her household from January 18, 1967, to October 4, 1974. She was charged with fraud and was told that her check was being reduced in recompense for the money which had been received on false pretenses.

Mrs. Gonzalez panicked. She telephoned me, and she telephoned a social worker whom she knew. She went to the welfare center to verify the situation and to find out how to combat the charges. On April 19, 1977, she requested a fair hearing. The hearing was scheduled for January 4, 1978.

By the time of the hearing, Mrs. Gonzalez had been receiving a reduced welfare check for nine months. She was very worried about being charged with fraud. When the local legal counseling service told her that no one would be available on the day of her hearing, she asked me to appear as her representative. When I arrived she told me that I would have to do the talking because she would lose her voice in front of the welfare officials. Since she was an articulate and intelligent woman and knew the case better than I did, I encouraged her to represent herself. She insisted, however, that she was too frightened.

When the state representative judging the case walked in, he remarked, "Fraud is a serious charge, you know. I hope you understand that." Mrs. Gonzalez turned white and began to shake. She told the official she could not talk because he made her so nervous.

On her arrival the prosecutor announced that the welfare department had no evidence. The only evidence had been included in the notice of intent and referred to the superintendent's allegations four years earlier.

The state representative suggested that if the welfare department had no evidence, the case should be closed and Mrs. Gonzalez's money refunded. The prosecutor maintained that she could not rescind the charges without speaking to her supervisor. She then remarked that the evidence was missing because the files for the period under consideration (1967–1974) had been placed in storage, and she had not put in a request to look at them. Again the state representative suggested that the hearing be cancelled, remarking: "Why harass this poor lady? . . . Why should we put her through the whole procedure when you have no evidence anyway? Why don't you just call your supervisor?"

The welfare prosecutor then remarked that her supervisor was new and had less knowledge of the case than she did. She said that she saw no point in speaking to her. Finally she telephoned her and explained the situation. The supervisor directed her to retain the charges and conduct the hearing although the department had no evidence whatever to support the charges. This inflexibility clearly reflects the lack of decision-making powers and severe constraints placed on officials in the lower levels of the welfare bureaucracy.

At this point the state representative turned on his tape recorder and began the hearing. He asked me to act as Mrs. Gonzalez's legal representative and gave me a paper to sign to that effect. Then he began to interview her. He questioned her about her marriage, her children, and her husband's occupation. She had to explain that her husband never gave her support, that he "forced his way into the apartment," and "always made a scene." If she did not let him in, he would "climb the fire escape or sleep in the hall." She reported that he had "no regular pattern" to his visits, "no job, and no money."

After forty-five minutes of interrogation, during which Joannie Gonzalez mentioned that her husband was presently in prison and unable even to visit, the state representative turned to the welfare prosecutor. The prosecutor handed the representative a copy of the original letter containing the landlord's allegations and repeated that she could provide no further evidence. The hearing was then called to a close.

One month later, Joannie Gonzalez was informed that the charges would be revoked and that the welfare department would refund the money that had been subtracted from her check for ten months.

The letter from the New York State Department of Social Services read:

Section 351.1 of the Regulations of the State Department of Social Services provides that a recipient of public assistance has the responsibility to provide truthful and accurate information on her needs, including household composition and rent, and her income and resources, including the amount received for support and the location and ability of responsible relatives to provide support. This information is necessary so that the agency can properly determine the need for assistance and the amount to be provided. The credible evidence and the record establishes that the appellant did not violate her responsibility in that the appellant did not report that her husband was a member of her household during the period January 18, 1967, to October 4, 1974, and did not report this support during that period because the appellant's husband was not a member of her household and contributed no support.

Mrs. Gonzalez's fair hearing illustrates why informants who were dependent on welfare assistance were afraid of the Department of Social Services. As it happened she had evidence, such as an order of protection against her husband and a record of trying to bring him to family court, that made it clear that she had been unduly suspected. But although Mrs. Gonzalez knew that her husband had not supported her for sixteen years, she was afraid of the hearing and of the serious charges made against her.

This case also demonstrates the harrassment practiced on clients by the welfare department. Although the hearing officer pointed out that the department had no evidence to back up its charges, both the welfare prosecutor and her supervisor continued the interrogation. The charge of fraud and the hearing caused tension and panic in the client for which the prosecutor could provide no justification other than "procedural requirements."

Joannie Gonzalez had no warning that her past history was under review and that she was to be challenged once again for charges that had been dismissed four years earlier. The unpredictability of the charges, combined with the fact that all the allegations had been dealt with previously, led to a situation that could only be described as harassment. In the light of such treatment, the anxiety of most informants about dealings with the welfare center can easily be understood.

In the last two chapters, I have shown how a public institution such as welfare assistance affected the conditions of life and responses of recipients. The rigidity of regulations and bureaucratic delays exacerbated and at times created difficulties in low-income life. Dependence on welfare assistance contributed toward fear and a sense of insecurity on the part of recipients. Such feelings were intensified by the belief of welfare officers that suspicion and harassment of clients were requirements of their role. One of the bases for the justification for the welfare bureaucracy was that welfare was a "last resort." In order to prove that assistance was essential, interrogation of clients, examination of their backgrounds, and suspicion of the information supplied were regarded as necessary procedures.

The atmosphere of disbelief and harassment discouraged clients from demanding their legal rights. Such a situation has to be understood in light of the job insecurity and unpleasant employment conditions described in chapter 3. Under such strains the fluidity of low-income life clashed with regulations of the New York State Department of Social Services and set the welfare client against the welfare officer. The fear and anger generated on both sides led to the inaction and noncooperation of recipients and the corresponding tendency toward harassment and unnecessary interrogation and inflexibility on the part of officers.

CHAPTER 6

Landlord-Tenant Relations

Landlords

Landlord-tenant relationships contributed to the atmosphere of fear and insecurity engendered by the welfare system. There were three types of landlords in Greenpoint-Williamsburg. The most common was the homeowner who rented out space in his or her own building. The second, more similar to those in Manhattan, was the absentee landlord. These landlords generally lived in Queens or Long Island and only arrived, or sent their representatives, to collect the rents. The third type of landlord was the New York City Housing Authority. One block of buildings, Woodlawn Projects, contained seven hundred apartments and was rented out at subsidized rents by the authority. Each type of landlord had varying interests in real estate and the future of the neighborhood and correspondingly different relations with tenants. The actions of the three types of landlords and their distribution in the neighborhood were related to the income level and ethnic composition of the tenants.

Homeowners

In most areas of New York City, banks would not lend money for the purchase of residential homes. Such investments were regarded as high risk, or simply not in accordance with other plans for city real estate. Where projects for urban renewal were a possibility, banks which regarded such developments as lucrative would be less likely to loan money for the purchase and rehabilitation of existing buildings. In areas such as Greenpoint-Williamsburg, this problem was exacerbated by close geographical association with Bedford-Stuyvesant, where the degeneration of a neighborhood had progressed much further and investments were not considered profitable. Bank loans, fire insurance, and loans for the renovation of buildings were extremely difficult to procure in Greenpoint-Williamsburg. As will be seen, such problems led to the further deterioration and neglect of apartment buildings and resulted primarily in worse living conditions for the poor.

Although local banks did not often loan money for the purchase of houses in the area, exceptions were allowed in certain cases. The director of one bank was trying to bring higher-income couples into the neighborhood to renovate a block of brownstone houses. The people who bought these houses had special access to loans. One couple, who were journalists moving from Manhattan, described their loan problems. The first time they requested a loan, they were flatly refused. They responded by contacting the local banker who had encouraged them to live in Greenpoint. He opened the way for them to obtain several different loans. The practice of withholding loans, known as "redlining," was tested by three women employed by CETA. They went separately to three different Williamsburg banks requesting housing loans, and all were turned down.

Except for the brownstones, which cost around $30,000, houses sold cheaply. People whom I interviewed had bought two-family homes for $16,000. One family bought a three-story house for $12,000. The buildings were not in good condition, and the houses were not spacious or well-designed, but they represented a major investment for low-income residents. An example of advertised rents follows:

Prices of Houses for Sale, September 1976
(as advertised by a realty company in local papers on September 23 and 30)

1 fam. store, $16,000
2 fam. gas heat, $34,500
2 fam. brick, $38,990
3 fam brick, $37,990
3 fam. St. Stan's parish, $34,990
6 fam.—a steal at $13,500
2–4 fam. brick
    good income $58,900
Maspeth: 1 fam. 8 rms
    plus fin. attic,
    many extras, redec. $62,900

As was true in many working-class neighborhoods even one hundred years ago (Thernstrom, 1964), a common practice among wage earners in Greenpoint-Williamsburg was to save their money to buy a house. A second method was to borrow from a variety of private sources at excessively high interest rates. A house represented security, saved money on rent, and was a possible source of profit if space could be rented out. Many neighborhood residents who owned houses and rented out apartments did not live far above the financial level of their tenants. In some cases an exorbitant proportion of their income went to paying off privately arranged loans.

Most low-income homeowners interviewed did repairs themselves in order to save money. For example, a man who worked in refrigerator maintenance, and whose wife had worked as a school-crossing policewoman before she retired, owned a building with three apartments. He remodeled his apartment and redecorated the others with inexpensive plastic-paneled walls and linoleum. In the same way as other homeowners, he did all the work himself.

A young construction worker married to an unemployed secretary took care of the maintenance of his father's building. His father also worked in construction. When the young couple moved into one of the three apartments, the husband completely remodeled it. He pulled old paint and plaster off the walls, tiled the floors, and painted all three rooms. He was also responsible for repair work in the rest of the building.

I knew four couples who completely renovated the interiors of their apartments. Three of them lived in buildings which they owned or which were the property of relatives. The fourth, a newly married couple, spent a month putting down linoleum and painting and tiling the walls in a building owned by Mr. and Mrs. Stavisky. However, the wife did not get along with Mrs. Stavisky. They would yell at one another in the hall. Just after the couple had carried in their new furniture, an apartment became vacant in an uncle's building, and they moved out. Renovating an apartment in someone else's building was a risky and expensive proposition, for money put into redecorating mainly benefited the landlord. Most of the people who conducted extensive remodeling were living in buildings where they kept the expenses among relatives.

Joe Gallo, whose father was born in Italy, owned a building with eight apartments on Norman Street. He worked in the local electrical parts factory, and his wife worked in the office there. His father and his four children shared an apartment with him. He kept the building in better condition than those without resident owners on the street. One spring and summer he even grew potted plants behind the iron railings on the sidewalk which marked his front yard. He was concerned about the upkeep of the block and was treasurer of the block association.

The Staviskys, who had arrived from Poland in the 1940s, also owned a house with eight apartments. They lived in the first-floor apartment with their twenty-seven-year-old daughter, a student at Hunter College. The wife managed the accounts with the help of her daughter, who wrote out the leases and the rent receipts for her. Although she had no problem keeping the budget, Mrs. Stavisky could not speak English well and could not write it. Her husband was a confirmed alcoholic who would not have been able to keep a regular job. He was responsible for building maintenance. Although he seldom appeared on time and took several weeks to finish simple jobs, Mr. Stavisky eventually managed to attend to most maintenance problems in the building. If the problem was complicated or involved electrical wiring, he would call in his son. It often took several months for the work to be completed satisfactorily, for his son worked as an electrician during the week and was only available on Saturdays. Thus Mr. Stavisky cut landlord costs by doing everything himself and calling in his son in emergencies.

Apartments in buildings owned by resident landlords were decorated in similar ways. The buildings were old, and the walls and floors were thin and uneven. A large part of the maintenance was directed toward putting plastic paneling on the walls and linoleum or low-cost carpeting on the floors in order to disguise the faults. Cheap, easily broken blinds were placed on the windows, and painting was often left to the discretion of the tenant. Although required by New York City law, a stove and refrigerator were not always provided.

Most of the homes in Greenpoint-Williamsburg were divided into two or three apartments. Even in small houses, a section would be partitioned by the owner and made into an apartment. As has been illustrated, homeowners included many people with regular wage-paying jobs as well as families with unemployed husbands and wives. Many homeowners spoke only Polish or Italian and had learned a bare smattering of English although they might have been in the United States for twenty years. Sometimes the sole income of the family came from the renting out of apartments in one building, for owning a house did not mean that a family was solvent.

Homeowners did not usually collect welfare. One of the requirements of welfare was that an individual not have money in the bank or outside resources such as a house (New York State Department of Social Services, 1976). However, many homeowners appeared at the local social service agencies to apply for food stamps. The problems of job insecurity and chronic unemployment affected such homeowners in the same ways as they affected their tenants.

Under such conditions contracts, rent, and credit arrangements were flexible. Rents were generally low but might be raised before a lease expired. Extra costs for heat and hot water, sometimes $10 per month, could be added to the rent. Leases were easily broken, and rent was sometimes owed for four to six months at a time.

When I signed a lease for Mrs. Stavisky, she said to me in broken

English: "Don't worry. You can leave. This is only for the city."
She took me to the real estate office across the street to notarize
the lease. She spoke with the salesman in Polish, introduced me,
gossiped a little, and paid 25¢ for the service. Mrs. Stavisky made
it clear to me that despite these formalities, the one-year lease was
not binding from her point of view. If I wanted to leave in six
months, as I had mentioned, then she would have no objections.
As I watched the turnover in the apartment next to mine, I
realized that a year was much longer than many tenants stayed
(although some people had lived in the building for over three
years). In the apartment opposite mine, two months was the
maximum period for any tenant over a period of a year. They
had all signed one-year leases.

Resident landlords generally used personal rather than legal
harassment against uncooperative tenants. Mrs. Stavisky resorted
to loud and vicious attacks on tenants who did not comply with
her requirements. One woman, who had installed an air conditioner
against Mrs. Stavisky's directives, moved out after one such shout-
ing match. When a family on welfare did not pay their rent for
four months, Mrs. Stavisky turned off the heat and hot water and
forced them to leave. Like their tenants, and unlike absentee
landlords, resident landlords do not have the financial resources
to hire legal assistance, and problems are generally settled in more
immediate ways.

Rents were negotiated on the spot. If the owner approved of the
applicant, he might lower the stated rent by $10. If he did not
approve, for ethnic, economic, or personal reasons, he might add
an extra $50 to the quoted rent. Mrs. Stavisky lowered the rent
$10 for me, since she welcomed having a single, white, educated
woman as a tenant. She raised the rent $35 for a Puerto Rican
couple who inspected the apartment next door.

In this situation instances of discrimination against categories
of tenants were numerous. In order to control the type of applicant,
many resident landlords did not advertise their vacant apartments
in the local papers. Instead, first preference would be given to
relatives. Next, notices would be placed in church bulletins and
perhaps in the Polish-American Center (a neighborhood office) or
in the office of the Italian-American League. If notices were placed

in the local paper, this did not mean that all applicants would be equally treated. The editor of one of the local papers remarked that notices would be repeated for weeks, not for lack of applicants, but because landlords "don't want all those people on welfare."

Blacks rarely came looking for apartments with resident landlords. No blacks ever came to Mrs. Stavisky's building. Black people whom I interviewed said that they would never risk the rebuffs they expected from homeowners in the area. A black woman who lived in the projects rented by the New York City Housing Authority remarked: "Oh, black people don't live across there, you know. We wouldn't go over there."

Resident landlords tended to make categorical decisions about tenants. If any blacks had applied, they probably would have been turned away, partly through landlords' fear of their fellows. Landlords had reason to be afraid of the reactions of other tenants and their neighbors. On Norman Street the building where a black family was renting an apartment was burned down. Neighborhood residents associated the arson with the presence of black tenants.

On a relatively better-off block, the sign "Niggers go home" had been painted in three-foot-high letters across the front of a house where a black family had stayed temporarily. The owner had tried unsuccessfully to wash off the paint. Blacks were periodically attacked on Greenpoint streets at night, especially when they associated with white ethnic and Hispanic women in the neighborhood. Thus even if landlords did not themselves have any inclination to discriminate, the pressures from local residents and the history of racial conflict led them to avoid trouble.

When a single, dark, Hispanic man came to inspect an apartment, Mrs. Stavisky showed him around and then said that she had another couple who had promised to bring the money the next day. She insisted that she could not promise him the apartment unless they changed their minds. When the man called back, she told him that the apartment had been taken, whereas it was not yet rented by the following week. She mentioned that he had been angry on the telephone and accused her of discrimination. Perhaps he had had similar experiences previously, or the reputation of the neighborhood led him to expect such practices.

On another occasion a Hispanic couple came to inspect an

apartment. Mrs. Stavisky again prevaricated and told them that she had someone else waiting. She then reminded them that she did not allow washing machines or pets. This upset the couple, who had a dog and needed the washing machine for their children's clothes. They said, however, that they wanted to take the apartment despite these drawbacks. It seemed that they had had a difficult time looking for a place. The next day the landlady told me that she had not rented to them. This apartment was not rented for at least another month. Finally Mrs. Stavisky offered an apartment to a Hispanic couple for $175 when she had offered the same apartment to me for $140 only six months previously.

People in need of housing often wandered around the area knocking on the doors of buildings which appeared to have empty apartments, attempting to circumvent exclusive advertising practices. Although she did have vacant apartments which were not bringing her any rent, Mrs. Stavisky complained to me that I had no curtains on my windows. She said, "The Spanish people comes around and asks me if the apartment is empty because you no put curtains on your windows. I no want trouble with these people. Just put on the cheap curtains, is O.K.?" She insisted on this despite the fact that the apartment next door to mine was empty and could have been shown to the inquirers at her door.

Landlords would explicitly turn away families with children. Notices in the local paper read:

> 5 rooms and bath, heat and hot water, adults preferred
>
> or
>
> 6 rooms, heat and hot water, stove, top floor, no children, no washing machine, adults preferred
>
> or
>
> 3 rooms, adults preferred
>
> or
>
> 4 rooms, heat and hot water, tile bath, adults preferred.

If notices were not as explicit as this about not wanting young children, landlords would prohibit washing machines, which were regarded as essential by mothers with young children:

> 4 rooms, heat and hot water, no washing machine.

Another method used by landlords to exclude unwanted tenants was the request for references:

4 large rooms, cabinet-lined kitchen, ground floor, references
or
Williamsburg, 2 rm. apt. w kitchen facilities, gd for single person. Ref. required.

Many landlords blatantly discriminated against prospective applicants who received welfare assistance:

4½ rooms in Greenpoint, no welfare
and
4 rooms 1st floor, shower, heat-hot water, no welfare, $150 mo.
or, perhaps slightly more subtly:
5 rooms on Russell St., 4th floor, newly painted for 2 or 3 hard-working people.

All of these announcements were taken from the classified section of the *Garden Spot News* for one day, September 23, 1976. This particular issue was chosen at random, and the announcements are typical of the apartment advertisements in the area. Of the twenty-four advertisements for apartments in the paper that day, six specifically excluded children and three refused to rent to people who received welfare assistance. Other landlords who were not as specific in their announcements, such as Mrs. Stavisky, also commonly acted with the same biases. For exclusivity apartments could also be listed with real estate agents, who labeled themselves, for example, "the oldest Polish real estate in Brooklyn." Such agencies would sift the clients before they even reached the landlords.

Although there were generally many vacant apartments in the neighborhood and rents were considerably cheaper than in most areas of Manhattan, it was often difficult for the inhabitants to find housing. Landlords varied in their behavior, but the economic circumstances, household composition, and ethnic status of prospective tenants were prime considerations. Thus it took Jenny Ferguson, as a mother of two children on welfare, a month to find an apartment. She eventually found one in a building with an absentee landlord.

Two modes of behavior were typical among landlords in the area. Resident landlords generally refused to rent to people who received public assistance, while absentee landlords raised the rent for welfare recipients.[1]

Mrs. Stavisky maintained that she had previously rented to welfare recipients and had been left several times with unpaid bills spanning three or four months. I had evidence of two instances where Mrs. Stavisky had not received rent. In one case the husband was unemployed, and the family was on welfare. In the second case a woman who lived alone with her child was employed and not a welfare recipient. Mrs. Stavisky insisted that she would rather accept lower rents than ever rent to a welfare recipient again. Her behavior, when she attempted to rent vacant apartments, appeared to conform to this rule.

On the other hand, I was told of several instances when a landlord quoted a low rent and then asked if the prospective tenants were on welfare. If they were the rent was raised, often by as much as $75 a month. A landlord might charge $110 a month for a four-room "railroad" apartment and raise the rent to $175 for a welfare recipient. Such behavior seemed to be restricted to absentee landlords, for homeowners took Mrs. Stavisky's position. They preferred security to extra money.

Homeowners were indeed often in a precarious economic position. A building was usually their one major investment, sometimes their sole steady source of income. They had a double investment: not only their money, but their daily lives and their friends and relatives were all associated with the neighborhood. It was not easy for them to leave the area and simply collect profit from the real estate. Unpaid rent and empty apartments were a direct threat to their livelihood. They also had a vested interest in the stability and upkeep of the particular area in which they

1. The economic underpinnings of this distinction, in terms of real estate investment, are discussed in Harvey (1973). I have not distinguished between small and large absentee landlords, although this too probably affects renting and maintenance practices.

lived. In all these ways, they differed from the absentee landlords who owned buildings purely for their value as real estate and were not necessarily primarily dependent on the rent.

The personal investment of resident landlords, as has been discussed, affected their behavior both positively and negatively. It led to greater concern with building maintenance, personal relations with tenants, the upkeep of the block, and, finally, the community life of the neighborhood. (It also affected politics, the subject of later chapters in this book.) But relative economic insecurity caused the resident landlords to discriminate categorically and harshly against people on welfare, both white and black, and against groups associated with poverty, such as black and Hispanic people, even when such families were not receiving welfare aid. And fear of damage to property through violence or arson kept them from accepting black and Hispanic people as tenants.

Through these processes the area became divided in the minds of its residents into "good" and "bad" blocks. Such definitions were recognized and accepted by residents on both kinds of streets. Homeowners' blocks ("good" blocks) were populated largely by white ethnic wage earners. The buildings were fairly well maintained, and there were flowers growing in the backyards. Building facades were decorated with colored tiling and often freshly painted in pastel colors. On "bad" blocks, such as Norman and Ealing streets, buildings were owned in greater proportion by absentee landlords. Here they were poorly maintained, and facades were often faded. Blacks, Hispanic people, and those on welfare assistance were forced to live in larger proportions on such blocks.

These differences are illustrated in the census figures, where income variation is clearly marked between each block. On the Staviskys' block (Dapper Avenue), the median income for a family was $6,000. On Norman Street it was $5,300 (U.S. Bureau of the Census, 1972). (These figures refer only to *blocks,* which I have selected, and not to the whole length of the street, where considerable variation according to block can be detected.) It is significant, however, that rents on the two blocks varied around the same figures. On both Norman Street and Dapper Avenue, rents ranged from $100 to $200. The variation depended more on rent control and particular tenant histories than on the block on which the apartment was situated.

An apt illustration of the varying attitudes and behavior of residents of different blocks occurred in the summer of 1976. Three blocks in Greenpoint requested play street supervision from the Police Athletic League (PAL). A relatively large proportion of homeowners lived on two of the blocks. Norman Street, the third block, had a greater number of absentee landlords. PAL sent a black director to organize all three play streets. Upon meeting the director, inhabitants of the two blocks with resident landlords immediately cancelled their request for the program. They sacrificed the advantages of play street supervision for their children in order to prevent a black man from organizing their blocks. Norman Street kept the program, and children and mothers participated enthusiastically in the project.

Absentee Landlords

Buildings in Greenpoint-Williamsburg owned by absentee landlords were not generally well maintained. The front doors were not locked, the stairs and bannisters were frequently in poor condition, the roofs leaked, and the heating was erratic. When such buildings burned down, as did one on Norman Street, the landlord was unavailable, and the responsibility and expense of sealing off the property often fell to the city.

Investment by absentee landlords in such decrepit buildings seemed to be based on the principle of little maintenance expense and low returns. The property served as a long-term investment or as a tax write-off. Whether the building was standing or the rents collected did not appear to be important considerations. Since the community planning board for Greenpoint-Williamsburg wanted to develop the area for middle-income residents, it was in the interests of such landlords to hold on to the property until it could be sold or developed at a profit. In the interim they rented to poor people who could find no alternatives and maintained the buildings with the minimum of expense. For these reasons blocks with absentee landlords developed bad reputations in the neighborhood.

Such buildings progressively deteriorated. Jenny Ferguson, evicted from Mrs. Stavisky's building, moved to an apartment with an absentee landlord. The roof leaked, and the plumbing never worked properly. When the Fergusons finally moved out, the apartment was in such bad repair that no other tenants would take it. It was empty for six months. Eventually a Hispanic couple with a two-year-old son moved in. No maintenance work had been conducted since the departure of the Fergusons, and there had been no heat through some of the most bitterly cold weeks of the winter of 1976. In the winter of 1975, there had been a fire in the factory behind the apartment building. The windows of each apartment facing the factory had been broken by firemen. The landlord took three weeks to replace the glass.

Absentee landlords were more likely to resort to legal means to evict tenants. Joannie Gonzalez, as described in chapter 5, was taken to court four times by a landlord who was trying to evict her from a rent-controlled apartment. She had fought and won every case and still lived in the building, where she was the only tenant to have remained for so long. Her brother, mother, and a friend were all evicted from other apartments there. Gloria Johnson responded to a series of eviction notices from an absentee landlord by moving out without trying to fight back.

Tenants were often months late with the rent for absentee landlords, just as for resident landlords. Similarly, they tried to establish a personal relationship with the rent collector (landlord or superintendent) in order to negotiate credit. Leases were broken, just as they were in homeowners' buildings.

The main distinguishing characteristics of absentee landlords were poor maintenance of buildings and less dependence on rent. They also discriminated less often than resident landlords against Hispanic people and people on public assistance, though they raised the rents for the latter to the limit of what they knew the welfare department would pay. Yet there were few apartments, even among those owned by absentee landlords, where black people were allowed to live.

New York City Housing Authority

Black people in Greenpoint-Williamsburg lived mainly in housing projects such as Woodlawn, with the New York City Housing Authority (NYCHA) as their landlord. Woodlawn, a group of high-rise apartments, had housing for seven hundred families. The city built these projects amid heated community protest since public policies preventing discrimination would operate in their renting patterns.[2] Rents were set according to income and subsidized by the city. Such apartments were not easy to obtain, and the waiting list was long. In 1976, 95 percent of the seven hundred families were black and Hispanic.

As in other forms of housing, residents of Woodlawn often owed rent for several months. Legal harassment and arbitrary shifts in rent due to changes in New York City fiscal policies were common. Rents for people not receiving welfare assistance were suddenly raised in 1976, with tenants given a month's notice of the changes. Despite organized protest by tenants, the rent raise remained.

Buildings were fairly well maintained, except that elevators were frequently out of order and stairwells were regarded as invitations to muggers. Certain buildings were less safe than others. Due to community efforts, a small gymnasium had been added on to the projects in 1977. Previously no provisions for youth activities had existed.

Fear Among Tenants

All three types of landlord-tenant situations provoked insecurity and fear among tenants, who were frequently unable to pay rent on time.

For example, when I asked Mary Sanchez why she did not complain to her absentee landlord about the lack of heat in her apartment, she told me she owed him money. He had raised the

2. Similar heated protest accompanied projects being built in 1977–1978 in the Hassidic section of Williamsburg, concerning the proportion of Hispanics to be housed there. This conflict was not the subject of extensive fieldwork and is not covered here.

rent by $6 per month the previous winter, and the welfare department had refused to pay the extra amount. Mrs. Sanchez did not pay it either. She also owed the landlord three months' back rent. If she informed the welfare department, they would be likely to cut her biweekly check for living expenses ($54) to pay back the debt and arrange a rent check that had to be cosigned by the landlord (Mrs. Sanchez had experienced this penalty on a previous occasion). Living in constant fear of eviction, Mary Sanchez brought no action against a landlord who left her household, which included two four-month-old twins, without heat in subzero weather.

Jenny Ferguson, who lived with her husband and two children in the apartment next door to Mary Sanchez, moved away. Her husband started working, and they could afford to pay rent regularly. Because of the deteriorated state of the apartment and the landlord's refusal to maintain it, the Fergusons withheld their last four months' rent. Since they could afford the rent for a better-maintained apartment, they were in a position to stand up to their previous landlord. Mary Sanchez did not have the means to be independent of her landlord. If she had looked for an apartment, she would probably have been turned down by many of the area's landlords simply because she was on welfare. If she had signed a new lease, she would have run the risk of eviction when unable to pay rent on time. These considerations militated against tenants demanding their legal rights. Since they could not maintain the requirements on their side, they felt helpless to demand the enforcement of regulations in their favor.

The actions of Gloria Johnson also illustrate a widespread fear preventing direct approaches to problems with landlords. Mrs. Johnson owed four months' rent on the apartment where she used to live and where her husband was still living. She received an eviction notice through the mail. Convinced that the notice was due to her owing rent, she hired a truck and moved the furniture out of the apartment. After she had left, she met a neighbor who informed her that because there was a rent strike in the building, the landlord had sent eviction notices to all the tenants as a scare tactic. The neighbor told her to ignore the notice, but by this time the move had taken place. If Mrs. Johnson had not been afraid to seek further information, she could have avoided losing the apartment. Scare tactics such as sending out eviction notices derived some of their effectiveness from the fear already present among low-income people. The fear was based on the reality that they had not and never would be able to live up to the financial demands placed on them by the wider society. For this reason they were always vulnerable and constantly afraid.

Similar fears were prevalent among tenants of the NYCHA. Gloria Johnson's experience with the NYCHA and its alteration of her rent subsidy shows how difficulties with rent and housing became intertwined with general problems and often inhibited people from taking any action at all.

Low-income tenants were constrained in many ways. They might owe back rent. They might fear that other landlords would refuse to rent to them. They might be old and unable to move. They might think that rents in better-maintained buildings would be too high for them to afford. Finally, they might fear that their own incursion, or imagined incursion, of legal requirements in other ways had forced them to forfeit their rights as citizens to demand adequate maintenance.

The combination of the discrimination against low-income tenants by homeowners and the absentee landlord's realization of the tenant's poor bargaining position contributed to the deteriorated state of low-income housing. No matter how poor the conditions, the tenants feared that they might lose the little they had. It was an economic rather than a cultural trap in which such tenants found themselves.

CHAPTER 7

Cooperation and Conflict in a Block Association

Norman Street between Bush and Oak streets was composed of a row of four-story apartment buildings largely owned by absentee landlords. The residents included a group of low-income families whose most numerous contacts and significant exchanges were concentrated on the street and a few surrounding blocks. It was by "hanging out" on the block for months at a time that I became familiar with their lives and problems. The Norman Street Block Association provided my own introduction into the social circles and kin networks of the street.[1] During my first week in Greenpoint, I met the president and founder of this association at a Polish-American Community Center shopfront where she worked part-time, and she invited me to attend.[2] Participation in this association was one of the few ways in which outsiders could become incorporated into the neighborhood social organization. Although the fieldwork expanded to include activities and people with no relation to the block association, it is probable that this initial contact helped form my view of the people on the block.

The block association was but one attempt by residents of

1. Block associations in New York City were generally formed in the interests of neighborhood improvement by a group of people living on one block. The citywide Federation of Block Associations was formed in May 1975.
2. The center was a community-service agency. In November 1975 most of its employees were funded by CETA.

Norman Street to influence their environment. In three years of interaction with the residents of Greenpoint-Williamsburg, I collected a mass of data which testified to the frequent involvement in collective action of working-class poor in urban areas. Although seldom successful and often not long-lasting, such persistent efforts to control the environment were a significant feature of low-income life.

A Meeting of the Norman Street Block Association

The block association meeting was held on the second Monday of every month at 7:30 P.M. At the first meeting that I attended, on November 17, 1975, Rosie Sheehan, the president, introduced me and explained that I was doing university research. I asked if there were objections to my taking notes. Nobody objected, and people did not appear offended although they expressed incredulity that someone should be interested in their activities.

Despite a friendly atmosphere, only Jenny Ferguson actually spoke to me. She was a member of a large family network and explained that two of her aunts (her mother's sisters) were at the meetings, that her brother was the vice-president, and her cousin (her mother's sister's son) was the little boy playing in the background.

At the time I found it hard to believe that so many members of one family lived on the same block. Later I learned that one of the other four women present was also closely linked through friendship with the same family. Ten people attended the meeting: six women, three men, and one little boy. The informal, undirected atmosphere is described in a short excerpt from my field notes:

During the meeting, which Rosie called to order about five minutes after I came, and which they told me was smaller than usual [although it never got any larger for the year that I attended], the little boy was sent continuously back and forth to fetch coffee and doughnuts. The women complained about their weight (which was quite excessive) and ate the doughnuts anyway. They complained about their landlords who fixed up the front of the house and the halls and did nothing about the apartments themselves. They talked about the vacant lot on Norman Street that they wanted to convert into a children's park and the problems with the man next door, who wanted them to put up a special fence to protect his wall. . . . Three people left, and the others went on slowly discussing things for about an hour. . . . Jenny's brother tried to sell some raffle tickets for a friend of his from the Bronx. . . . I asked if people minded my coming, and they said no—it made the meeting look bigger.

Since they will play central roles in the analysis of social relations on Norman Street, a brief description of the ethnicity, employment, and interrelationships of the nine adults at this first meeting follows.

1. Rosie Sheehan, president of the block association, claimed that she was Polish despite her Irish married name. Her friends and acquaintances considered her Polish and referred to Polish characteristics of her personality. Both her parents, however, had been born in the United States and lived in Greenpoint. Their parents had come from Poland. Her married sister lived on a different block in Greenpoint. Rick Sheehan was considered Irish by his wife Rosie and others although he too had been born in Greenpoint. Mrs. Sheehan, who was thirty-four years old, had worked as a low-level accountant for Schaeffer Brewing Company in Williamsburg for six years. After the company moved away, she became unemployed. At the time of the meeting, she was employed part-time in two neighborhood agencies funded by CETA. She and her husband owned a house on Norman Street and had four children ranging in age from ten to sixteen. Rick Sheehan was a supervisor in a machine factory, although he was later laid off.

2. Anthony Sanchez, the vice-president of the block association, was nineteen years old and had been born in New York City. In 1975 he considered himself Puerto Rican. Despite his Hispanic last name, he did not look Puerto Rican: his skin was light, and he had a Brooklyn accent. He mentioned to me several times that in previous years he had been ashamed to admit that his father was Puerto Rican. His mother was born in Williamsburg. Her father's family were from Greenpoint-Williamsburg and were at

least fourth-generation Americans. Her mother's family had emigrated from Germany in the 1920s and had some Swedish ancestors. Mary Sanchez's maiden name was Brock.

Anthony's choice of ethnic identity was further complicated by the fact that his white American relatives on his mother's side, who had raised him, were very poor. His father had connections with a Puerto Rican association in the construction industry which had on occasion helped Anthony to find employment. Anthony's father owned a house in the suburbs and appeared to have much more money than his estranged wife and children.

In Anthony Sanchez's family, the stereotypical American pattern of the poor Puerto Ricans and the established whites seemed to be reversed. In claiming Puerto Rican identity, Anthony may have been opting for his own opportunities for social mobility, or, just as logically, for the rights of an oppressed minority.

At the time of the block association meeting, Anthony had been unemployed for almost a year and was still receiving compensation. He had earlier worked for a construction company in the Bronx. It had taken him three hours by subway and bus to get to work, and he had been forced to leave the job through a combination of illness and exhaustion. He shared an apartment with his mother, Mary Sanchez. In November 1975 nobody else was living in the apartment, and Mrs. Sanchez was receiving welfare payments for herself and her daughter Jeannie, who was living with a pregnant sister in Greenpoint.

3. Joe Gallo, treasurer of the block association, was born in America, but because his father was born in Italy, people on the block regarded Mr. Gallo as Italian. He worked in the local electric parts factory, where his wife worked as a secretary. As mentioned earlier, he owned a building with eight apartments on Norman Street. Joe Gallo shared an apartment with his wife, two children, and his sick father. When I first met Mr. Gallo, I thought he was Hispanic because he was dark and, although born in Brooklyn, had a foreign accent.

4. Jenny Ferguson was Anthony Sanchez's oldest sister, twenty-one years old and married to John Ferguson. They had two children and in November 1975 lived in an apartment next door to Mary and Anthony Sanchez. Mrs. Ferguson did not claim

any ethnic identity but was considered white American by most block residents. John Ferguson claimed an Irish background. All his grandparents had been born in the United States, and his mother's mother still lived in Greenpoint, as had his parents until both died of alcoholism. All Jenny's family (sisters, aunts, mother Mary and brother Anthony) lived in Greenpoint. She had worked in a Greenpoint factory when she first got married but had quit after her husband joined the army. She had left high school in the twelfth grade, after she became engaged, but she and her husband had later passed an examination which was considered equivalent to high school graduation. This was unusual among the members of the block association. In November 1975 she and Mrs. Sheehan were the only two members to have completed high school.

5. Davida Delgado, age twenty-eight, was born on the Lower East Side of Manhattan, where her mother still lived. She came from a Jewish background and had relatives in New York and New Jersey. Her relatives were regarded as "rich," which meant that they had more money than people on Norman Street generally did. They helped Mrs. Delgado with her more outstanding debts. Mrs. Delgado identified herself as Jewish and attended bar mitzvahs and other ceremonies organized by her relatives. Her husband, Jeff, grew up in Puerto Rico. They had two children, born in Greenpoint. Mr. Delgado's three children, from a previous marriage in Puerto Rico, lived with them in their four-room railroad apartment on Norman Street as did his brother and mother. None of the Hispanic relatives who lived in the apartment spoke much English, although the teen-age daughters were rapidly learning the language. Davida Delgado cooked Puerto Rican food, especially rice and beans, as the staple diet of her household. Her husband worked as a hotel dishwasher.

When my Israeli relatives came to visit, Mrs. Delgado asked me about them and said that she would be interested in meeting them because they were Jewish. In the limited environs of Norman Street, being Jewish was exceptional.

6. Cecilia Berette was Mary Sanchez's youngest sister and Anthony's aunt. She was thirty-four years old and lived on Norman Street with her adopted one-year-old son and her husband,

who worked loading trucks in the neighborhood. Cecilia was a Brock, of Swedish-German heritage. Her first husband had been Puerto Rican, and her second had an Italian last name. Judging by her name, a common practice in Greenpoint, people would assume that she was Italian. Her husband was also American-born.

7. Arlene Brock was the middle sister in the Brock family, younger than Mary Sanchez and older than Cecilia Berette. At the time of the block association meeting, she had an apartment on Norman Street, but she soon moved to Ealing Street, three blocks away. Although she had been employed continuously until the birth of her second child, at the time of the study she and the children lived on welfare assistance. She had never been married and retained her Scandinavian maiden name.

8. Roy Farrano was unemployed and in ill health. He lived with Maureen Jones and her five children in an apartment on the street. The household was supported with welfare assistance and occasional informal trading organized by Mrs. Jones.

9. Julie Berry was married with five children. She worked in a CETA-funded community agency as a secretary. She and her family were evicted from their apartment in November 1976 for owing back rent. Her husband drove a truck. Mrs. Berry claimed no particular ethnic identity other than white American.

10. Sharon Bianco, Anthony's younger sister, was not present at the November 1975 block association meeting because she then lived with his youngest sister Jeannie on Ealing Street. Later, when she and Jeannie moved in with Mary and Anthony Sanchez, Sharon became an active member of the Norman Street Block Association. She was married to a serviceman whose parents had been born in Puerto Rico, although he was born in Williamsburg. Sharon claimed no particular ethnic identity. Her first son had a Hispanic name while her two sons, born while her husband was away in the army, were both given American names.

A History of the Association

An important factor in the formation of the Norman Street Block Association was the favorable attention paid to self-help organizations by Mayor Abraham Beame's administration between January

1974 and December 1977. At a time when reduction of essential neighborhood services was the administrative solution to New York City's fiscal problems, efforts to form voluntary groups that might replace paid workers were openly encouraged.[3] The community relations officer of the local precinct was responsible for the development of block associations, and the Greenpoint chapter of the New York City Federation of Block Associations met in the precinct house on the corner of Norman Street.

A more immediate factor in the origin of the association was Rosie Sheehan's employment in an active community agency in which her supervisor rated employees by the degree to which they organized their neighbors. Mrs. Sheehan had been hired in May 1975 when a friend telephoned to inform her that CETA openings were available at the Northside Neighborhood Committee (NNC).

When the block association was formed, Mrs. Sheehan participated in a Parent-Teacher Association at a Roman Catholic school attended by her children and was also active in her church. Nonetheless, she was encouraged by her supervisor at NNC to start a block association on Norman Street. She was expected to organize activities for the association during work hours and was not initially required to appear at the NNC office full-time.

Having contacted the community relations officer from the nearby precinct and Anthony Sanchez from Norman Street, Rosie Sheehan scheduled a first meeting of the Norman Street Block Association in June 1975. Two of her coworkers at NNC came to this meeting to help explain the purposes and methods of a block association. Norman Street residents, resenting the presence of a police officer at early meetings, scheduled the association meetings to clash directly with those of a community organization at which the presence of the community relations officer was required. After Mrs. Sheehan's two coworkers ceased attending

3. Deputy Mayor John Zuccotti presided over the annual conference of the citywide Federation of Block Associations on April 2, 1976. In June 1976 the mayor's Volunteer Action Center cooperated in the distribution of brooms and dustpans to neighborhood residents for the sweeping of their own streets. The equipment was funded by the Citizen's Committee, a nonprofit organization for distributing information about elections and political representatives.

meetings in September 1975, only Norman Street residents, most of whom have been described above, were to be found there.

By November 17, 1975, the third meeting since the summer break, meetings were being held at a wooden dinner table in the back hall of a local chapter of the Knights of Columbus. Rosie Sheehan had arranged the meeting place, which was also used by a scout troop and several other organizations. Each member was supposed to contribute one dollar per month, whether or not they attended. However, most members owed dues. They paid the dollar when they had the money, and as the year progressed, this occurred less frequently. Coffee and doughnuts were regularly provided from the funds of the block association.

Procedures of the Association

At the beginning of each meeting, association members waited for Rosie Sheehan, who was usually about thirty minutes late. She was relied on to direct the meeting. People seemed to expect a president to initiate procedures. Anthony Sanchez chaired a meeting one night when Mrs. Sheehan was not able to attend, and afterwards he mentioned how poorly he thought he had supervised the event. It had appeared to me to be similar to other meetings, but he felt that only the president was capable of conducting a meeting.

An effective public speaker, Mrs. Sheehan had little sense of group dynamics. Meeting agendas were not followed, and the same topics were discussed repeatedly. Long silences were common. Mrs. Sheehan made no attempt to converse with newcomers at meetings. Such inhospitable behavior did not contribute to the expansion of the organization.

Although members often discussed the need to enlarge the association, no new people joined between November 1975 and August 1976, when it disintegrated. Block residents would appear once and never return. On one occasion two Korean men attended a meeting. At other times a Puerto Rican woman and a Polish woman came. For reasons which will be discussed, neither joined the association.

Issues Raised at Association Meetings

Association members were concerned with three major issues. The first problem was a vacant house in the center of the block which had remained open to vandalism since a fire occurred there on April 28, 1975. The second issue was an attempt by association members to create a children's park in the vacant lot on Norman Street. The third issue, a topic of constant conversation, concerned preparation for a Norman Street Block Association dance to be held in July 1976 to raise funds for the organization.

At each meeting Rosie Sheehan would raise the problem of the burned-out house. Members would discuss the danger of a deteriorating building to children who were able to enter and play as well as its potential as a future fire hazard. Mrs. Sheehan would mention that she had called the New York City Housing and Development Administration (HDA) and that nothing had been done. Other members would suggest contacting state Senator Bartosiewicz or Representative Richmond, the political representatives with whom they seemed most personally familiar. However, letters were not actually written.

The apparently simple question of boarding up doors and windows was in fact difficult to resolve. As emerged in an April 1976 interview at HDA offices with administrators responsible for sealing unsafe buildings, no money had been allocated for this purpose since New York City was threatened with bankruptcy in June 1975. HDA policy was that no buildings would be sealed. If an edifice was in a state of dangerous collapse, which was not the case on Norman Street, funds would be allocated for demolition. No maintenance measures were to be funded. The inability of Rosie Sheehan or Anthony Sanchez even to locate an agency which would take responsibility for boarding up the burned-out house may have reinforced the inertia observed at block association meetings.

A sense of futility was also engendered by the results of an earlier effort to make use of an overgrown, garbage-strewn vacant lot on Norman Street. Rosie Sheehan, Anthony, and numerous neighborhood children had spent the summer cleaning out the lot in order to prepare it for use as a playground. They had been informed by a city councilman that the lot was to be auctioned off by the city and that they would be able to buy it for the nominal sum of $1. However, association members were not informed of the date of the auction. In the fall of 1975, the cleared space was sold to a private investor who turned it into a parking lot.

The loss of the vacant lot demoralized association members and was often recalled by them as one more instance of betrayal by a political official. The councilman's failure to inform them of the auction date was further evidence that politicians could not be trusted to effect any improvements for poor people like themselves. This incident discouraged them from attempting to gather political support or from utilizing channels of local patronage to achieve their goals.

A third topic frequently raised at Norman Street Block Association meetings was the organization of a summer dance. Tickets for a fund-raising dinner-dance in Greenpoint-Williamsburg often cost $15 to $20 per person, and the dance constituted an important social event. Well-known people were generally invited, annual announcements were made, and in most cases awards for service in the organization or other contributions were presented. Such an event usually began at 8:00 P.M. with an hour for cocktails and, frequently, hors d'oeuvres. Although the main meal was standardized, hors d'oeuvres tended to reflect ethnic preferences, offering a choice of dishes including lasagna, sausages, and sauerkraut. At the dinner, which was served to people seated at tables (seating arrangements having been carefully worked out beforehand), a small fruit dish was followed by watery noodle or onion soup. Next, a few slices of roast beef, gravy, potato, and canned vegetable arrived. Cake and coffee were served for dessert. Alcohol was plentiful throughout. Generally two quarts of hard liquor (gin, vodka, or scotch whiskey) were placed in the center of each table of ten people. Soda and mixes were provided. A live band played a mixture of ethnic music (particularly Polish and Italian), rock music, and waltzes, depending on the composition of the party. The band entertained the guests with jokes, accepted requests from the floor, and supervised special dance steps. Guests danced between courses and continued after the food had been served. The hall was usually closed at one in the morning.

The magnitude and significance of the planned event caused several problems for the members of the association. On the one hand, they wanted to organize an impressive dinner dance which would be recognized as such by other neighborhood residents and which would establish their effectiveness as a block association. On the other hand, they realized that neither they nor other potential ticket buyers would be able to afford to attend such a grandiose event. These unresolved issues led to difficulties in preparing for the occasion.

At every meeting, renting a hall, catering, printing tickets, and scheduling the dance were discussed. Questions apparently resolved at one meeting would be opened up for discussion again the following month. Directives were seldom carried out between meetings. Mrs. Sheehan agreed to order printed tickets but did not actually do it. Anthony accomplished assigned tasks, but his efforts were generally stymied at the next stage. For example, on three occasions he telephoned caterers to compare prices for the dinner and dance. When he reported to the group, prices were regarded as too high, and they suggested that he call a different set of places. Decisions about the dance hall, the date of the dance, and the number of guests were announced, but arrangements were not completed.

No compromise over the cost of the dance was reached, and in June, less than a month before the event was scheduled, Rosie Sheehan unilaterally cancelled it. She maintained that too much work was involved, and "anyway, it's too late to sell tickets." One might speculate that she feared the dance would be a failure, along with the efforts to construct a children's park or to promote administrative action over the abandoned building.[4] In terms of tangible results, block association meetings had yielded little. In fact, they tended to contribute to a sense of hopelessness among the members as to the possibility of improving their environment.

---

4. In September 1976 a new landlord with interests in renovation bought the burned-out house and sealed up the building.

The Association Street Fair

Partly in reaction to the cancellation of the dance, Anthony decided to put all his energies into a street fair. This fair had been suggested by Mike Jensen, an articulate young man who came to only one meeting of the association. Before moving to Norman Street in January 1976, he had lived in Brooklyn Heights (a predominantly middle-class area with strong links to Greenwich Village and the artistic atmosphere associated with it) and had worked on Wall Street. Mr. Jensen had large-scale ambitions for a block association in Greenpoint-Williamsburg. He explained enthusiastically that in Brooklyn Heights they had had floodlights, music, and a children's fairground machine. They had attracted a large number of people and made a lot of money for their block association. However, this event had occurred in an area where people had money to spend on a street fair. Norman Street residents were well aware of this difference. They did not speak out at the meeting at which Mr. Jensen presented his proposal, but later they talked about it among themselves.

Mike Jensen was disliked by the regular members of the block association and also by other Norman Street residents. He was beaten up three months later by a neighbor who claimed that Mr. Jensen had hit his child on the stairs. He moved away from Greenpoint soon after.

Despite the hostility toward the man who had made the proposal, the idea of having a street fair was raised several times after Mr. Jensen's departure. The proposal may have persisted partly because it was voted on and approved at the February meeting at which it was suggested. Perhaps some of the impetus for the fair came from the fact that it had been proposed by an educated middle-class man who was different from the people on the block. Although they were hostile to him personally, he had status in their eyes. They were convinced he must know something they did not know. Rosie Sheehan remarked to me, "He's very intelligent, you know." I asked why she thought so, and she answered; "Well, he reads the *New York Times.* I've seen him carrying it down the street. You have to be intelligent to be able to read that." I replied that I did not feel that reading the *Times* proved anything. Her answer was, "Well, you're intelligent, too; you read it."

Remarks such as these reflect the indicators of status noted by people on the block and some of the significance attached to them. In fact, although he bought the *New York Times,* Mike Jensen showed numerous symptoms of actual mental instability. The residents of Norman Street did not miss this, and they talked of him as "weird." Yet his opinions still carried weight. He talked about a franchise that he owned for the development of a mobile supermarket. He even offered to employ Rosie Sheehan and Anthony in March. Both of them considered the offer seriously and talked about it for some time. But as the months passed and the date for the opening of the supermarket shifted from March to May to June to September, their belief in the possibility of the job diminished.

As will be shown later, low-income, poorly educated people such as those of the Norman Street Block Association are often vulnerable to manipulation by members of the educated middle class. Of all the people in the association, Mrs. Sheehan alone had completed high school (although Mrs. Ferguson had passed the high school equivalency examination). They are open to manipulation partly because of their own ignorance and partly because they believe that anybody with education or money must know better than they. Such people have little faith in their own understanding of their situation. Here was an example of a newcomer with little knowledge of the area and no special organizing skills, but with an educated "presentation," who suggested a project which Norman Street residents were prepared to accept as eminently practical.

The street fair held on August 14 and 15, 1976, was the only planned event to come to fruition during the year-long existence of the Norman Street Block Association. Although the fair was under discussion from March 1976, the decision to hold it and actual preparation only materialized in June. At that point Anthony began collecting old clothes, books, and other potentially marketable goods. He stored them in the basement of his apartment building. Anthony and Rosie Sheehan also prepared a flyer which she copied on the mimeographed machine at the NNC office and distributed to mailboxes along the block.

At the end of July, a group of Norman Street residents led by Anthony and Mrs. Sheehan began to meet once a week on Mary Sanchez's front steps to discuss detailed preparations for the street fair. All the members of the association who had been present at the November meeting were involved in preparations, and Mary Sanchez and several other women also became active participants. As will be discussed in the next chapter, the involvement of material resources in block association activities, such as the potential for making money at the fair, brought participants who did not attend normal association meetings. Along with Cecilia Berette pushing her son in a baby carriage, I visited the stores along the main commercial avenue to ask for donations. Stores offered goods ranging in value from 50¢ to $10, with a greater number in the lower range. Storeowners looked askance at the idea of a Norman Street fair because of the reputation of the block. This was further reason why the association wanted to hold the fair and why the impressive dance had been important— to redeem the reputation of the block.

Few people attended the fair, and little was sold. After many hours of work put in by more than fifteen people, the association just managed to break even. When the cost of food that was cooked and other expenses were reimbursed, no profit remained. Over the entire two days, receipts totaled only $105.

The disappointment of this defeat destroyed the Norman Street Block Association. After the strain and tension of that weekend, no further meetings were ever held. Anthony and Rosie Sheehan discussed scheduling meetings several times but never managed to gather people together. They too seemed to have lost interest.

Underlying Problems in the Norman Street Block Association

Class Factors and Charisma

The problem of "educated" middle-class people exerting unwarranted influence over low-income Greenpoint-Williamsburg inhabitants described above, appeared in other contexts too. Thus, a man with a bachelor's degree who was a social worker for an agency offered group therapy to the mothers in a local Parent-Teachers Association. Eight women participated and became personally involved with the "therapist." Two of them told me that they became so infatuated with the man that they believed every word he said. He told one of the women that she was an alcoholic and suicidal. Understandably, these accusations upset her considerably. When I met this woman, about six months after her "diagnosis," she drank only at parties or on social occasions, and then not excessively. She was a capable mother of three children; managed a full-time job, housework, and community activities; and sometimes became depressed. A year later she was a leading organizer of a slate for the school board election. There was little to indicate any extreme mental disorder such as that described by the man who appointed himself a therapist.

The opinions of people on the block and those with a similar lack of education seemed to the people on Norman Street to carry less weight. Insults were laughed at, and snubs were often ignored among the women. Individuals would frequently retaliate immediately, and they rarely brooded over the import of remarks. They easily became angry but did not generally accept criticisms or personal slights as valid evaluations of their characters. However, the pronouncements of individuals with a higher level of education and broader social contacts had a more disturbing effect.

In the conviction of their own ignorance, therefore, the poorer members of the Greenpoint-Williamsburg community were led to accept ideas that they might otherwise have examined more closely. As in the case of the fair, this sometimes had negative effects on their attempt to organize among themselves and sometimes even damaged their ability to cope with daily problems. In some cases a welfare worker or legal adviser who had not paid much attention to the case he was dealing with led individuals astray. Residents of Norman Street seldom judged the efficacy of "expert" advice with the same harshness with which they examined a less-educated person's remarks.

Participation and Residence

Although people from throughout the neighborhood helped with some events, residence on the block appeared to be a determining characteristic for attendance at block association meetings. When Jenny Ferguson, Anthony's older sister, moved off the block, she stopped coming to meetings. When Arlene Brock moved to Ealing Street, she stopped attending, even though she came back to Norman Street every night to visit Davida Delgado and her older sister, Mary Sanchez. Cecilia Berette continued to attend meetings for some time after she moved into her mother's apartment but was still paying rent on Norman Street. When Sharon, Anthony's younger sister, moved back on the block, she started to attend meetings.

In involving Anthony, the vice-president, in the group, Rosie Sheehan brought in a set of contacts which remained the basis of the organization throughout the year. If her relatives or friends had lived on the block, Mrs. Sheehan might have been able to mobilize a different network of people. Her two sisters and her parents lived in the neighborhood, but not on Norman Street. She had been born in the area and had always lived there, but did not play an active part in the social interactions and reciprocal relations formed on the block. Since the development of a block association by its nature restricted the territory for recruitment, Mrs. Sheehan could not rely on her own kin connections.

Social Interaction on the Block

Like Rosie Sheehan, Joe Gallo was not part of the strong informal gossip network. The other seven people who formed the core of the association participated daily in social interaction on the block. They knew many of the people in the surrounding apartments, details of their family lives, and information about their relatives. When any of these acquaintances walked down the street, members of this group could often predict where they were going. They knew what time people came home from work, and where to wait if they wanted to speak to them. Acquaintances were spoken to on the street; it was only on rare occasions that neighbors would knock on someone's door or enter their apartment. Even though Rosie Sheehan had a telephone, Anthony would wait for her outside when he wanted to discuss the affairs of the association. This method was often ineffective; Mrs. Sheehan did not always come straight home from work. If he missed her, Anthony would simply wait for her again the next night. Sometimes he would have to wait for several weeks before he could see her.

A woman might specifically visit the apartment of a good friend. More often, she would send a child around to let her friend know she wanted to meet her in the street, or simply to take a message. People would visit an apartment to play cards in the evening or if invited for a baby shower or other special occasion. One or two good friends would wander into each other's apartments to sit, gossip, and watch television. Whenever the weather permitted, instead of watching television, residents sat out on the stoops until late at night to watch people on the street.

In winter groups congregated in one of two kitchens belonging to apartments close to the street. Families who had had their electricity turned off because they had not paid the bills went to their friends' apartments to watch television. If a household could afford it, women went bowling once a week during the winter and to bingo frequently throughout the year. During much of the cold weather, women stayed in their own apartments watching television while their children amused themselves. Men also often stayed home and watched television. They went bowling and to bingo, sometimes in separate groups and sometimes with the women. They were, however, more likely than women to spend evenings with friends at local bars. Because of this bias toward street life, especially among women, the seven individuals whom I met at my first block association meeting were not a discrete action group, apart from their neighbors. Nor were they lacking in wide local contacts. In recruiting Anthony, Rosie had tapped a channel of local energy with many possible ramifications.

There were also limitations set by this mode of daily and seasonal organization. Interactions on the block were dominated by women. Although several men appeared at different times at block association meetings, and Anthony and Joe Gallo were regularly present, no network of male friendships was ever mobilized in relation to the association. Partly because he was unemployed, had not joined a street gang, or found friends in a bar or through drug-related activities, Anthony was not a good source of further male contacts. The block association became largely a concern of local women and children. Husbands and boyfriends would "help the women" quite frequently, but they seldom made public appearances at block functions or monthly meetings.

Male friendship groups centered upon work, local bars, and for the young boys (often in trouble), street corners. Some also frequented social and political clubs. There was an active teen-age street-corner gang on Norman Street. Its members were infamous among other youths throughout Greenpoint-Williamsburg. There were also bars at each end of the block. One, which served both Norman Street and the commercial street with which it intersected, was notorious for its drunken clientele, who would wander down the block in various stages of intoxication. The other bar was less unruly and was frequented mainly by men and women from the block, one of whom was a part-time bartender.

The women in the block association made no attempt to recruit either the boys in the street gang or the clientele of the corner bars for their projects. Sometimes they were harassed by the street-corner gang, which was widely feared. Gang members carried knives which they held threateningly visible upon occasion. Nevertheless, the women of Norman Street scolded and yelled at these youths, whom they had known since they were children, and appeared to exercise considerable control over them. When fights occurred the women did not run away but came out into the street. On several occasions during the summer that I lived in the neighborhood, these women appeared to have prevented violent outbreaks from escalating into major street riots. One hot Saturday evening, for example, they resorted to throwing garbage can lids and rolling the cans themselves at a group of fighting youths. Women also placed themselves between a band and a street gang at the Norman Street fair. In spite of their familiarity with and degree of influence over the youths, no attempt was made to involve them in block activities. The gang was regarded as a source of trouble rather than of aid.

Frequenters of the "bad" corner bar were also regarded with

apprehension. During the summer this bar organized barbecues, and there were often as many or more young people in the street around the bar as in the bar itself. The women of the block association and their friends were familiar with the company and occasionally spent an evening in the bar, or at the least, bought a late-night pack of cigarettes there. However, resentment against the notoriety of this bar and the bad publicity which it gave to the block was often voiced at association meetings. Remarks such as, "They don't even live on Norman Street, and we get blamed for it" were common at every meeting. It was one of the stated aims of the association to have the bar closed. This objective, however, was never acted on in any way.

The hostility of block association members to the bar was justified. Most of the youths and young women who hung around did not live on the block, although several of them once had. Fights outside the bar were common. One evening two black men (one of them the boyfriend of a pregnant woman on the block) were assaulted in front of the bar. One lost an ear, and both were badly beaten. The assailants were known to residents of the block and identified as bar clientele. However, their names were not reported to the police.

Similar incidents involved several well-known bars in the neighborhood. The previous summer the Puerto Rican boyfriend of a Jewish woman resident was attacked. When the woman's father pursued the attackers, he was murdered. Such brutal events were the basis for the resentment of local women toward the bar on their corner, yet they had difficulty implementing any action against it simply because it was also an integral part of their own social life. If they did not go there often, their daughters, husbands, or boyfriends did. Because of their close contacts, they were well informed about events occurring in the environment of the bar while remaining powerless to do anything about them.

Racial Conflict on Norman Street

The teen-age youths in the street gangs and the men of all ages who gathered in the local bars directed much of their violence and hostility against black and Hispanic men, whom they saw as a personal threat. Women in the association and their friends on the block often expressed quite different attitudes toward blacks and Hispanics. Some were part or wholly Puerto Rican themselves; others were married to Puerto Rican men or had black or Puerto Rican boyfriends. One white family of two parents and four children had adopted a black child. Although the women on the block made outraged statements in open disapproval of the men's behavior, they were also torn by their loyalty to their white male acquaintances and relatives who were likely to have been involved in the racial incidents.

One woman remarked to me that she thought all people should be treated equally regardless of race. She referred to the fact that her father, who had left her mother, was Puerto Rican, and that two of her sisters were living with Puerto Rican men. However, when her husband, a white truck driver, came home, he gave me a drunken lecture on "how they had to be beat up—before they get to you. They are always the enemy. Just you wait and see. When we were kids, that was one thing, everyone was together. But now, that's just the way it is. You've got to get them." His wife did not reiterate any of her previous remarks about the equality of members of different ethnic groups in front of her husband. She did not remind him that her own father was Puerto Rican.

Another man was subpoenaed to appear in court to testify about a murder of a Hispanic man which had occurred during a bar brawl. When he failed to appear, his wife told the prosecutors that he had left home. Such a reaction to court proceedings was a stated policy among the men who received subpoenas. This man knew who had been involved in the fight but told me that he was unwilling to incriminate his friends. He may also have been afraid of group retaliation, although he was not explicit about this.

Although the members of the association and several other residents on the block maintained social contacts with individuals from all ethnic groups, they functioned within the shadow of violence from their own friends and relatives. As mentioned earlier, several ethnic groups were represented on Norman Street. There were Poles who still spoke only Polish, Koreans who spoke only Korean, Puerto Ricans and Dominicans who spoke only

Spanish, and several people of mixed ethnic backgrounds who had grown up in America and were at least conversant in English. There were no people who were classified by the residents as black living on Norman Street. Many of the Puerto Ricans were dark-skinned, but they were regarded as "Spanish," not "black," by the local inhabitants. The absence of black residents was not fortuitous, nor was it due to housing discrimination alone. We have seen that a black family had lived in an apartment building in the middle of the block until that building was burned down in a fire attributed to arson. This became the only burned-out site on the street, and the arson was ascribed to racism by local residents. In view of the other violent incidents in the neighborhood, this was a likely although unverified explanation. A few people accused the black tenants of setting fire to their own building, although the motives for such behavior were not discussed.

Some incidents of racist behavior on the part of Norman Street residents were more clearly verifiable, as was the effort by other individuals to counter them. One such episode occurred when a band was needed for the block association street fair. Anthony telephoned several groups in the area to invite them to play. Every group turned the offer down because of the reputation of Norman Street as a rough street with a dangerous gang. Finally, I telephoned the leader of a rock band that I knew in Williamsburg, and he agreed to play. When I called back to make more specific arrangements, however, he told me that other members of his band (Hispanic residents of the South Side of Williamsburg) refused to participate when they discovered that the engagement was for Norman Street. He, a white man raised in Brooklyn of Jewish parents, had been unaware of the problem and surprised at the response.

Eventually a mixed white, black, and Hispanic group from Manhattan's Lower East Side—one with no knowledge of conditions in this part of Brooklyn—agreed to perform. The block association organizers were pleased to have acquired the group but apprehensive about the response of their neighbors to a band which included blacks.

They were right to be apprehensive. When the group arrived to play, the apartment owner in the middle of the block who had agreed to allow them to hook up to his electrical outlet changed his mind. The performers had to carry their equipment to the end of the block where Rosie Sheehan arranged for them to plug into outlets in her house. The atmosphere on the block was tense although the entertainment was much appreciated and people leaned out of their windows to listen to the music. It was significant, however, that few came directly out into the street.

As the performance continued, a group of youths from the street gang on the corner began to congregate nearby. Block association women gathered between the group and the street-corner youths. Rosie Sheehan informed me later that residents believed that as long as she and another woman, Linda McGill, who had grown up on the block, stayed between the band and the hostile youths, nothing would happen. Linda sat on the steps with her baby in the carriage, watching the events.

Fortunately, perhaps, it soon began to rain, and the band started to pack up its equipment. By this time the gang had been joined by several older men, one of whom lived in the next house. The youths had taken out knives and were holding them in view of the people on the street and the band. The members of the band remained cool and unhurried. They loaded their truck with equipment and got into their cars, ready to go. Women from the block association brought them food which they ate sitting in the cars. They then left quickly.

This incident illustrates both the problems that the block association had to overcome in relation to any event that it organized and the divisions among the residents themselves with respect to racial attitudes. Racial conflict inhibited the unity of the association and the cooperation its members could expect even from neighbors of their own ethnic groups.

Organizers were aware that without the help of black neighborhood groups and of the band, whose services had been donated, the street fair would not have been possible. Anthony and Rosie Sheehan had borrowed stoves and tables for stalls from a black tenants' association in Woodlawn. This assistance was more significant in light of the fact that the supervisor of the Polish-American Community Center had refused to help out. They had also received much advice about how to prepare for the event from members of the tenants' association, who had themselves organized a similar activity. Yet residents on the block who had not helped organize the street fair and who may or may not have been aware of the nature of this outside help registered their racial hostility in overtly violent ways.

Racial conflict was also evident when a black man was hired to teach gym at a YMCA close to Norman Street. He was a competent teacher, and his classes were well attended. He was, however, often seen with a married white woman who was a student in one of his classes. A rumor circulated that they were "seeing each other," and the woman and the YMCA director received several threatening telephone calls. The instructor was fired the following week, and a young white man hired in his place.

On another occasion, a Woodlawn group organized a circus outing for several hundred children from the project. Norman Street residents, although invited, refused to send their children. Having learned how to buy cheap tickets at group rates from the black tenants' association, Anthony Sanchez had to arrange a separate set of tickets in order to bring Norman Street children on a different date.

Episodes such as these, which made organizing of any kind a problem, were exacerbated by the multi-ethnic composition of the block. Once a Puerto Rican woman who lived on Norman Street and whose children were among my acquaintances asked if she could come to a block association meeting. I took her and her two children with me. I introduced her to the members, who already knew her from the street. Rosie Sheehan ignored her during the entire meeting. Afterwards I asked Mrs. Sheehan if this was intentional hostility. I assumed that a community organizer would want to recruit as many residents as possible. She answered that she had not meant to neglect the woman or put her in an uncomfortable position. She simply did not know her and therefore had no reason to speak to her. Since I had observed people of other ethnic backgrounds ignored in similar situations—and had experienced the same treatment myself on occasion—I did not interpret Mrs. Sheehan's behavior as necessarily racist. But the woman against whom it was directed may have come to that conclusion. She did not attend another meeting, and her acquaintances on the block, most of whom were Hispanic, made no attempt to join the organization. Little effort was made to recruit them, other than the distribution of announcements for meetings. Even this was half-hearted. One afternoon, when I was helping Mrs. Sheehan distribute some leaflets, I noticed that she had missed a group of women and children standing on the corner. She consistently avoided handing leaflets to certain women. On being questioned she replied, "Oh, you know, they're the Spanish, they wouldn't understand anyway." She decided not to hand them leaflets without ascertaining whether or not these particular Hispanic women understood English.

The block association, it will be remembered, was started by a policeman in cooperation with several community workers. The New York Police Department was carrying out a mayoral policy of encouraging block associations through the Federation of Block Associations sponsored by the city administration. Its objective was to initiate self-help programs aimed at reducing maintenance costs for a city caught in a fiscal crisis. Although begun with police assistance, the Norman Street Block Association did not become a flexible tool in the interests of the New York City administration. Meetings attended by police were oriented toward complaints against residents (such as discussions about the gang at the street corner). The people who joined the association were able to direct discussion toward protest against city neglect. Discussion at block association meetings tended to reflect members' own preoccupations rather than those of the police or the municipal administration.

As the members of the association began to implement their projects, they came in contact with black groups having similar goals. We have seen in the process of organizing, members of the association received support, both in the form of materials and through advice from black groups. Contacts with these groups and experience with the problems of collective action led to a diminution of the distrust between some members of the block association and the black tenants' association.

But cooperation between community groups was slow to develop into more advanced collective activities because of the threat of violence on Norman Street. The black tenants' association in Woodlawn was far better organized and had more experience with recruitment, the management of events, and protest action than did members of the Norman Street Block Association. The neighborhood's history of racial conflict prevented the association from profiting fully from the knowledge and experience of other poor working-class people living under conditions very similar to their own.

Although the Norman Street Block Association led to some cooperation across racial barriers, major organizing problems derived from divisions of class, race, and gender, institutionalized in housing, employment, and educational opportunities. In addition to the racial problems, for example, a depreciated sense of self caused residents to adopt ideas put forth by "educated" people, and a poor sense of group dynamics on the part of leaders exacerbated an already delicate situation. Sex role divisions among residents caused problems in recruitment and task assignment. Thus, policy and recruitment problems which on the surface appeared to be related to inefficiency or lack of organizational skill were found on further analysis to be rooted in institutional divisions of the larger society. In the next chapter we shall examine the issues around which successful events were organized and the way in which successes were also closely related to the class position and material needs of the Norman Street residents.

CHAPTER 8

Making Things Work

Two programs which involved the distribution of resources on Norman Street stimulated interest among block residents and were successfully organized: a summer lunch program and a play street. A third project, decorating for the Bicentennial celebrations of 1976, was also completed as planned.

The Summer Lunch Program

People on Norman Street generally ate their main meal at dinner, around 5 P.M. every evening. If an individual's work hours conflicted with this, his dinner time would be changed to fit his work schedule. Sometimes dinner would be as late as 10 P.M. or as early as 3 P.M. When Anthony Sanchez worked a night shift, he had dinner at 2 A.M., when he arrived home in the morning. Dinner typically consisted of a little meat combined with a large amount of sauce and rice, spaghetti, potatoes, or bread. Lunch was not a formal meal unless structured by school or work. Sometimes ham or bologna sandwiches were eaten. Breakfast often consisted of a cup of tea or coffee and a bowl of cereal. Meals were supplemented by frequent purchases of ice cream, small prewrapped cream and chocolate cakes, packets of potato chips, and similar cheap prepackaged food high in sugar and other carbohydrates. Free food, such as doughnuts and cakes, often provided at neighborhood events, was eaten in large quantities. These high-starch foods constituted an inexpensive method of building up calories to assuage hunger. The purchase of vegetables, which supplied fewer calories, was regarded as a luxury and only occurred on special occasions such as Thanksgiving or Christmas. Poor working-class Greenpoint-Williamsburg residents were often excessively overweight and subject to diabetes and high blood pressure, probably as a result of eating habits conditioned by the high price of food and the economy of postponing hunger with the purchase of sweet, high-carbohydrate foods. People on Norman Street were aware that highly caloric foods contributed to weight and health problems, but they could not afford the luxury of dieting. The summer lunch program, funded by the federal government, was a welcome addition to the food supply of many households. The provision of cold-cut sandwiches, packaged crackers, and cookies suited the habitual diet of the low-income Norman Street residents.

Beginning in 1972, from May to September the Food and Nutrition Service of the United States Department of Agriculture provided free breakfasts, lunches, suppers, and snacks to children from low-income areas. In 1976, when the events on Norman Street described here took place, food was funded through grants to the New York State Department of Education. Two percent of the grant was allocated for administrative costs.[1] In 1976 sponsoring agencies made up of public and nonprofit private service institutions applied for funds from the New York State Department of Education. Caterers were then allowed to bid for contracts to supply food to the sponsoring agencies, which in turn chose vendors and coordinated the distribution of the food. In 1977, due to accusations of the acceptance of excessively high bids in 1976, the bidding for contracts by vendor corporations was initiated by the New York State Department of Education rather than left to the sponsoring agencies.

Representatives from the sites at which summer lunches were to be distributed applied for food through the sponsoring agencies. Sites included day care centers, play streets, and community

---

1. In 1978 the state Department of Education claimed that administrative costs were too high, and the program was afterwards administered directly by the federal government.

service centers. The sponsoring agencies determined the eligibility of the requests and notified the New York State Department of Education of the number of lunches and their costs.

Before a site was approved, it was inspected by the Department of Education for adequate facilities, provision for inclement weather, and the availability of refrigeration for unused food. Food allocation was not directly conditioned by individual need in 1976. If one third of the children to be served were low-income families, all children at the site were entitled to free lunches.[2]

In the summer of 1976, articles appeared in the *Daily News,* the *New York Post,* and the *New York Times* denouncing the misuse of food from the summer lunch programs. Several articles attacked the distribution among the poor; most of these articles did not investigate the quality of the food and the inadequate facilities for transporting it to the needy. Both newspapers and television news claimed that people were taking more than they needed and that the program was not well monitored.

In May 1976 Anthony Sanchez, with the encouragement of Mary Sanchez, requested free lunch delivery for the children on Norman Street. He registered with the Italian-American Committee as sponsoring agency, not because of any institutional connections but because an acquaintance of his worked there and provided him with the necessary forms.

To meet the requirements of the program, Mary Sanchez and Davida Delgado, both residents of Norman Street, arranged for an old refrigerator to be moved into the Sanchez basement. Since the food had to be brought to a house with a telephone, Mrs. Delgado agreed to accept the daily deliveries at her apartment. This was convenient since she had a ground floor apartment and was always home. In contrast to the failure of coordination and participation in block association events described previously, when the food did not arrive on schedule, Davida Delgado immediately telephoned to complain.

After the summer lunch program started, block residents arranged a system to distribute the lunches. Seven women, some of

2. In 1978 regulations were changed. Only children from low-income families were entitled to the free food.

whom were association members and who also formed a friendship group, became involved in the task.

All seven of the organizers—Mary Sanchez, Davida Delgado, Cecilia Berette, Arlene Brock, Sharon Bianco, Rosie Sheehan, and Sonya Garcia (a Puerto Rican woman who lived upstairs from Mrs. Delgado with her husband and two children)—took enough lunches to feed their households. They also collected milk cartons sufficient for all household uses. Whenever I or any other personal friends of the organizers appeared on the block, we were offered a lunch packet. Three or four lunch packets were always saved for the household of Elizabeth Brock, Mary, Arlene, and Cecilia's mother. Carol McGill, a grandmother in her forties, lived in the ground-floor apartment next to the Delgados. She was a longtime friend of Mary Sanchez, and her daughter had been friendly with Anthony Sanchez since they were children. Mrs. McGill collected lunch packets for herself, her husband, her two adult unmarried daughters, and her two grandchildren, although her daughters had moved to an apartment three blocks away from Norman Street.

The lunches were delivered to the Delgado apartment at any time between 7:30 A.M. and noon. The recently supplied refrigerator, a regulation requirement, was not in functioning order, and milk and orange drinks were transferred into an insulated icebox. From 11:30 A.M. onwards, little children began arriving, requesting lunches for their homes. Sometimes children picked up one or two lunches, but generally they would ask for five or six. Since the women distributing the food were familiar with most of the children and knew the size of their families as well as whether certain members were away that day and why extra food was sometimes requested, they could evaluate whether or not a child's demands were excessive and allot food according to their own criteria.

Despite the infamous reports of the free lunch program in the New York press, food on Norman Street was not wasted. Extra food was seldom seen scattered on the ground in the fashion described in the papers. Although lunches were distributed to children, they were eaten by families; food which was not eaten was due to the quality of the catering rather than to the profligacy of the receivers since much was exceptionally poor. Lunches were composed of one slice of meat such as olive loaf, two pieces of white bread, a packet with a few cheese crackers, a carton of milk, and a piece of fruit. The olive loaf was sometimes replaced by a slice of bologna, and occasionally there were a couple of small pieces of cold fried chicken. When chicken was served, the people on the block commented on the improved quality of the food. The food did not seem fresh, and the bread was often stale. One morning Davida Delgado received a special emergency call from the caterers. They informed her that the meat had turned green and ought not to be eaten. She and the other women on the block had already noticed this and had only distributed the milk and crackers.

In many cases the summer lunch program appeared to provide a major portion of a family's nutrition. The lunches often were stored in people's refrigerators until later in the day. Among families closely associated with the organizers, the substitution of summer lunch sandwiches for the evening meal seemed to be common practice.

Elizabeth Brock, fifty-seven years old, lived partly on food saved from the summer lunch program. She had worked from the age of eighteen until she was fifty-five as a cleaning lady in a factory and intermittently on assembly lines. For the last two years her arthritis had been getting progressively worse, and by 1976 it was impossible for her to lift anything. She also had difficulty walking. She would have been eligible for free lunches distributed to the homes of disabled persons but had not applied for such assistance.[3] Instead, her family helped her with whatever resources were available to them.

Carol McGill earned approximately $100 a week at Leviton Manufacturing Company, where she had been working full-time on an evening shift for two years. Her husband, who had been working longer, brought home a little more money. Since Mr. McGill spent a considerable amount of their meager income on

3. Since the age for senior citizen status and its provision of free lunches was sixty years, Mrs. Brock was under the impression that she was not eligible for any free lunch program.

alcohol, the free lunches constituted an important part of their domestic economy. One evening as I was sitting with a group of women and children on the steps outside her apartment, Mrs. McGill came out to gossip. She often emerged about half an hour before she had to leave to work the midnight shift at Leviton's. In the course of the conversation, she mentioned that she had been hungry and had eaten her lunch packet. She complained in a joking way that now she would have no food to eat during her eight hours at work. She said that the second lunch packet was for her husband to take to work, and that she had to leave it for him. It appeared that they had arranged their expenses for the week around the provision of free food. If they diverged from the plan, there was no extra cash to buy ingredients for another meal. This was a common pattern among all the households involved in the distribution of free lunches.

Before the start of the summer lunch program, Anthony and Mary Sanchez often went for several days without an evening meal. When they had food, they would give some to Cecilia Berette. She and her husband often lacked the money to buy dinner and would rely on her mother or sisters, Mary and Arlene, to have something for them to eat. If there was nothing at her mother's house, the Berettes would borrow money or else go without dinner. The lunch program supplemented the Berette family's food supply over the summer months.

It was over this general use of the food that a dispute arose among the women on the block. The conflict made clear which women were in control of the situation and their attitude toward the summer lunch program. It also illustrated the effectiveness with which these women could collaborate when actual resources were put at their disposal. The people on Norman Street read accusations against the organization of the summer lunch program practically every day in the *Daily News* ("the paper," as they referred to it) and watched the program vilified almost every evening on television. Public criticism of the program provided a setting for grievances among women on the block to be expressed.

Maureen Jones was an unemployed mother of four children, with a fifth child whom she and the unemployed man with whom she lived had adopted. They lived largely on welfare assistance, although the man of the house worked intermittently at various jobs. Both were extremely overweight, and he had a weak heart while she had diabetes. Their unemployment was due to ill health as well as the state of the job market. Although the Jones children collected five free lunches a day, Mrs. Jones felt that she was entitled to more. She was aware that close friends of the organizers collected enough lunches to feed adults as well. She knew that they divided the packets left at the end of the day among themselves, and she complained several times that she was not allocated more food.

Mrs. Jones threatened to inform the city authorities that food was being distributed among adults. In retaliation, and also out of fear of the authorities, Mary Sanchez immediately telephoned the Italian-American Community Center and cancelled the lunch program. This action was taken after a joint decision with Davida Delgado. Once they had decided on this course of action, they had no difficulty implementing it. The process was remarkably different from the long pointless deliberations which had occurred at block association meetings.

With the cancellation of the lunch program, and the obvious demonstration of power by the two women, the dispute was quickly resolved. Nobody wanted to lose the lunches altogether. It was clear that Mary Sanchez and Davida Delgado were responsible for the fact that the food arrived on the block at all. Mrs. Jones apologized to Anthony Sanchez and explained that she recognized the amount of work that they had all put into improving conditions on the block. Another woman had been making a collection to help Anthony financially, and she mentioned to me and to Anthony's mother that Mrs. Jones had contributed a dollar to the fund. This may not seem like a large amount of money, but to a group of people who might receive a welfare check of only $60 to $70 every two weeks, and to Anthony, who then had no income at all, it appeared a significant contribution.

Two days later Mary Sanchez again telephoned the Italian-American Community Center, and the lunches were restored. After this demonstration of their power, the methods of distribution organized by Mrs. Sanchez and Mrs. Delgado were no longer questioned, although they remained carefully scrutinized by their neighbors.

While they were not explicit about their policy, it was clear that Mrs. Delgado and Mrs. Sanchez more or less guaranteed free lunches to certain adults. Yet they never deprived any children of meals, no matter how much enmity might exist between them and the parents. Such practices would probably have caused open rebellion by other parents on the block. It was always possible for dissatisfied block residents to make a few telephone calls and precipitate investigation either by newspaper reporters or, less speedily and with less certainty, by the city agency responsible for the program. In spite of the danger of this happening, certain adults invariably received lunches, which sometimes formed the main meal of the day.

Thus the free lunch program, although not conducted legally, became an essential resource on the block. Food was not limited to young children, but it was rarely wasted. The importance of the program to the people who received it was reflected in the energy that they expended in maintaining it. In contrast to less concretely rewarding block improvement projects, street cooperation and efficiency in the organization of the lunch program were at a high level. Such behavior highlights the demoralizing aspect of the Norman Street Block Association's efforts. When there was some possibility of success and a direct improvement in life conditions was a goal, decision-making and collective action became effective. A second consequence of the availability of resources was the enlistment of leading women on the block into the coordination of the project. This too facilitated the functioning of the program, resulting in further involvement and a greater sense of control and accomplishment.

The summer lunch program brought Mary Sanchez and Davida Delgado and several other women into active cooperation with Rosie Sheehan and led to a more cohesive group, able to undertake other activities on the block. One such activity was the organization of a play street, which was in operation through the summer vacation.

A Play Street

On a play street the passage of cars is blocked, and children are allowed to play safely in the street. In areas of New York City where parks are scarce, such arrangements are common for poor children who remain at home during the long hot summers of the school vacation. A play street could be authorized through a request to the mayor's office. If the request was approved, barriers would be placed at each end of the street to prevent the passage of cars during determined weekday hours. The mayor's office did not provide play equipment or supervision.

In 1976 play streets with child supervision and equipment were organized by the Police Athletic League (PAL). Generally a resident would contact a community relations patrolman who would contact PAL. PAL officials would survey the street to make sure it complied with minimum requirements. The street had to serve only one-way traffic, could not be on a route used by the New York City Fire Department, and could not serve too many businesses or factories. The condition of the street and the number of children involved in the program were also considered. The approval of residents on the block was required. PAL officers claimed that income was not a criterion for the creation of a play street but that they only received requests from low-income areas.

Norman Street had been authorized as a play street by the mayor's office for three consecutive summers before the summer of 1976, when Anthony Sanchez and Rosie Sheehan requested assistance from PAL. The play street was in operation for the same period as the summer lunch program, and it came to be supervised by the same group of Norman Street residents.

PAL sent one paid supervisor to the Norman Street block several days a week and supplied ropes, balls, bats, and other game equipment for daily use. Markings were painted on the street for the boundaries of different games. A Norman Street adult resident had to sit with a checklist at an equipment table to write down the names of children using equipment from midday until 8 P.M. and to oversee the collection of equipment at closing time. Davida

Delgado, Mary Sanchez, Rosie Sheehan, Sharon Bianco, and Cecilia Berette alternated shifts in order to conduct the supervision.

At least fifty children appeared on the block, entering skipping competitions, playing volleyball, and participating in other activities. The children ranged in age from one to twelve years, with the majority around six, seven, and eight. They did not all reside on the block, and they came from many ethnic backgrounds. A large proportion were from Hispanic families. The adults who supervised the play street knew most of the children by name.

If the Norman Street residents who organized the play street felt that a woman was not sufficiently helpful, they would let her know. They would make remarks behind her back, and when she appeared, they would ignore her. At one point Mary Sanchez and Davida Delgado and finally Anthony became angry with Rosie Sheehan because they thought she should be doing more work. When she approached the group, people would stop talking. Mrs. Sanchez eventually shouted at her. Mrs. Sheehan continued to appear on the block and to carry out part of the work. She sat on her own at the corner with a small portable television for company. After a week of punishing Mrs. Sheehan, Norman Street residents became involved in organizing the street fair, and Mary Sanchez remarked that she thought Rosie had done her share of the work. Organizers began talking to her again.

The play street required several other activities besides the doling out of equipment. The most difficult task was to keep residents from parking cars on both sides of the street and to prevent other cars from driving through during the period that the street was closed. Parking regulations were displayed on the block, and it was the job of the local police to enforce them. In other parts of New York City, cars are ticketed mercilessly. In Greenpoint-Williamsburg, however, tickets are rare and seldom distributed off the main commercial avenue. Drivers tended to ignore parking regulations on Norman Street, and it was left to residents themselves to enforce them.

Barricades were requested when the play street opened. This was a standard procedure. But the week the play street was organized, police officers informed the Norman Street Block Association that all the barricades in the city were being used for a Democratic convention being held in Manhattan.

A major consequence of the convention for Greenpoint-Williamsburg was a reduction in city services.[4] Services were then running at such a low level that the slightest alteration or exceptional demand led to a diminution of standard provisions in parts of the system. While the press reported how much the delegates enjoyed city life and how much Manhattan businesses appreciated the delegates, residents of Greenpoint-Williamsburg cursed the convention. They resented their loss of services, and they could see no advantage accruing to them from the temporary influx of tourists and political officials. One of the women on the block suggested that "somebody should go down there and shoot the whole lot of them." Although most remarks were not quite so explicitly violent, her words reflected a general attitude. This was not to say, however, that Greenpoint-Williamsburg itself was not a heavily Democratic district.

Since police barricades were not available, the women on the block improvised. Mrs. Sanchez, Mrs. Sheehan, and Mrs. Berette placed boards over garbage cans at the end of the block. Whenever a car started to break through the barricade—which happened frequently—one of these three women would run down the street and loudly reprimand the driver. The cars generally backed out of the way. Even after the police provided official barricades a week later, such episodes were frequent, and the residents had to keep constant guard over the entrance to the play street. Continual vigilance was necessary since most of the very young children, who had previously been trained through slaps and scoldings to avoid stepping off the curb, had lost their recognition of street danger. This was another area in which collective action among the parents was both essential and effective.

4. The Bicentennial celebrations in New York City on July 4, 1976, had similar consequences for regular municipal services. The sanitation men failed to collect the garbage for a week. Norman Street residents noted this with resentment. It was a further illustration of the limits on municipal resources and the priorities of the city administration. Gala events were organized to raise the prestige of New York City while services in low-income areas were reduced.

The Bicentennial

In 1976 the Bicentennial became a focus of nationwide publicity. All over the country, mayors and other municipal officials were encouraging the painting of hydrants, lampposts, and telephone poles red, white, and blue. A presidential Bicentennial speech was scheduled for Philadelphia on the Fourth of July. In New York City, a sailing-ship regatta up the Hudson, fireworks, and other special events were planned for the same weekend.

In Greenpoint a Bicentennial Barge was organized by the Civic Council. The local newspapers offered a prize to the child who painted a hydrant in the best way. Publicity for the Bicentennial was widespread. In January the members of the Norman Street Block Association started to discuss painting a mural on Norman Street. It was generally agreed that the mural should be painted in red, white, and blue and that it should be a traditional representation, perhaps of people arriving in a ship or of the signing of the Declaration of Independence.

In March Anthony Sanchez made a collection door-to-door on Norman Street and received $40 to decorate the block for the Bicentennial. He invested the money in red, white, and blue flags and paint. In April he began painting the hydrants, lampposts, and telephone poles. Several young children helped him, but for the most part Anthony painted the whole block by himself. His work was much admired by block residents. A month later a collection was taken up to pay Anthony for some of the work he had done. This time the total came to $30.

In May Anthony hung flags diagonally across Norman Street, in a zigzag from house to house down the block. Five apartment owners refused to allow flags to be hung from their buildings, and the flags were arranged to miss those particular walls. On Saturday, May 21, and on several weekends following, Anthony mobilized his sisters and several of the younger women on the block, as well as about seven children, to paint a mural. Contrary to the original plans, the mural was not painted in red, white, and blue but in many bright colors, including yellow and green. It became, through the combined and unplanned efforts of all the people working on it, a representation of a cherry tree surrounded by yellow and red flowers with rabbits jumping through the air and a large yellow sun in the background. On one side was inscribed "We the people . . ." from the opening words of the Constitution. This painting may have represented aspirations and needs of children and young adults living on Norman Street. Its connection with the Bicentennial celebration appeared tenuous, and it may be seen as a metaphor for the tenuous relationship poor working-class residents of Greenpoint-Williamsburg felt they had to mainstream America. The mural was closer to a spontaneous expression of Norman Street class consciousness than to a patriotic participation in the celebration and propaganda associated with the Bicentennial.

Anthony himself, despite his energetic efforts to decorate the block, displayed a marked ambivalence toward the planned patriotism and national publicity. Until Independence Day he was still uncertain whether he would join a demonstration which was to take place in Philadelphia at the same time as President Ford's speech. The demonstration which interested Anthony and several of the Norman Street residents who were painting the mural was organized by Vietnam veterans and was billed as the "Get the rich off our backs" protest march. In the end Anthony did not attend, but his sympathies were definitely with those critical of government policies toward the poor.

Norman Street residents enjoyed the sailing-ship regatta, visited the Bicentennial Barge, and contributed money toward decorations on their street. However, they were generally skeptical about the nationwide propaganda in relation to the Bicentennial. They spent little time decorating their street or spontaneously demonstrating their views. At the point where collective activity was successful, the results did not represent patriotic attitudes but rather highlighted their sense of deprivation. If there were no trees, flowers, or rabbits on their block or anywhere in the vicinity, at least they could paint them. The sign "We the people" may have expressed an identification with revolutionary fervor for equality and peoples' rights more than an uncritical acceptance of sentiments expressed in the national and local official publicity for the Bicentennial. Without the general excitement precipitated by the national Bicentennial celebrations, however, the mural would probably not have been painted.

This project was successful partly because of the nationwide and local publicity, which may have encouraged people to donate money for decorations. Anthony Sanchez's main concern in painting the hydrants, lampposts, and telephone poles was to raise the status of the block. Once the money had been collected and the paints bought, painting the mural served as a focus of entertainment and an opportunity for spontaneous expression welcomed by many of the young people on the block. The red, white, and blue formal decorations for the Bicentennial did not arouse the same enthusiasm. Anthony painted them alone.

Possibilities for Success on Norman Street

Many instances of both successful and unsuccessful collective activity occurred among poor working-class residents of Norman Street. They were evidently a persistent phenomenon of daily interaction. The history of activity on the block preceded the block association and, although oriented around its members, activity was not led by regular participants at association meetings. The Norman Street Block Association, which might have been expected to be the prime manifestation of community spirit, was, as we have seen, a product of the influence of a local community organizer and the CETA job she procured. The significant events which were organized for the benefit of block residents were carried out and directed by local leaders who had not attended the monthly association meetings. However, their activities were initiated and supported by association members. Anthony Sanchez might not have arranged for the summer lunch program or the play street without the aid and encouragement of Rosie Sheehan, the president of the association. In the year following the dissolution of the association, neither a summer lunch program nor a PAL play street was organized.

Successful projects were also those for which public funding or assistance from nonprofit agencies (such as PAL) was forthcoming. In addition, without the stimulus of some formal organization such as the block association, ambitious projects were not initiated.

It seems that the success of a local project was integrally related to the external resources available, the existence of a local organization, and the degree to which residents on the block were able to cooperate.

Mary Sanchez, a major organizer of the play street, the street fair, and the summer lunch program, never attended a block association meeting. She did, however, attend organizational meetings once programs had been scheduled and specific tasks had to be managed. In December 1975 Mrs. Sanchez maintained that she was not interested in politics. She told me, "I'm not political. Ask my son—he knows how long it is I've not been registered to vote. I don't believe in it." She equated the block association with politics. When invited to attend, she remarked scornfully, "Oh, I wouldn't get mixed up with those things. I only go to bingo, you know. Ask my sister Arlene—she might go. She used to do all sorts of political things like that. She's very argumentative." However, when Mrs. Sanchez recognized that the control of resources for the block was involved, she immediately slipped into an organizing role. When issues became important to her, Mrs. Delgado, and Mrs. Brock, they did not leave the field open so that Rosie Sheehan could utilize their networks in order to conduct projects. They took over, using their leadership positions among the women on the street to distribute goods and encourage cooperation. Once involved, they worked long hours and committed themselves to the success of an enterprise. Thus although the Norman Street Block Association was introduced from outside, the only projects effectively carried out were those which became linked with a network of cooperation and leadership that predated the association. This network continued to affect a variety of forms of collective action after the block association became defunct. The basis of the cooperation between women on the block will be examined in detail in the next chapter.

CHAPTER 9

Kinship, Friendship, and Support

In order to meet various social and economic demands, households in Greenpoint-Williamsburg have developed a high degree of cooperation. This has allowed them to deal flexibly with the fluctuations of employment and unemployment, changes in the welfare system, the variable support that may be gained from federal agencies, and rising rents and food prices. The flexibility of Greenpoint-Williamsburg residential and cooperative arrangements complicates the concepts of household and family and leads one to question their utility in an analysis of social organization or as a basis for social policy.

A household is generally regarded as a group of people under one roof who share eating, sleeping, and financial arrangements and the care of young children. Among poor working-class residents of Greenpoint-Williamsburg, several different types of households and many forms of cooperation, both domestic and financial, must be considered. Norman Street inhabitants shared many aspects of their lives with kin and neighbors, sometimes staying for long periods in the households of relatives. Such findings suggest that a support network or some other wide grouping is the underlying basis of the interactions, dependencies, and obligations of poor working-class people.

The large number of individuals incorporated in such a support network represented an efficient method for relieving hardships caused by fluctuating employment and inadequate welfare assistance. If one person were badly in need of money for a short time (a week or a month), he or she had a wide circle of people from whom to draw small amounts of support. This wider selection of people might include at any one time more employed individuals than chance would produce in a narrow family constellation. Thus in a large group of cooperating individuals, those without jobs or adequate income could be carried along more effectively than if they became the sole burden of a small household.[1] Since everyone was existing on the margins, there seemed to be a general acceptance of the fact that each should give a little to the others. In that way, when any one person lost a job or needed assistance for some other reason, somebody would be there to help out a little.

Cooperation Between Households on Norman Street

To demonstrate the extent of cooperation between households on Norman Street, we will examine three households of the Brock-Sanchez family and one unrelated household which formed part of the same support network. This network included three other households—those of Elizabeth Brock, Arlene Brock, and Sharon Bianco—which are discussed as they interact with the four described in this section. Since Mary Sanchez played a major role in the success of activities on the Norman Street block, her household and its support network also illustrate how the networks aided the development of collective activity.

Mary Sanchez's Household

The Sanchez family lived in a fourth-floor walk-up apartment in a row of tenements. In November 1975, when I first visited them, Mary and her son Anthony were sleeping in one apartment while Mary's oldest daughter, Jenny Ferguson, and her husband and two children were living in an adjacent apartment on the same floor.

Jeannie (seventeen years old), Anthony's youngest sister, had

---

1. Carol Stack (1974) makes this argument in her description of poor black families in a northern city, and my findings suggest that the same strategies are used by poor white families in New York City.

a bed which was designated as hers in her mother's apartment. However, in November 1975 she was staying with her older sister Sharon Bianco (eighteen years old) on Ealing Street. Sharon's husband Carlos had enlisted in the army and lived in Georgia on an army base. Jeannie was keeping Sharon company and helping to look after Sharon's one-year-old son, Tommy.

Mary Sanchez received $54 in welfare assistance every two weeks and an allowance of food stamps. Jeannie was listed as her dependent, and Anthony collected weekly unemployment checks. Welfare funds paid the rent for the apartment, $104 a month.

Sharon received $216 a month from the army as a supplement provided for military wives. Sometimes her husband sent her an extra $100 out of his wages. Welfare assistance paid her rent, and she received a biweekly check. She had registered for welfare assistance before she had become pregnant for the second time, and she and the father had decided to get married in order that she might qualify for an army supplemental income. At this point in November 1975, Mary Sanchez's household was in better financial condition than it was for the entire year following.

In the living room, which one entered on coming through the front door of her railroad apartment, stood a large color television set. Anthony had bought this on installment for his mother when he was still employed as a construction worker. In early December this one luxury item was reclaimed by the store because of lapsed payments. In this room also were a rundown couch and an armchair.

Above the television was a set of shelves covered with photographs of young children. The first time I entered the apartment, Mary Sanchez was wearing a housedress and slippers, smoking a cigarette, and sweeping the floor. She was a considerably overweight woman with unkempt long red hair. My original impression was of a gray, worn-out woman in her fifties. This impression was further borne out when she informed me that the photographs on the shelves were all pictures of her grandchildren. Later I discovered how wrong my first impression had been. Mary Sanchez was thirty-eight years old, an energetic, intelligent, strong-minded woman, who as I came to know her better seemed to have a solid, cheerful appearance.

In the alcove adjoining the living room was a double bed where Mrs. Sanchez often slept. The next room, a small alcove which also served as a corridor through the apartment, was Anthony's. Past Anthony's the front room, with windows on the street, had two beds. Jeannie slept there when she was home. Sometimes Sharon and her son Tommy slept there, and sometimes Mrs. Sanchez moved back into it. The kitchen and bathroom were at the end of a narrow passageway leading out of the living room in the other direction. This was a typical railroad apartment, and its description would suffice, with a few minor variations, to depict the living quarters of any of the persons in tenements on Norman Street.

In November the Brooklyn Gas Company turned off Mary Sanchez's gas for failure to pay bills. The event was taken without much excitement, and she proceeded to cook meals on Jenny Ferguson's stove, which was still functioning next door. After Jenny moved out in September 1976, Mrs. Sanchez continued to cook on the stove of the now vacant apartment. In December 1976 the gas company turned off the gas in the Ferguson's old apartment, and Mrs. Sanchez was forced to resort to other measures, including buying precooked food.

The Ferguson's had a telephone which the whole family made use of. Sharon telephoned her husband long distance, and Anthony made local calls for the Norman Street Block Association on this phone. Previously, when Anthony and his mother had a telephone, Jenny had made and received calls on that. In April, when Mrs. Sanchez's electricity was shut off, an extension cord into Jenny's apartment provided current for a lamp and a small television.

After her electricity was turned off, Mrs. Sanchez did her laundry at her friend Julie Berry's and at Davida Delgado's apartment. Mrs. Sanchez had a new washing machine, bought while Anthony was working, but money was lacking to run it. When the electricity was turned on again eight months later, the pipes had rotted, and the machine no longer worked.

Tommy, Sharon, Jeannie, Mrs. Sanchez, and Anthony often ate together. Sharon and Jeannie would walk over to their mother's house with Sharon's son Tommy and eat hamburgers and french fries or sausages and peppers on a hero sandwich, or whatever else Mary had prepared. On Friday nights they would all eat at the apartment of Mrs. Sanchez's mother, Elizabeth Brock, a few blocks away. They also used Mrs. Brock's telephone as frequently as they used Jenny's. When Cecilia, Mrs. Sanchez's sister, had no money, Mary Sanchez would feed her and her husband and one-year-old son.

In May 1976 Sharon, Jeannie, and Tommy moved into Mrs. Sanchez's apartment. Sharon was five months pregnant and already excessively heavy and awkward. Jeannie was planning to get married to a Puerto Rican man who was away in the army. She had had a shower for her engagement and was waiting to hear from him about marriage arrangements. Sharon moved in with her mother for help with babysitting, since Jeannie planned to leave town after she got married. As it turned out, however, Jeannie did not get married and stayed in the apartment until late August when her boyfriend returned from the army and they went to Florida. In February 1977 Jeannie came home from Florida to live with her mother and to have her own baby, which was due in June. She planned to move back to live with her boyfriend after the baby was born.

When Jeannie scheduled her first departure date for May 1976, Mrs. Sanchez informed the welfare department that she was no longer dependent on the household. From this point Mrs. Sanchez received only the amount of assistance allotted for one person on welfare. She never again received money for any dependents although Jeannie remained in the apartment for extended periods after this and was fed and kept on whatever funds were available.

Shortly before Mrs. Sanchez took Jeannie's name from the list of household dependents, Anthony's unemployment checks stopped coming. He had been out of work for a year and by then had already exceeded the period for which support was provided. Although the government later extended the period, Anthony was not eligible for an extension. From January until July 1976, when he was temporarily employed by the Police Athletic League, and from September 1976 until May 1977, Anthony was financially dependent on his mother's welfare check combined with whatever money he could borrow from his mother's sisters, his grandmother, and their neighbors and friends in the vicinity. Since he had frequently provided his aunts and several of his friends with small sums of money when he was working, they gave him money and cigarettes when they could.

Thus from May 1976 Mary Sanchez's apartment had no gas or electricity and was inhabited by Anthony, Mary, a pregnant Sharon, her son Tommy, and Jeannie. At that time they were still using the gas and electricity from the adjoining apartment where Jenny Ferguson lived. In September Jenny and her husband moved to a new apartment. He had found a full-time job and was also working part-time as a bartender so that they could afford a more expensive apartment ($200 a month).

In September Sharon gave birth to twin sons, and her husband took leave from the army and came to Mrs. Sanchez's apartment to stay. The extra provisions which had to be made for the newborn children were scattered through numerous apartments, as were facilities to meet the daily requirements of the adult inhabitants. Milk and water for the babies' bottles were heated on the stove next door. Disposable diapers were used to reduce the laundry load, which was distributed between the Berry and Delgado apartments. A friend of Sharon's who lived on Norman Street gave them five large boxes of baby food which she no longer needed. A neighbor knitted winter sweaters and caps for the babies, and Jenny Ferguson's old crib and other equipment and toys from her babies were brought into the front room, where Sharon's family was established. Numerous other household items ranging from jars of coffee to babies' bottles were brought over by people from the block. Clothes were ironed at the apartments of Davida Delgado, Jenny, and Elizabeth Brock.

After the electricity from Jenny's apartment was no longer available, Mrs. Sanchez would often go with her whole family (laying the twins on the floor) to watch television at the Berry's or Delgado's for the evening. If they stayed home they were obliged to sit in the front room by candlelight, a hazardous situation exacerbated by the presence of three young children in the house. The lack of heat and electricity had a devastating effect on the family. When I came to visit, Anthony and his mother would be sitting in the half-dark with blankets wrapped around them for warmth. It was a shock to me to walk into such a depressing scene in what was usually a lively, noisy household.

Mrs. Sanchez, Anthony, Jeannie and her newborn baby, and Sharon and her three children might be regarded as semipermanent residents of Mrs. Sanchez's household. However, Arlene Brock, Mrs. Sanchez's sister, and her two children seemed to regard the apartment as a form of second home. Mrs. Brock had lived with her sister when she first moved to Greenpoint in 1964 until 1972, when she and her children moved into an apartment of their own in the same neighborhood. Although Mrs. Brock now lived on Ealing Street, her social network still carried her frequently to Norman Street, and she would spend nearly every evening gossiping on the block. Since she kept a strict watch over her two children, they had to come with her to visit friends on Norman Street. They would often fall asleep at Jenny's or Mary Sanchez's apartments (sometimes on the stone steps of the apartment building), and Mrs. Brock would frequently stay at her sister's rather than wake the children long after midnight when the social evening was over. She would put her children's clothes through the washing machine at Jenny's and iron them on her ironing board. She and the children were as accustomed to staying with Mrs. Sanchez as to sleeping in their own home.

After Arlene Brock's gas and electricity were turned off (for the all-too-common reason of failure to pay the mounting bills), her visits and the periods that she stayed at her sister's increased. They decreased considerably during the winter, when Mary Sanchez's apartment had no heat and her method of connecting to the adjoining apartment's electricity and gas supplies were no longer effective. Nobody except the semipermanent residents stayed with Mrs. Sanchez that winter when she, Anthony, and Sharon were attempting to look after newborn twins in an unheated apartment by candlelight.

These circumstances were not unusual in Greenpoint-Williamsburg nor were they restricted to families where the husband was unemployed or the household totally dependent on welfare. Among low-income families, evictions for nonpayment of rent and the loss of essential utilities because of debt were common. Telephones would come and go, as would gas and electricity. The ability to buy food and cigarettes was never certain, nor was the ability to maintain an apartment. Personal situations and economic viability were constantly fluctuating. As they varied, so did the household composition and the distribution of domestic tasks among any group of kin-related or friendship-linked individuals.

Cecilia Berette's Household

Cecilia Berette's household provides another example of the effect of indebtedness on social organization. Her experience contrasts with that of Mary Sanchez, since throughout their difficulties Mr. Berette was fully employed as a loader for the Gallo Wine Company. Mrs. Berette, it will be remembered, was Mary Sanchez's sister. Her husband, Jerry, acted as a guarantor for several of Anthony's installment purchases since Anthony was under age. When Anthony did not have the money to pay, his uncle was held responsible. However, the Berettes were too deeply in debt to deal with these additional problems.

At one point Mrs. Berette, who was the treasurer of the Riverside Bowling League, spent a night in prison for embezzlement. It was found that $600 was missing. She had spent the money in small amounts, allowing her sisters and nieces to bowl without immediately collecting the money they owed. Unfortunately, none of them were able to pay her.

The Berette's and their one-year-old son lived in their own apartment on Norman Street. In April 1976 their gas and electricity were turned off for nonpayment of bills. To cope with this situation, they spent the evenings at the apartment of Elizabeth Brock, Mrs. Berette's mother, three blocks away. In July they gave up their Norman Street apartment and moved their belongings and furniture permanently to Mrs. Brock's home. Already living in this apartment were Elizabeth Brock and her son, Jim, Cecilia's older brother. All five people shared food, although there was some controversy over who was to buy it. Jim Brock claimed that he always bought enough for the Berette's but that by the time he came home they had finished whatever they had cooked.

While Mrs. Berette was living at her mother's, she spent most of her days on Norman Street. She was, as we have seen, active in the events organized on the block. She took a major role in the summer lunch program and in the street fair. She was not an organizer, but in the face of complaints and cutting remarks from her sister Mary, she assisted in each project. Anthony Sanchez commented, "Cecilia only looks out for herself. She asks for everything, but she doesn't help." Mrs. Sanchez observed, "Cecilia's lazy; she doesn't help." In response to such criticism, Mrs. Berette worked extra hard on the street fair. She also profited from the summer lunch program. Since she was dependent on the good will of the block residents, especially her sister and her sister's friends, she tried to dispel the image of herself as unhelpful and did not simply ignore disapproving remarks.

The boundaries of Cecilia Berette's living space were indeterminate. When gas and electricity were cut off in her apartment, the Berettes were not sure whether they would be able to save enough to restore service. During this period their living quarters were divided between Elizabeth Brock's and the apartment on Norman Street. Later, when it became clearer that their finances were not improving, Jerry and Cecilia Berette moved permanently to Elizabeth Brock's.

Moves in and out of the apartments of parents, in-laws, and other relatives in times of financial stress were part of a general subsistence pattern in Greenpoint-Williamsburg. But Norman Street residents did not necessarily move in with their mothers' relatives, as happened in the case of Cecilia and Jerry Berette. Jenny Ferguson relied on her father-in-law when the Fergusons needed a home.

Jenny Ferguson's Household

Jenny and John Ferguson were married at an elaborate wedding paid for by Jenny's father, who was not living with her mother, Mary Sanchez. After the Fergusons were married, they moved into John's father's house, which was also in Greenpoint. Mr. Ferguson could not get a job and enlisted in the army, leaving his wife at his father's house. When he came back from the army after an absence of a year, the Fergusons moved into their own apartment in Greenpoint. However, Mr. Ferguson was again unemployed after he returned from the army. Although she was pregnant, Jenny Ferguson did not move into her mother's apartment, and her husband took care of her when she became ill and was hospitalized early in the pregnancy. After they failed to pay rent in their apartment for four months, the landlady evicted them. Partly because of a shortage of space, Mrs. Sanchez refused to take them into her apartment. They went to stay with Jenny Ferguson's aunt, Arlene Brock, for a few months and then moved back with Mr. Ferguson's father. After a few months there, they moved into the apartment next door to Mary Sanchez, who knew the landlord and negotiated the arrangement. By this time the Fergusons had two children. As discussed in chapter 6, families who were on welfare and who also had children had difficulty finding apartments in Greenpoint-Williamsburg. Jenny Ferguson told me that she had walked all over the neighborhood looking for an apartment and that most landlords refused to let her into their buildings.

Davida Delgado's Household

The Delgado household on Norman Street was similar to those of the Berettes, Fergusons, and Mary Sanchez, although the Delgados were not related. Through 1975 Davida Delgado lived with her husband, Jeff, who was Puerto Rican, their two sons (aged eight and one), and Jeff's younger brother (who spoke little English and tried to find a job several times, unsuccessfully).

Mrs. Delgado, an extremely heavy woman who had difficulty walking far because of her weight, also appeared older than her thirty-four years. Her husband was smaller than she was and often absent at work or elsewhere. His orders, however, carried impact, and on several occasions Mrs. Delgado was unable to go out in obedience to his edicts.

Perhaps to compensate for her long periods at home, Mrs. Delgado always had a kitchen full of people. Friends and relatives watched television in the middle room while little children wandered through the apartment and young boys peered out the front window. Often her mother-in-law, who spoke no English, was to be found at the kitchen table preparing the evening meal, while her two granddaughters leaned shyly against the hallway door, listening to conversation they only partly understood.

In the summer of 1976, Jeff Delgado's mother had brought two daughters and a son from his previous marriage in Puerto Rico to stay with them. His mother had been keeping them in Puerto Rico but was about to relinquish the task. After a few months she returned to Puerto Rico, leaving her three grandchildren with their father. Thus eight people (three adults and five children) lived in an apartment the same size as that of Mary Sanchez.

Although shared arrangements between relatives were closely connected to financial necessity, in some cases, as when Sharon and Jeannie went home to their mother's apartment for help with their children, financial need was combined with child care problems and a desire for companionship. Especially when boy-friends or husbands were in the army (a situation itself connected to unemployment since men often enlisted because they could find no other work) or when a woman had separated from the father of her children, women moved into apartments with other relatives.

Thus in Mary Sanchez's generation, Arlene Brock, who had never lived with the fathers of her two children, moved into Mrs. Sanchez's apartment after Mr. Sanchez deserted his wife and four children. The two sisters lived together for many years and assisted each other with child care, domestic tasks, and expenses. The cooperation evident on a daily level between these two apparently separate households was due to the fact that both constituted part of a wider, shifting support network that had grown up over time. Fluidity in household composition, in adjustment to financial and personal stresses, could be detected in the flexible relations between apartment residents manifested on a daily basis. It was also evident from an analysis of the changes in household composition which occurred over extended periods.

Child Care

Child care was not a cooperative venture in the sense that women took turns watching each other's children. Generally, babysitting was only shared among relatives. However, child care was the basis for social mingling on the street.

Babysitting for Others

Assistance with young children was widespread among relatives on Norman Street, although brothers and uncles who helped watch children were much rarer than sisters, aunts, and grandmothers, who took these responsibilities as a matter of course. Yet despite the generality of this phenomenon, the time spent watching other peoples' children was strictly measured, and often resented, by those involved. Remarks such as: "My mother babysits for my sister much more than for me. It isn't fair the way they treat me," and "I sat for them two nights last week; the least she could do is take my kids tonight," or "She always dumps her kid on us—but try asking her to help you!" present the level at which such obligations were calculated. These evaluations were remembered over long periods of time. Arlene Brock remarked, "Sharon helped me such a lot when she was a teen-ager. My two were a real problem. That's why I don't mind taking Tommy for her." I never saw anyone ask for help babysitting unless it was from a relative. Kin were constantly being asked, although they often refused outright. Perhaps it was the freedom which allowed relatives to refuse that made it possible to ask them so much.

If a woman appeared to be overwrought and perhaps liable to abuse her children, it was common for a sister or her mother to offer to take the children for a while. Sometimes relatives would intervene when a mother was hitting her child excessively. People who were not close relatives would not have attempted to interfere.

When a woman considered taking a job, she generally thought of her kin acting as babysitters for free, or else of paying a baby-sitter. Two child care centers were located in the neighborhood, but both had long waiting lines and stringent regulations. When Cecilia Berette went for a job interview in a local factory, she told me that she would leave her child with her sister. Other women left children with grandmothers or aunts, whether or not these relatives lived in the neighborhood. They might leave a child with a sister who lived in another borough and only see the child on weekends. Alternatively, they might pay a woman to watch their children, although this seemed rare as a full-time expedient.

The day care center required that both parents (if there were two) work and that their income be less than $10,000. This excluded mothers on welfare and discouraged women with working husbands from job-hunting since their salaries might bring the parents' joint income above $10,000. Women often lied about their situation, sometimes on the advice of social workers at the day care centers, and in this way entered their children upon the center's rolls.

Child Supervision and Daily Interaction on Norman Street

Although child care itself was not a cooperative effort, women who were watching their children spent many hours together. They did not leave their children with one another for long periods, but they cooperated in projects and everyday activities. Neighbors also kept an eye out for every child in the vicinity, although they did not take full responsibility for someone else's child.

The constant hours spent together watching their children play on the sidewalk and teaching them not to stray into the street, or to wander down the stone steps where the garbage cans stood, formed the basis for strong friendships among the women on Norman Street. This time was the ground on which other levels of cooperation and reciprocal aid were formed and reinforced in daily interaction.

Mothers of young children on the block tended to bring their children out of the apartments to play nearly every day of the long summer months. Apartments were cramped, and from the first pleasant day of the year, usually in April, until the last possible moment in October, mothers and children spent their days on the front steps of the apartments and on the sidewalks.

Sharon Bianco, for example, would bring her twins and three-year-old Tommy out around 10 A.M. every morning. Another person would help her to carry the twins' large baby carriage down four flights of stairs, and they would wander over to Davida Del-

gado's steps to spend the day in the street. Around 5 P.M. Mary
Sanchez would organize something for supper, and Sharon would
bring her children up the stairs, leaving the carriage by the outside
front door. After dinner everyone would go out onto the street
again and sit around and talk until around midnight, sometimes
even later. The children would stay out as late as the parents.
They would often fall asleep, without complaint, in their carriages
or on the steps.

Since the Bianco and Ferguson apartments were both on the
fourth floor of walk-up buildings, the women usually brought
down everything that they needed for the day. Disposable diapers,
bottles, and rugs were stuffed into the baby carriages. If something
extra was needed, an older child was sent upstairs to get it. The
mothers did not run up and down the stairs all day but more or
less set themselves up on the street. Mrs. Delgado, who lived on
the ground floor, made coffee for everyone and provided a bathroom and an indoor base for rare necessities.

The daily pattern was followed so closely that if the weather
was bad, mothers and children still came down to the street. When
it rained they sat in the hallways for protection, and as soon as
the rain stopped, they were out on the steps again.

People seldom went in for lunch. They ate snacks, candy, and
soda out on the street. In the evening women would treat the
group to a round of coffee or cake, if anyone had money to spare.
Such behavior seemed to be in repayment for small favors. In
the daytime Mrs. Delgado would make coffee on her stove. In
the evening Mrs. Sanchez would pay for coffees to be brought
from the all-night shop on the main street.

I have emphasized that mothers with young children followed the
pattern outlined above. However, groups were not restricted to
such women. Mary Sanchez, as a grandmother who had constant
child-watching responsibilities, was on the street almost every day
of the summer of 1976. Davida Delgado, a mother of two sons
aged eight and one year, was on the block every day that summer.
Sharon Bianco was on the street almost every day until she went
into the hospital for childbirth. Pregnant women, who had no

children yet born, would also sit out on the steps, sometimes accompanied by their young boyfriends. In all three of the cases of such women, the expectant mothers were under eighteen and not married to the fathers of their children. I did not hear this remarked upon disapprovingly by other women on the street.

Cecilia Berette brought her one-year-old son out on Norman Street every morning and stayed until late in the evening. After the family moved to Mrs. Brock's, Cecilia's husband stopped by the block on his way to and from work at 5 P.M. and 12 P.M. He often came back during his lunch break, which was in the evening. When Jerry Berette was not working or when he was watching the child, he too would be on Norman Street. He would give the local children rides up and down the block on the back of his three-wheel bicycle.

Linda McGill, whose mother lived on Norman Street, often brought her daughter and her sister's daughter to play on the block. Although not a frequenter of the steps (she would sometimes stay indoors and watch television), Jenny Ferguson often brought her two sons downstairs.

Maureen Jones, with her five children, would sit at her end of the block all day. There was another group of women who sat around her rather than on the Delgados' steps. Julie Berry, Mary Sanchez's best friend (according to her reports), who lived with her two daughters and boyfriend in Maureen's building, usually sat on Maureen's steps. Maureen had the ground floor apartment as did Davida Delgado and this seemed to lead to each forming a group around her own steps. Maureen Jones, like Mrs. Delgado, usually had a telephone. Her boyfriend, Roy, was also a common presence on her steps, and he was one of the few active male members of the block association.

A woman entering the block at one end would stop to talk with Maureen Jones and the people on her stoop. She might then walk on to Mrs. Delgado's stoop and settle down there. Each woman appeared to have her own spot, to which she would return daily. Someone who normally sat on Maureen's steps would stop on her way past to talk to the women on the Delgados' stoop and then keep walking until she reached her own group. Relations between the women in the two groups of baby watchers were amicable, although, as mentioned above, a dispute occurred over the distribution of the summer lunch program. The lunches were distributed from Mrs. Delgado's steps, and the women around her apartment had control of the extra food.

As they sat on the block every day, women traded information about their money problems. They compared electricity and telephone bills. They discussed the methods that they used to obtain Medicaid benefits, whether or not they were eligible. They discussed what they were going to make for supper and their problems with feeding their children and husbands. They calculated whether they could scrape together the money to go to bingo. They also kept a general watch on everything that people on the block were doing. The young mothers were given advice by the women with more children and constantly teased about their pregnancies and their boyfriends. The older women joked about nonexistent affairs. When the mailman or the garbage men came around, they were greeted with familiarity, and sometimes they joined in the general conversation. If they did not appear or were late, this was noted critically. The mailman was a familiar acquaintance of most of the women on the street. Since he delivered checks which were not safe in the mailboxes, it was important for residents to know when he arrived. Women were often waiting anxiously to see if the money would be available before they could go to the store, and the mailman's appearance was generally welcomed. Good relations with the mailman were an asset in dealings with the New York City Department of Social Services. Because of the numerous irregularities and variations in addresses, the department sometimes sent checks to a woman's previous address. If the mailman was aware of this, which was often the case, he had a choice of delivering the check or returning it to the post office, creating problems for the client. When Sharon Bianco moved out of her apartment on Ealing Street without informing the income maintenance center, it was thought that her checks for the next three months were pocketed by the mailman. When a new mailman was assigned to the beat, her checks began to arrive again. Because she was not completely within the regulations in her welfare registration, she was not able to report this incident or demand any form of reparation. Such occurrences made good personal relations with mailmen and other officials an essential aspect of survival.

We have seen that poor working-class residents of Norman Street assisted one another in a variety of areas, including small financial loans and the sharing of laundry, cooking, shopping, and baby-sitting. Individuals and families moved from one household to another in response to changes in their economic or family situations. The existence of a support network in which each individual provided small amounts of assistance was combined with a high degree of flexibility in household structure. Although assistance was limited and shared household situations often fraught with conflict, such adaptations helped families to provide for members under periods of stress and adverse economic conditions. The reciprocal relationships which developed also formed the basis for the action groups organized around the block projects described in the last two chapters.

In the next two chapters, the analysis will be extended beyond the affairs of the block to the larger political issues of the neighborhood. The connections between the strong personal links described in these three chapters and the progress of local political events will be examined.

CHAPTER 10

Save the Firehouse!

We have analyzed unsuccessful efforts to obtain concessions from the city administration and a block association which functioned effectively only when concrete resources were at stake. In the dispute about to be described, a highly valued and significant resource—a firehouse—was threatened. Despite their daily problems and their fear of retaliation from employers, landlords, and city bureaucracies, residents of the area participated in a long-term protest action to oppose the closing of a Williamsburg firehouse.

On November 22, 1975, after a four-month reprieve, New York City Fire Commissioner O'Hagan again proposed the closing of Engine Company 212, which was located in the Northside section of Williamsburg. Local residents, objecting to the loss of protection, gathered outside the firehouse to protest the removal of the engine. This became the first episode of a long struggle on the part of Northside residents to win back a fully equipped and functioning firefighting company.

The Northside, in the northern section of Williamsburg, is separated from other parts of Greenpoint-Williamsburg by the Brooklyn-Queens Expressway along its eastern border and by 15th Street in Greenpoint to the north. It is bounded on the west by the East River and on the south by Grand Street.[1] The North-

1. These boundaries have been given their actual street names, and the engine company retains its official number.

side is a predominantly Polish neighborhood with a high proportion of older people, while the population becomes progressively
more Hispanic on the other side of Grand Street. Although the
Northside borders on Greenpoint and is situated within ten blocks
of Norman Street, several rows of factories in the intervening
blocks tend to limit interaction between residents of the two areas.

Locally mobilized protest action around the firehouse illustrated
several aspects of life and behavior for residents in this low-income
section of New York City. Four specific concerns will be considered in the following pages. First, the danger of fire and the
importance of fire protection in New York City in the 1970s must
be emphasized. Residents were well aware that entire sections of
the city such as the South Bronx had perished through fire. Such
issues were especially significant in ghetto areas and sections such
as Greenpoint-Williamsburg bordering these neighborhoods, as it
was there that fire hazards were concentrated.

Second, the dispute over the firehouse closing in the Northside
was not an isolated incident. Opposition to the removal of a fire
engine occurred in all eight locations to which the city's November
1975 closing orders applied. The case of the Northside illustrates
a common response of local people to New York City's administrative policy of reducing protection at a time when the risks of fire
and arson were increasing.

Third, a continuous struggle for political articulation by the
urban poor, both white and black, had been taking place in New
York City.[2] Organization to protest the closing of the firehouse
was based on relationships and knowledge similar to the networks
described for Norman Street, built up over a long period of
involvement in community issues.

Finally, since the issue involved the employment of firemen,
local residents were also able to mobilize strong union support for
their activities. Union interest, combined with the efforts of local
politicians and church representatives, contributed both to the
persistence and effectiveness of the firehouse movement.

The reduction of fire protection in New York City was part of a
stated policy of "planned shrinkage" (*New York Times,* November

2. For descriptions of other community-organizing efforts in New York
City, see Cloward and Piven (1975, pp. 141–60).

14, 1976). The Northside's response was part of an effort to maintain low-rent housing and a viable neighborhood. The protest provides a case study of an attempt by low-income people to influence policy decisions imposed on them with the justification of a municipal "fiscal crisis." The firehouse struggle demonstrates the efficacy of direct action in such cases as well as the failure of less drastic methods for the articulation of working-class needs.

Fire Protection in the City

During the early and mid-1970s, the number of firemen employed by New York City was reduced, and the crew required to man an engine was cut from five to four. In 1939 there were 40,000 fire alarms in New York City and 10,500 firefighters. In 1975 there were 400,000 alarms and only 8,900 firemen.[3] The problem became most visible in November 1975, when 900 firemen were dismissed (*New York Times,* November 23, 1975).

When a fire is reported in New York City, the information is processed through a computerized dispatch center. On receiving the call, the dispatch officer contacts the closest or most readily available engine and orders it to the scene. A large fire generally requires three or four engines, each of which arrives from different neighborhoods. Thus any reduction in fire protection in one area puts greater demands on all the surrounding firehouses and leaves other parts of the city unprotected.

The reduction in the number of men assigned to a team exacerbated the problems of engine coverage. As retired Deputy Chief George Freidell reported at a hearing organized by several state senators:

> To handle fires of a certain size we have to call in extra people, not for relief but just to fight the fire. We had a fire in Brooklyn where a building collapsed. . . . We had to use people, not machines. We had to use police, who don't have equipment.

3. When officers were included, there were 10,900 firemen in the New York City Fire Department (*New York Times*, November 23, 1975).

I have an insufficiency of men so that I have to call multiple alarms [call in extra *engines*]. . . . It's wasted equipment. We needed *men* to operate the pumps, not to use their own equipment. (New York State Senate Finance Subcommittee, 1976)

Complaints about the replacement of men by machinery are common, especially in unions interested in job protection. Yet when extra machinery is rushed around the city in order to provide sufficient men to deal with an emergency, such claims seem justified. Response time is a crucial factor in the effectiveness of fire protection. If engines are tied up in other parts of the city, response time is increased. The deputy chief who taught fire technology explained:

A fire burns very slowly until it is preburned. Then the fire grows. The rate of burning doubles with an 18°C rise in temperature. The more it burns, the faster it burns until the fire becomes uncontrollable. . . . In 10 minutes the fire may become uncontrollable. (ibid.)

Mike Higham, a retired member of the fire department, wrote:

Adding to an already-serious housing shortage, fires that would, heretofore, have damaged only one apartment, are now consuming whole buildings and, resultantly, more families have to be relocated at considerable expense to the city. (Higham, 1976), p. 3)

As the fire commissioner stated in reference to the announcement of firehouse closings in 1975: "In the last analysis the cuts will result in an increase in loss of life and property" (*New York Daily News,* November 21, 1975).

At the same time as cuts were being made in the New York City Fire Department, the rate of "suspicious" fires and arson was rising at a precipitous rate. It was during this period that large sections of the South Bronx were devastated by fire and burned-out buildings on the Lower East Side and in Bedford-Stuyvesant became a familiar sight. Arson was the commonly accepted explanation (for example, *New York Post,* January 27, 1976), although few arrests or convictions were made.[4] Firemen interviewed in Greenpoint-Williamsburg claimed that arson was the obvious cause of most of the fires they had fought in the South Bronx. They even identified a ring of arsonists which they were convinced was responsible. Convictions in city courts confirmed that arson (which, if undetected, allows landlords to collect on insurance policies) was a major factor in the fires that have broken out in poor areas of the city. In one case a realtor bought a building and took out a $25,000 insurance policy. Two days later he attempted to hire an undercover police agent posing as an "arsonist-for-hire" to set fire to the building and its tenants (ibid., March 17, 1978).

Not all of the increase in fires was due to arson. Abandoned tenements constituted a common fire hazard, for children and vagrants shelter in such buildings and, as occurred on the Northside, tend to cause fires through carelessness. From September 1975 through 1976, the Housing and Development Administration refused to seal abandoned buildings.

In April 1976 an angry group from Greenpoint-Williamsburg staged a sit-in at the HDA until officials agreed to answer their questions. A staff member stated there was no money to seal buildings, but that the HDA would act to demolish buildings in an "emergency":

Staff Member: A collapsing building is an emergency. That's our criterion.

Northside
Community Worker: A building which is a fire hazard right next to our homes is just as much of an emergency.

4. As Clark Whelton points out: "Arson is a difficult crime to prove, not only because the evidence usually goes up in smoke, but also because a torched building provides plenty of money to both the people striking the match and the people investigating the fire. . . . In a declining area collecting fire insurance may be the only way for an owner to realize money on otherwise worthless rental property" (1977, p. 1). Whelton suggests that complexities and loopholes in zoning regulations may also supply an incentive for arson in some areas.

Staff Member: We agree—but if you're talking about all the four thousand unsafe buildings—we haven't got the money.

Second Staff Member: As serious as your condition is, there are at least one dozen other neighborhoods with the same problems. . . . Last time I was in your neighborhood, about six weeks ago, I saw twenty to thirty buildings that needed to be sealed up or demolished.

At the end of the interview, a staff member promised: "We'll make a determination today. It depends on the borough office. We have to consider hundreds of other buildings which need to be demolished—but we'll lean toward 'emergency' classification."[5] In response to pressure from this community group, three buildings were demolished.

The cooperation of the city agency was coerced in this particular instance. The remarks recorded above indicate, however, that the problem was much wider than could be solved by demolishing three buildings. The confrontation shows the efficacy of direct action techniques for eliciting a response from beleaguered city agencies, but, it did little to change administrative priorities. As already noted, despite a housing shortage in New York City, through 1975 and 1976 there was no policy to assist in the rehabilitation of abandoned buildings. If the landlord did not repair dwellings, they were allowed to deteriorate to the point where they became a fire hazard and a danger to the community. No effort was made to seal the buildings and thus preserve them for future use. When buildings began to collapse of their own accord, the city would intervene and tear them down.[6] Often this

5. The meeting was held in the HDA office in Manhattan on April 14, 1976. The quotations are from my notes. In June 1978 an official of the newly created New York City Department of Buildings (which replaced the HDA in August 1977) confirmed by telephone that demolition rather than sealing was still administrative policy.
6. If a landlord could not be contacted to take responsibility for the taxes or maintenance of a building, it became the responsibility of the HDA. The HDA hired contractors to demolish the property after presenting a case for the necessity of the action to the state supreme court. A lien

policy became economical since the buildings would burn down before the city was required to bear the expense of demolition.

Staff members at HDA recognized these problems and suggested that the community mobilize residents to seal the buildings themselves. This would save both the landlords and the city expense. The Northside community group present in the office did not embrace the proposition, although some groups in a neighboring section of Brooklyn had sealed buildings themselves.

The city's policy was perhaps best stated in a November 14, 1976, *New York Times Magazine* article by HDA director Roger Starr:

> Throughout the city, consistent density is a necessary part of building or block survival. It is better to keep one building full than two half-full, better to have one full block than five occupied at 20 percent of their capacity. . . . More important, the city can provide services much more efficiently to fully populated areas. Large parts of the Bronx south of the Cross Bronx Expressway are virtually dead—they have been so reduced in population that block after block of apartment houses stand open to wind and sky, their windows smashed, their roofs burned, their plumbing pilfered. . . . Yet the city must still supply services to the few survivors, send in the fire engines when there are fires, keep the subway station open, even continue a school.

In his outrage against the fiscal irresponsibility of providing services to devastated neighborhoods, Starr neglected to recognize the role that the city administration itself had played in precipitating such deterioration. The failure to seal buildings or to force landlords to maintain their property and the reduction in fire protection were two obvious factors contributing to the destruction of neighborhoods he so vividly described.

Starr proceeded to complain about efforts at rehabilitation:

> In some of these sections, under the pressure of a local official or a single community group, the city is pressed to make new

---

placed on the property for the cost of demolition was payable by the landlord on reclamation of the land. If no claim was made, further procedures allowed the city to auction the land.

investments in housing rehabilitation or street improvements whose chances of long life are limited by the surrounding decay.

He might have added that the chances of survival were also limited by the failure of the administration to follow through on such stopgap projects. Starr continued:

> [Apartment houses] must be occupied fully . . . if they are to remain in decent condition. The stretches of empty blocks may then be knocked down, services can be stopped, subway stations closed, and the land left to lie fallow until a change in economic and demographic assumptions makes the land useful once again.

From this perspective, it becomes clear why the HDA failed to receive money to seal buildings but could finance their demolition. Such a policy corresponded also with the closing of firehouses in poor areas of New York City.

The Closings: July 1975

Greenpoint-Williamsburg, it will be remembered, lay on the margins of Bedford-Stuyvesant, an area notorious for the devastation of its buildings and the poverty of its inhabitants. Parts of the southern section of Williamsburg were already covered by rubble and unoccupied houses. Whole blocks of apartment buildings had been burned down. Abandoned homes had broken windows and were surrounded by garbage and glass. This deterioration was beginning to take place within four blocks of Engine House 212 and the inhabitants of the Northside. The policies of the HDA and the Fire Department posed real threats to the survival of a functioning neighborhood, and it is in the light of the immediate and visible risk of housing destruction that the drastic and prolonged firehouse struggle can be appreciated. One Northside resident, Jeff Poulaski, told me:

> They've been killing this neighborhood since the Brooklyn-Queens Expressway knocked down that beautiful Italian church. . . . The 92nd Precinct was closed three years ago. Where there used to be three fire engines—215, 212, 238—two were closed.

Mr. Poulaski also pointed out that new housing was not necessarily going to save the neighborhood:

> Greenpoint got new housing built. So did the Southside—got money to remodel.[7] The South Bronx was remodeled and burned down; it was done over twice and burned down by landlords for insurance money.

Fears such as these promoted action on the Northside where many landlords, themselves resident working-class men and women, combined with apartment dwellers to protect the buildings of the area and to fight to maintain city services.

In the conversation recorded above, which I had with Jeff Poulaski at the firehouse in December 1975, he mentioned that an organization of Northside residents was trying to renovate an abandoned building for use as a community center. A month later the building, which the community group had received permission to renovate, burned down, the fire spreading also to two adjacent inhabited buildings. No one was hurt, but the occupants had to stay with relatives for months. Despite neighborhood efforts to renovate the area, such chronic problems continued to stand in the way of improvement.

Reactions to Firehouse Closings

From 1972 to 1975, the Fire Department closed down seventeen engine companies and relocated seven others into areas of lesser fire incidence than their original location (Wallace and Benway, 1976). This was a direct reversal of the city's policies in the 1960s: from 1968 to 1969, thirteen new firehouses had been built. In July 1975 Mayor Beame announced that twenty-six firehouses were to be closed in New York City. Local residents circulated petitions in the vicinity of the doomed firehouses, and in several cases firehouses were occupied by protestors who refused to let the firemen out or to allow them to remove the engines.

7. The Southside was a name for the southern section of Williamsburg, whose population was predominantly Hispanic.

One of the firehouses scheduled to close was in the Bushwick section of Brooklyn, a predominantly Hispanic neighborhood on the borders of Williamsburg. The events which occurred there were recounted in a report by Lt. Eugene Welischar from Engine Company 218, the firehouse in question (1975). He described the demonstrations of community residents on July 1, 1975, the day before the firehouse was to close. On the following day, when official announcement was made that the firehouse was definitely to be closed, Bushwick residents surrounded it and refused to allow firemen or their engine to leave, even to answer alarms. Demonstrators were afraid that once the engine was removed, it would never be brought back. Eventually Commissioner O'Hagan responded to community pressure and agreed to reopen the firehouse.

The report presents a detailed account of the sixty hours during which firemen were detained as hostages by local inhabitants. It is clear that the firemen, many of whom were to be laid off when the firehouses closed, were willing hostages. The Tactical Police Force was disposed nearby, but no action was taken against the crowd. As July 3 came to an end, a building behind the firehouse was firebombed. Commissioner O'Hagan had previously informed the demonstrators that he had no alternative but to close the firehouse since "the city just does not have the money." Soon after the bombing, however, the Fire Department announced that all the firehouses were to be reopened, although the firemen stationed in them would not be rehired.

Less militant demonstrations had taken place at other firehouses scheduled to be closed, including Firehouse 212 on the Northside. Apparently the strength of local protests, perhaps combined with the threat of summer riots, led the commissioner to reopen the firehouses and to postpone further action until late in November.

In July 1975 Bushwick residents were able to win their firehouse back in three days of protest. As will become evident, the fight to reopen the Northside firehouse was more prolonged. On November 22, 1975, the New York City Fire Department announced that in spite of the reversed decision in July, financial exigencies required that eight engine companies would indeed be dissolved, and four firehouses closed.[8] Demonstrations broke out again in all boroughs where the eight engine companies were located, but after a one-and-one-half-year struggle, only the Northside's Engine Company 212 was reopened.

The Occupation: November 1975 to April 1977

To appreciate why the Northside was the sole community able to retain its firehouse, it is necessary to examine the neighborhood's recent past. In 1972 S&S Corrugated Paper Machinery Company planned to expand its factory over two blocks of the Northside. Nineteen houses, the homes for ninety-four families, were to be torn down to make place for a new wing. Residents of the Northside, mobilized by community activist Pat Newton, who lived in the area, organized resistance to the destruction of their homes. A protracted struggle culminated in "direct action" as people obstructed the bulldozers brought in to destroy the buildings. The community group eventually won a concession from the city administration. Fourteen three-story homes, designed to house forty-one families, were to be built by New York City on a nearby block. These residential units were classified as "moderate income cooperatives" and had to be purchased, not rented. Of the ninety-four families displaced by the factory, nineteen moved into the new apartments, which, although subsidized, required a larger financial outlay than the $50 average rents they had paid for homes on the demolished block. Nevertheless, this protest action was regarded as a major victory by many Northside residents. It was significant that these new houses were among the first three-story subsidized dwellings that the city built. When I moved into

8. The closings were part of an $8.31-million budget cut implemented by the New York City Fire Department. Firehouses at 788 Union Street, Brooklyn; 3730 Victory Boulevard, Staten Island (built in 1972); 173 Franklin Street, Manhattan; and the Northside Firehouse (136 Wythe Avenue, Brooklyn) were closed and their engine companies dissolved. Four other companies were dissolved with their firehouses remaining open to serve other companies: Engine Company 294, 101-02 Jamaica Avenue, Queens; Ladder Company 171, 402 Beach 169th Street, Queens; Ladder Company 10, 100 Duane Street, Manhattan; and Ladder Company 53, 169 Schofeld Street, City Island, the Bronx (*New York Times*, November 23, 1975).

the area three years later, the new houses were occupied but the factory had not achieved its planned expansion. The row of homes had been demolished for as yet no practical end.

Following the demonstrations at S&S, Pat Newton, assisted by Northside residents, politicians, and community agencies, applied for federal funds to establish a community center. The Northside Neighborhood Committee (NNC), a board of community residents, was composed partly of people involved in the S&S protest and partly of local Democratic party activists. This board was strongly influenced by Pat Newton, who helped interview and select the new director of the center. After a community organizer was hired, a shopfront opened, and regular meetings scheduled, she became involved in other projects, and her role on the Northside diminished.

A second strong source of support for the firehouse protest came from the senior citizens' center. Since the center itself was new and had been obtained through community efforts, senior citizens had established forms of collective organization. They participated in demonstrations, spent time in the firehouse during the day, and kept other neighborhood residents informed about events there.

In May 1975 the Northside Neighborhood Committee was assigned some of the 296 CETA positions which had been brought into the neighborhood by the Greenpoint-Williamsburg coalition of community agencies. Most of those hired were previously unemployed local residents, many of whom had heard about the jobs and application procedures through involvement with local organizing campaigns and the NNC.

The Community Unites

In May 1975 firemen circulated rumors that the Northside firehouse was to be closed. The firehouse in which Engine Company 212 was stationed had two floors. On the ground floor was a large hall in which the engine was housed, with a small kitchen in the back. On the second floor mattresses were laid out for sleeping, and bathroom facilities were provided. Local residents had been accustomed to congregating at the firehouse to socialize in the large hall. The captain of the engine company had spent twenty of his twenty-eight years as a fireman on the Northside and was familiar with many of the inhabitants. In response to the rumors, neighborhood residents immediately circulated petitions. Four hundred names were collected. The petitions were brought to the board of the NNC, which decided to take up the issue. In July 1975 about three hundred people attended a rally outside the firehouse to protest the threatened loss of protection. In November 1975 the engine company was officially closed.

The firemen assigned to guard the firehouse promised local residents to sound the siren if they expected the engine to be removed. At 6 P.M. on November 21, 1975, the siren was sounded. The numerous organizations and associations in the area filtered the news among residents by telephone, and within an hour two hundred people surrounded the firehouse. For twenty hours the engine and twenty-four firemen sent to remove it were held hostage, with many of the demonstrators staying all night.

About fifty policemen were sent down to the firehouse, along with Fire Department representatives including chiefs, the borough commander, and his deputies. The police informed the crowd that they would be arrested for "misdemeanors." Seventeen people inside, including Jeff Poulaski's sixty-year-old grandmother, were told that they would be arrested for kidnapping and grand larceny. Unintimidated, the demonstrators stayed, and eventually a compromise was reached between them and Commissioner O'Hagan. The firemen were set free, and the engine remained with the community. However, it was not put back into use until one and a half years later, after a long struggle.

After the occupation of the firehouse, the walls were covered with posters and statistics on fire protection cutbacks as well as a calendar of weekly events. In a ritual performance, the demonstrators renamed the building People's Firehouse No. 1, and this was painted in red on a huge sheet hung over the entrance. In front of a large gathering of neighborhood residents, reporters, and political leaders, seven women put on the protective raincoats and hats of firemen and claimed to be in training to take over protection for People's Firehouse No. 1. The women dressed as firemen were greeted with enthusiasm by the crowd and seemed eager to assert their significant role in coordinating and participating in the demonstrations.

The success of the struggle was due partly to the fact that an accident had left an interested neighborhood resident free to join in a long-term protest action. Jeff Poulaski had been injured on a factory machine and laid off work the week the firehouse closed. Thus he was available to live there until the issue was resolved. He received an income of $90 a week in disability compensation from the insurance company for the soda factory where he had worked.

As on Norman Street, a single extended family lent continuity and stability to community activities. Jeff Poulaski and his wife and children moved into the firehouse along with two community workers-in-training and several other neighbors. About 200 people from the Northside visited or stayed overnight at least once a week, and the same number or more could be counted on to attend a demonstration, whether or not it was previously scheduled. CETA workers from the NNC were assigned to take eight-hour shifts through the day and night. An aide to a local politician was paid to stay at the firehouse twenty-four hours a day, but he departed after a month. Those involved also included a few small business-men, factory workers, unemployed men and women, older people, teen-agers, and children. Most of the participants were from white ethnic groups, and Polish people were especially evident. Other Northside residents helped the family with the laundry, collected the Poulaski children from school, and assisted Sandra Poulaski with the cooking.

On an afternoon at the firehouse, one would have come across several older people engrossed in a game of chess; a group of young boys playing around the steps; several young mothers, often in their teens, wheeling baby carriages up to gossip and see what was happening; and perhaps a meeting in progress in the back room with community organizers, the Poulaskis, and other local residents considering the next step in the campaign. The telephone rang frequently, and Jeff Poulaski was always willing to inform inquirers of the course of the protest.

On a cold evening in mid-December soon after the firehouse

was occupied, about fifty participants, including many young children, wrapped up in gloves and coats and set out to go carol-singing. The procession trailed through the neighborhood collecting singers as it went. There was no air of protest around this scene, as people sang old, familiar carols that many had known since grade school. The fun and camaraderie engendered by the event culminated in the warmth of the firehouse hall as shivering carolers drank the hot punch provided on their return. Such unpretentious community activities kept the spirit of the campaign alive.

Christmas Eve was celebrated with a large feast at the firehouse, and parties were held throughout the year. At such parties food would be cooked by neighbors, with, kielbasi (Polish sausage), pirogi (stuffed pastry), and sauerkraut predominating and sold in paper-plate portions for a dollar. Sometimes various arts and crafts, such as decorated boxes, dishtowels, and other goods would be displayed and sold around the edges of the large hall. Later the music would start, a mixture of contemporary rock and roll and polkas, to which many people of all ages danced with equal enthusiasm. Such dances did not bring in a large amount of money but served to maintain community interest in the campaign, provide entertainment to attract supporters to spend time at the firehouse, and strengthen bonds between residents.

Various people visited the firehouse every day and stayed on certain nights, but Jeff Poulaski was a fixture. His wife cooked evening meals in the firehouse kitchen, and his four children played around the engine and in the upstairs dormitory. His mother spent her evenings drinking coffee with her friends in the firehouse kitchen, and his brothers visited on weekends.

Jeff Poulaski, aged thirty-nine, was born on the Northside, as was his father. His father's parents came from Poland, and his mother was from Pennsylvania. Mr. Poulaski considered himself Polish. He had been working in factories for over fifteen years; first in a meat factory, and when the factory closed he moved to a lower-paying job in a soda factory. His wife was born on a farm in Germany and came to America as a young woman to look for work. She too had worked at the meat factory and later helped her in-laws with a luncheonette while she watched her four young children. At the time of the firehouse takeover, she was again working at a meat factory. It was around this family that the organization of the firehouse protest clustered.

The organization to save the firehouse profited from the correspondence of interests of firemen and neighborhood residents. Chiefs, dispatchers, and firemen attended meetings held at the firehouse. They provided information to the protesters and had warned them when they were about to lose the engine. The firemen appointed by the city to guard the firehouse and the local people who occupied it ate dinner together every night. They maintained friendly relations and were of considerable assistance to each other. In September 1976, when an arbitration committee was appointed by Mayor Beame, the president of the Dispatchers Union testified. He criticized the Fire Department in strong terms:

> New York City has an increasingly serious fire problem. Brooklyn has always been the busiest borough. Eleven fire companies in Brooklyn have been closed. . . . Response time is a charade, a lie —alarms get delayed up to six minutes in the dispatch office— sometimes dispatch alarms are ignored. . . . There were *six* fatalities this month in New York. *Five* of the people were in areas where they had closed the fire companies and *all five* were minority people. (New York City Mayor's Task Force on Fire Protection, 1976)

With support and information such as that provided by the firemen and the Dispatchers Union, it was difficult for local politicians and the city administration to ignore the demands of the protesters.

Several politicians made sporadic appearances at Firehouse 212. This generated extensive media coverage both for them and the firehouse occupants. Prior to his election, a local Puerto Rican Democratic Brooklyn councilman promised support for the firehouse demonstration. After he was elected, he sent an aide to stay in the firehouse. Although the aide returned to other political interests after a month, he had helped to establish media contacts. A New York State senator running in the middle of the term appeared at the firehouse several times before he won the election. After the election he was seldom seen there, although he was later instrumental in utilizing union interests to introduce a bill to increase the budget of the Fire Department. During the Democratic presidential primary elections, two candidates visited the firehouse and used it as a base for their campaigning in the community. Senator Birch Bayh of Indiana and Senator Fred Harris of Oklahoma gave speeches there. It might appear significant that the candidate supported by the local Democratic district leader and his workers, Senator Jackson of Washington, did not visit the firehouse. Yet the local Democratic party officers were not opposed to the firehouse action. The powerful district leader appeared along with his officials at several large meetings, but despite these appearances, these city politicians did not use their influence to help reopen the firehouse. Letters addressed to the borough president of Brooklyn were answered, but no assistance was forthcoming until August 1976, nine months after the firehouse was closed. At a time when the political mood in New York City was changing and after state senators had held hearings, the deputy mayor had entered into negotiations, and the firehouse had received national media attention, the borough president wrote to the fire commissioner:

> The closing of Engine Company 212 has not only been a loss in the matter of fire protection but it has proved to be a demoralizing factor in the life of the community.
>
> I would appreciate it if, in the light of recent events, you will take a new look at the situation in the Greenpoint-Williamsburg area with a view to restoring service to the area formerly serviced by Engine Company 212. (*New York Daily News*, August 1976)

This statement was greeted with surprise by one community worker at the firehouse. He remarked that until that point, the borough president had shown relatively little interest in the problem. But the letter was sent shortly before the elections in early November, which may have been of some concern to the borough president.

Eventually, interviews with the deputy mayor were arranged through a reporter with political connections. Meetings were scheduled and rescheduled in the fall of 1976 with little result.

The mayor offered the community a roving squad car with firemen but without equipment, while residents demanded a fire engine.

The Northside firehouse managed to gain recognition from state senators, partly through the local state representatives and partly through the influence of the Patrolmens Association in cooperation with the Uniformed Firefighters Association. During 1976 a controversy in the state legislature surrounded a measure known as the Stavisky Bill. Senator Stavisky, with the strong backing of Albert Shanker and the United Federation of Teachers, managed to pass a bill preventing any further cuts in the city's education budget. The state legislature had taken over a large part of the control of the city budget following the threatened default in 1975. In the wake of Stavisky's victory, several state senators attempted to develop a bill to prevent budget cuts and layoffs in the police and fire departments. Hearings were scheduled at the Northside firehouse in conjunction with the campaign in support of this bill. Although the bill was eventually defeated despite major police strikes and demonstrations throughout the city, the hearings at the firehouse provoked extended media coverage and placed pressure on the mayor and the fire commissioner to concede to the firehouse protesters' demands.

Throughout the year and a half that Northside residents occupied the firehouse, militant protest actions continued. These included such measures as picketing a mayoral dinner at the New York Hilton Hotel; picketing the home of the fire commissioner; holding a mock funeral parade through the neighborhood; and, most spectacularly, blocking traffic on the Brooklyn-Queens Expressway during a morning rush hour. The last demonstration, held on April 14, 1976, had a marked effect on traffic before protesters were ordered off the highway by the local police (who may have had some interest in allowing the protest to continue as long as it did).

Mayor Beame had promised to reopen Firehouse 212 on December 25, 1976, as a "Christmas present." This publicity stunt backfired when a nearby engine company in Queens was closed down instead of Firehouse 212. Northside organizers accepted this arrangement. Residents in Queens, however, occupied their own firehouse, again forcing the city administration to confront community protest. On March 3, 1977, the Northside firehouse was finally reopened and service resumed.

A Resident Is Radicalized

The Northside's history of collective protest influenced the participants in the firehouse demonstrations and was reflected in their own comments. Jeff Poulaski remarked:

> I supported the housing campaign. It was the first time in history the city ever bought a three-story apartment building. . . . Never had nothing like that in the neighborhood before the NNC.[9] I was always fighting for stuff. For years we were fighting with the parks department for lights in McCarren Park.

Laura Dancheski, also a Northside resident, was a quiet, retiring woman who dressed in plain, serviceable clothes and looked older than her twenty-eight years. She had worked in various local factories since she graduated from high school in 1965. Her father had worked for sixteen years as a rigger in the S&S factory, and she too had worked there for a while. Both of them had attended some of the protest demonstrations against the destruction of housing. Her father attended some NNC meetings and heard about the arrival of the CETA jobs. Laura Dancheski applied for a CETA job, and when the firehouse issue emerged, she asked to be stationed there. She described her gradual involvement in community activities to me on one of the many nights that she spent at the firehouse:

> I was at the demonstration when they knocked down the house for the S&S factory with a bulldozer. There was smoke all over the street. There were hundreds of people all over the street singing "God Bless America" with a flag, and the police pulled them away. The way they pulled that elderly man away—I wanted to kick the cop. The whole trouble here is that a lot of

9. Mr. Poulaski became a member of the NNC board after the S&S demonstrations.

people are really law-abiding citizens. You need someone really radical—then you'd get a lot for the neighborhood. I was afraid to be arrested, so I stayed outside. If I ever got arrested my mother would kill me. My mother is 100 percent behind the firehouse, my father is pro and con. They have heavy fights.

Laura Dancheski was not in any community organizations but had been attending Northside Neighborhood Committee meetings for about a year. Her father had also attended. She remarked that the NNC had "opened her eyes" and continued:

I was around on the day they took over the firehouse, but I wouldn't come near. I heard about the Williamsburg Bridge arrests [over a reduction in welfare assistance] and how people were bodily searched and I've been thinking about it ever since. . . . Now that I've become more community-minded, I would work for something—might even be arrested.

Laura was like other local residents who spent time at the firehouse. Her grandparents on both sides were from Poland, and her parents were born in Greenpoint-Williamsburg. Her parents, whom she lived with, owned an eight-family apartment house in which they occupied one apartment. They were unable to obtain loans to improve the house, and her father paid over $500 a year in fire insurance. Her grandfather rented an apartment in the building and had contributed money to buy the house twenty-six years earlier when the family could not obtain a mortgage. As with many other participants in the firehouse movement, Laura Dancheski had developed her views through the series of protest actions which had previously taken place in the neighborhood.

The firehouse action contrasts sharply with the frequently unsuccessful attempts of the Norman Street Block Association. Although the protest was based in the same area as Norman Street and built on similar forms of interaction among residents, other factors enabled it to develop into a wider cause. In particular, a history of collective action among Northsiders was combined with the connections and knowledge of trained community organizers. The movement, many of whose members were prepared for militant action, was also assisted by those whose livelihood was most at stake, local firemen supported by their union.

Through the contacts of a councilman's aide and the community organizers, wide media coverage was available from the initial takeover. Using the vulnerability of politicians during political campaigns and the influence of the police and fire unions, the firehouse protesters were able to pressure the city administration from the state level.

The organizers of the firehouse movement took an eclectic approach. They approached politicians at all levels and from both parties. Eventually, after sustaining a movement for one and a half years and utilizing media coverage and union influence to pressure the city administration, they achieved their goal. Yet fear that the firehouse might be closed again still prevailed. During 1977–1978, several rumors were circulated that Firehouse 212 might lose its engine or that firemen would be laid off. Throughout the year following the victory, the protest organizers and other Northside residents continued to meet weekly to guard their interests.

The Northsiders had managed to reverse one aspect of New York City's policy of "planned shrinkage." But as Roger Starr pointed out, the city administration may capitulate to a few community leaders without changing the overall project for the "de-development" of large areas of New York City (Starr, 1976).

Two points still remain to be considered. First, it should be evident that ethnic differences were not an issue in this movement for the preservation of a neighborhood. Many of the participants were low-income white Americans with mixed ethnic backgrounds, predominantly Polish. Although black and Hispanic people did not participate in the Northside protest, an identical occupation had taken place the summer before in a largely Puerto Rican and black neighborhood and had received similar support from firemen. During the period in which the Northside firehouse was occupied, I interviewed several black people who lived in Woodlawn Housing and were served by a different firehouse. They were in full support of the Northside action. When Jeff and Sandra Poulaski visited an all-black community meeting in the projects, they were met by a standing ovation. Similar sentiments were expressed in Hispanic areas of Williamsburg, as symbolized by the support of the Puerto Rican councilman and his aide (who was also of Puerto Rican origin).

Second, the problem of deteriorating neighborhoods in New York City cannot be simply related to racism and poverty. It derives from the policies of an administration which deprived low-income areas of adequate services and maintenance. Although in this particular instance the Northside won its case, the circumstances in which it did so suggest that such groups have few methods by which to make their demands heard. Influential political events, which included union and state intervention and national media attention, were required before the city administration agreed to reopen the Northside firehouse. Because such a massing of political influence is not common to most neighborhood issues, similar protests are likely to be defeated. The necessity for this level of mobilization in order for a working-class neighborhood to retain essential services indicates that "planned shrinkage" was a strongly entrenched city policy.

The events at Firehouse 212 demonstrate the continuous struggle of working-class people to maintain their political and social rights. The residents won back their services, but despite their present vigilance they may lose to the constant forces of deterioration in the long run. Only a combination of interests between the locality and other groups such as occurred in the isolated incident of the firehouse can prevent the decline of the neighborhood's services and the standard of living of its inhabitants.

CHAPTER 11

The Sources of Political Control

Decision-Making and the "Fiscal Crisis"

Major decisions affecting Greenpoint-Williamsburg and the rest of New York City did not involve local politicians. Decisions about a 43-percent rise in the New York City transit fare, the abolition of a century of free tuition at City University, and the drastic reduction in municipal services were imposed upon the elected representatives of New York City by powerful banking interests and the refusal of the federal government to grant aid. In June 1975, when New York City was on the verge of bankruptcy, the Municipal Assistance Corporation (MAC) was created to convert the city's short-term debt into long-term bonds and to oversee its financial problems.[1] MAC was responsible for auditing the city's expenditures. Jack Newfield and Paul DuBrul claim that the concept of MAC was worked out by bankers:

> The concept, structure and power of the Municipal Assistance Corporation was worked out, according to most accounts, in a meeting held on May 26 (Memorial Day), 1975, at the Greenwich, Connecticut, home of Richard Shinn, president of the $33-billion Metropolitan Life Insurance Company. The participants included investment banker Felix Rohatyn, and several commercial bankers, including Frank Smeal, the municipal bond expert at Morgan Guaranty Trust. There is no transcript, [sic] no min-

1. A precedent for this procedure was set in 1933 (Darnton, 1977).

utes are available of this informal meeting that changed the history of New York City. (Newfield and DuBrul, 1978, p. 178)

Five of the original nine members of MAC were picked by the governor of New York State and four by Mayor Beame. Eight had banking or brokerage connections (Newfield and DuBrul, 1978,

Table 1 The Original Municipal Assistance Corporation, 1975

Name	Affiliation
Felix Rohatyn	Partner in the global investment-banking firm of Lazard Frères; director of six corporations including ITT, Engelhard Minerals, and Pfizer
Simon Rifkind	Corporate lawyer; former federal judge; director of the Sterling National Bank
Robert Weaver	Director of Bowery Savings Bank and Metropolitan Life Insurance
Donna Shalala	Professor of political science, Teachers College, Columbia University
Thomas Flynn	Partner in Arthur Young and Company, an accounting firm; director of Household Finance Corporation; trustee of the American Savings Bank
William Ellinghaus	President of New York Telephone Company; director of Bankers Trust Corporation; trustee of Union Dime Savings Bank; chairman of Regional Plan Association; trustee of New York Racing Association; director of J. C. Penney
John Coleman	Senior partner in Adler, Coleman and Company, a stock brokerage house; former board chairman of the New York Stock Exchange; had influence with New York Archdiocese of the Roman Catholic Church
Francis Barry	President of Circle Line Sightseeing Boats; president of Campbell and Gardiner, a brokerage firm; chairman of city's Council on Port Promotion and Development; fund raiser for Bronx Democratic organization
George Gould	Chairman of Donaldson, Lufkin, Jenerette Securities; associated with Citibank "revolving letter of credit"

Source: Newfield and DuBrul, 1978, pp. 179–81.

p. 179). It was this board which decided in closed meetings during 1975 that the transit fare should be raised from 35¢ to 50¢,
that city workers should be laid off, and that tuition should be
charged at City University. David Rockefeller, chairman of Chase
Manhattan Bank, and several other bankers and brokers were
also present at the meeting where these suggestions were put for-
ward (ibid., p. 184). Newfield and DuBrul remark: "Everything
the commercial bankers and Rohatyn discussed at this meeting
happened within a year" (ibid, p. 186). Despite opposition from
members of Congress and the state legislature, the transit fare was
raised and service cuts and tuition instituted (ibid., 1978, p. 189).

In September 1975 the Emergency Financial Control Board was
created, with greater powers than MAC, to deal with the city's
increasing fiscal problems. The EFCB was made up of two elected
officers, Governor Carey and Mayor Beame, along with New York
State comptroller Levitt, New York City comptroller Goldin, and
three business representatives—Felix Rohatyn, William Ellinghaus,
and David Margolis (president of Colt Industries) (Newfield and
DuBrul, 1978, p. 182). Thus the major decisions involving New
York City services and development continued to be strongly influenced by a small group of bankers.

It has since been proposed that the major city banks contributed
to New York City's fiscal emergency. Starting with Chase Manhattan and followed a few weeks later by Morgan Guaranty Trust
Company and Continental Illinois Bank and Trust, banks began
to unload thousands of shares of New York City bonds onto the
stock market between October 1974 and March 1975 (ibid., p.
39; Tabb, 1978, p. 254). The action flooded the market and
precipitated the panic in June 1975. In reaction to the panic,
bankers took over a large part of the decision-making in New
York City. Up until this time, an enormous municipal debt
accumulated by ex-governor Nelson Rockefeller, ex-mayor Robert
Wagner, and others had allowed financiers immense power behind
the scenes in municipal politics. This power was enhanced by the
connections between New York politicians and real estate speculators, and the banks' control of mortgages and construction loans.
Operations were simplified by a system of "graft" within the law,

often and well documented in New York (Steffens, 1904; Caro, 1974; Newfield and DuBrul, 1978). In the summer of 1975, with their participation in MAC and the EFCB, the power of the banks in New York City became visible.

Although power was effectively removed from the province of local politicians, they had important roles to play in implementing policy. On June 26, 1975, William Simon, secretary of the Treasury under President Ford, outlined the position of New York's elected representatives. Mr. Simon recognized that Mayor Beame had to rely on his constituents for reelection, but he did not regard the demands of certain voters as legitimate considerations in the face of the fiscal situation in New York City. Mr. Simon's concern was with banking interests. The secretary stated that Mayor Beame would receive no federal aid (as indeed he did not) until these interests were taken into account.

In Mr. Simon's view, the banks and the capital markets would be able to withstand a default by New York City. There was no concern voiced for the living conditions of the inhabitants in such a situation. As long as the economy could withstand the shock, the federal administration was prepared to risk bankruptcy of the municipal government. Secretary Simon concluded by enumerating other cities where services had been cut, suggesting that in the light of the refusal of federal assistance, the mayor of New York would have to follow suit (Newfield and DuBrul, 1978, pp. 65–67).

There was no mention in federal directives or decisions by MAC and the EFCB of the collection of back real estate taxes, unpaid by landlords. There was no consideration of the backlog of federal funds owed to the city and the state (Melman, 1977, p. 182). Funds concealed by the Port Authority and other large interests were not examined. The thrust of the directives was toward service cuts and an increase in unemployment and consumer expenses for city residents. This was the plan which the city's politicians had to sell to their neighborhoods. The campaign methods local politicians used as a result of their restricted influence are remarkable examples of maneuvering in an austere political environment.

Local-Level Politics
in Greenpoint-Williamsburg

Although local political representatives had to implement un-
popular fiscal policies, they were also dependent on their constituencies for reelection. Four cases from Greenpoint-Williamsburg
illustrate the way officials dealt with these contradictory problems.
These cases all show the attempt of established political coalitions
to maintain their control of municipal resources and to ensure
the election of selected candidates. The first case, "The Election
of a State Senator," demonstrates the use of "neighborhood
chauvinism" and the possible manipulation of racist feeling as
the fundamental issue in campaign propaganda. It also provides a
public illustration of cooperation between Republicans and Democrats when the question of neighborhood control was at stake.

Case 2, which concerns school board elections, displays racism
in a more blatant form in a campaign. It also provides instances
of what I believe must be called political repression and indicates
how competitors not backed by the local leadership were dealt
with.

The third case involves subsidized senior citizens' housing. It
shows the response of different sections of the community to the
possibility of introducing new federally funded housing.

The fourth case, labeled "the Red invasion" by a local newspaper, provides an opportunity to analyze repressive practices outside the formal channels of political parties.

The situations described in the last three cases also illustrate
the nature of conflct within Greenpoint-Williamsburg. Its working-
class people did not accept unquestioningly many of the sacrifices
that were imposed upon them. The exercise of political control
documented in these cases was a response to the discontent and
division within Greenpoint-Williamsburg itself.

The Election of a State Senator

The majority of state political officials were selected from the
Republican and Democratic parties. Since areas tended to be

overwhelmingly represented by one party, primary elections within each of the parties were of major importance. Within both parties (although more so among the Democrats) were reform movements whose candidates competed, sometimes successfully, with the regular candidates in the primaries. New York City Liberal and Conservative party organizations generally endorsed Republican or Democratic candidates, although occasionally an independent was nominated. The Socialist Workers party organized statewide campaigns, but its candidates were not successful.

The election of Senator Thomas Bartosiewicz provides case material for an analysis of the use of election propaganda in Greenpoint-Williamsburg. Mr. Bartosiewicz was the son of a prominent businessman who was a member of several influential boards in the area. His mother was on the County Committee of the Democratic party. Mr. Bartosiewicz was in his early thirties and had a law degree from an Ivy League university. When a New York State senatorial seat became vacant in early 1976, he was selected as the candidate of the Democratic club whose head was the district leader, the equivalent of the "ward boss" in the Democratic party. He was also the designated candidate of the powerful leader of the Democratic party in Brooklyn.[2]

An opening campaign statement by the Democratic district leader Frank Creta was quoted in a local paper:

> The plain truth is that Bedford-Stuyvesant and Bushwick control a majority of the Senatorial district. Unless we stand together in support of one candidate and one candidate only, we'll lose this fight to an outsider.

The same newspaper article continues:

> In 1974, the Legislature redrew the lines in the district in order to encourage minority representation. . . . Thomas Bartosiewicz was reported to be working overtime in the battle to prevent someone from outside the district from taking over the Senate seat. Former State Senator Waldaba Stewart and Carl Butler, both

2. For a description of the power of Meade Esposito in New York City politics, see Newfield and DuBrul (1978, p. 80).

residents of Bedford-Stuyvesant, are reported to be the main
challenges for the County Committee's designation. (*Garden
Spot News*, January 8, 1976)

Next to a map which demonstrated clearly the wide geographic
area to be represented by the state senator, including the poorer,
predominantly black and Hispanic neighborhoods of Bushwick
and Bedford-Stuyvesant, an article in another Greenpoint newspaper states:

> Our neighborhood's fight to maintain its representation in the
> State Senate, however, is expected to meet a stiff challenge from
> among a number of candidates from outside the district includ-
> ing Waldaba Stewart, a former State Senator from Bedford-
> Stuyvesant, and Victor Robles, who was described on the front
> page of last week's Amsterdam News as the "Top Aide to Con-
> gresswoman Shirley Chisholm" (D., Bedford-Stuyvesant). . . .
> Greenpoint and Williamsburg have faced several tough challenges
> in the past. A community united in its purpose—We've done it
> before and we're ready to do it again! (*Greenpoint Gazette,*
> December 30, 1975)

The two newspapers firmly endorsed Mr. Bartosiewicz for the primary elections, and his opponents' names were rarely mentioned
again in either paper. Both papers, which are widely read in the
neighborhood, devoted pages to Thomas Bartosiewicz and his
activities every week until the elections.

In every article relating to the campaign, the writer's strong
emphasis on the fact that the other candidates came from Bedford-
Stuyvesant implied that these candidates were probably black. An
emphasis on Greenpoint, by contrast, suggested that the candidate
was white. Another indicator of ethnicity was the last names of the
candidates. Mr. Bartosiewicz was construed as a Polish representative. Thus the newspaper writers expected their readers to be
instinctively sensitive to subtle innuendoes.

Besides his "Greenpoint" credentials, the campaign statements
of Mr. Bartosiewicz concentrated on his support for community
protest actions:

He has served this community in the fight to move the homes on the Northside against the expansion of S&S Corrugated. He has served on the committee to keep Greenpoint Hospital open. He is currently active in the fight to keep Engine Company 212 on the Northside. (*Garden Spot News*, January 8, 1976, p. 1)

Support for the firehouse movement and other protest actions were among the community activities for which Mr. Bartosiewicz was cited, and he was, in many ways, a progressive young politician. Although selected as the candidate of the regular Democratic party, he had never before held elective office. He had been employed as an assistant to Mayor Beame and was closely connected with a Democratic party political club. Thus he had not worked his way up the electoral ladder to the position of state senator.

In the month before the elections, Mr. Bartosiewicz attended many neighborhood functions and had his photograph in each weekly edition of the local newspapers several times. He attended breakfasts, lunches, and dinner dances every weekend night, and he was photographed with members of the community at every function. He seldom made speeches but simply appeared and chatted to a few people at each event. After his first election in 1976, he opened an office on the main commercial street in Greenpoint.

Because of the recent alterations in the boundaries of the senatorial district, the election of Thomas Bartosiewicz was of critical importance to the retention of political power by established Greenpoint politicians. A local newspaper stated the matter this way:

The reason for our precedent making decision is the urgency of the issue at stake. . . . The resignation of State Senator Straub [who had been accused of questionable practices], which became effective the first of the year, left this area without representation on a state level in the Senate. This situation cannot be tolerated. Greenpoint and Williamsburg must have a voice in the Senate and that voice must belong to a Greenpointer who is acutely aware of the needs of the people of this area. (*Garden Spot News*, January 8, 1976, p. 1)

At the time of the national elections in November 1976, the matter of retaining control in Greenpoint became so crucial that Republicans and Democrats joined in support of the same candidate.

Stressing "Greenpoint" and the importance of retaining control in the area, the Bartosiewicz campaign received strong support from financial interests. An influential local banker wrote:

> Wright is determined to see a Bedford-Stuyvesant man run for the Senate spot, regardless of who that man is, as long as he is a Bedford-Stuyvesant man. All Greenpointers would not gain, in fact, they would lose much should the Senate seat go to a man in the lower end of the district. It is in the interest of every citizen in this district, particularly Greenpoint and Willamsburg, that they vote [for Thomas Bartosiewicz in the primaries]. (*Greenpoint Gazette,* September 7, 1976, p. 1)

With the support of the local Democratic district leader, the Brooklyn Democratic party, and local Republican and financial interests, Mr. Bartosiewicz conducted a personalized campaign directed toward the small section of his electoral district with a predominantly white ethnic population. As a result he won two primary elections and two general elections within one year.[3]

Throughout the campaign in Greenpoint-Williamsburg, the attack on "outsiders" from Bedford-Stuyvesant was interpreted racially by many residents. In this way the Democratic party manipulated the issue of racial competition in the area. Interestingly, on higher levels of representation in New York City, such as congressional elections, the Democratic leadership supported black candidates. Perhaps this campaign might be interpreted simply as part of New York City's ethnic politics. I believe, however, that the black population was seen as a threat by Greenpoint-Williamsburg residents, who coalesced across ethnic groups in order to exclude them. Propaganda with racist overtones was used by established members of the Democratic party to retain electoral support in a neighborhood where their personal positions were

---

3. One election was held in mid-term due to the resignation of the former state senator. The second election was held at the beginning of the next senatorial term.

threatened and in which there was to be found a conveniently located black population.

It has been suggested that on the higher levels of New York City government, distinctions between the two parties do not operate: "It is important to understand that above a certain level of power, at the level of permanent power, there is no party politics. There are no Democrats and no Republicans" (Newfield and DuBrul, 1978, p. 112). Apparently the same is sometimes true in local politics, especially under conditions of stress when entrenched power is threatened. Thus in Greenpoint-Williamsburg, when an alteration of district boundaries threatened the district leader's control of the state Senate seat, cooperation between the Democratic and Republican parties was combined with racially tinged propaganda to ensure incumbent politicians success in the elections.

A School Board Election

Since 1969 New York City has been divided into 132 local school boards under the central supervision of the New York City Board of Education. The first elections were held in May 1970, and members took office on July 1, 1970. Elections were held every two years until 1974, when the period between them was increased to three years. Each school board was composed of nine members elected by voters within its district. Candidates had to collect petitions containing two hundred valid signatures from neighborhood residents in order to have their names listed on the ballot. Voters numbered their choices from one to nine, and candidates' final scores were computed through a complicated process which took these numbered preferences into account. Greenpoint-Williamsburg was represented by New York City School Board District 14, and the elections described below took place in May 1977.

The Greenpoint-Williamsburg school board was important for two reasons. It distributed a large budget for the district, and it provided a platform for further political endeavors. Budget control allowed board members, although they themselves were unpaid, to make decisions about hiring and firing teachers, principals, and paraprofessionals in the area's schools. Where employment was at a premium, such decisions gave school board members considerable power and influence.

At least two members of the 1976 Greenpoint-Williamsburg school board competed for political office in the Brooklyn Democratic party during their tenure. Both were members of the same faction, which was challenging the supremacy of the incumbent district leader. The school board, with its municipal resources and connections, served as a base from which to attack the leadership from within the party.

One of the board members, who worked as an assistant in the office of the resigning senator, unsuccessfully challenged Thomas Bartosiewicz for the King's County designation for state senator. A second board member, Peter Dellaiacono, with the wife of a third member as his co-runner, challenged the district leader himself. Although he lost the election, it is important to understand that connections with other politicians and large amounts of anti-poverty money in a neighboring district, as well as connections with the head of the Brooklyn school board, provided Mr. Dellaiacono with a base from which to challenge a faction of established political influence.

Because of their authorization to make budget decisions, individuals on the school board were of interest to unions whose members worked in the district schools. Both District Council 37 of the American Federation of State, County and Municipal Employees and the United Federation of Teachers provided support and campaign funds for favored candidates.

District Council 37 offered a small amount of money and advice to candidates who requested its sponsorship. The UFT, on the other hand, played a major and apparently decisive role in the election of school board candidates. Its representatives approached candidates for the 1977 board elections and offered to fund elaborate propaganda as long as the candidate agreed with UFT views and ran on a slate picked and funded by the UFT.

The United Federation of Teachers, with Albert Shanker as president, was a powerful force in New York State politics and offered a base for challenging the district leader. (It did not, however, represent a challenge to the methods and control of the Brooklyn Democratic party as a whole.) Peter Dellaiacono was constantly seen in consultation was the UFT district representative, Robert Germino.[4] Mr. Germino hired a work force to man the polls during the elections and assigned more than fifteen people to supervise the vote-counting. As a result the UFT team was able to count the total number of votes cast before the municipal employees doing the official count were able to calculate their own total.

The slate funded by the UFT and supported by most incumbent board members used racist propaganda more blatantly than had the Bartosiewicz senatorial campaign. As in the Senate campaign, the distribution of leaflets and electioneering were concentrated on white voters in a few enclaves of the district. Although two members of the slate were Puerto Rican and had Hispanic last names, their names were incorporated into the racially biased propaganda circulated by the UFT slate.

An excerpt from one of the most widely circulated campaign statements of the UFT slate exemplifies the literature used. For several weeks both Greenpoint newspapers ran a full-page advertisement entitled: "Yes, we also have roots!!" The advertisement appeared while the famous television drama "Roots," about the black heritage of African slaves in America, was showing. This program was watched by both black and white residents of Greenpoint-Williamsburg and excited a considerable amount of discussion.

> Yes, some of us have roots in Poland from where our ancestors worked the land and finally came across the ocean so that we could have a better life than they—And some of us have roots in Ireland . . . and the fighting spirit we inherited enabled us to climb up from poverty to a bit better kind of life—yet we never forgot home and friends . . . and the church. . . .
>
> Some of us have roots in sunny Italy . . . and our fathers knew music and art and philosophy . . . and our mothers knew about family and respect . . . and they taught us well—and we love them for it.

4. The organizer of the successful slate for the school board elections, Robert Germino, was appointed president of a local Democratic club in 1978, when the previous president, the district leader, left New York City.

Some of us have roots in Germany and our ancestors knew science and mathematics and they had music . . . and when the barbarian Hitler swept through Europe, we turned our guns on him because we are Americans and we love this country.

Now there is a school board election on May 3rd this year. In a peculiar way this election is not only about books and education.

In a sense it's about our roots.

You see, the major goal of any educational system is to continue the social mores and values of its people. That is what it's all about. We want to make sure that the values of our parents, and their parents before them, are the values taught in the schools. Values like respect for adults, family, marriage, religion, patriotism . . . respect for property and working for a living . . . and taking care of the children, the family.

The advertisement then proceeds to attack an opposition which is labeled "the radicals" and concludes:

The radical group goes to school board meetings causing disruption and threatening, violence. They make ethnic slurs. They discriminate against us. And, if they had their way there would be no Italian, Irish, Germans, Jewish or Polish teachers and principals. There would be no Pledge of Allegiance. There would be just jobs . . . for them.

Well, we too, have roots. On May 3rd we will show them as we have shown them for 3 elections . . . just what our roots are.

There is little or no substance to the suggestion that opposition to the school board was part of a move against white ethnics. In April 1976 a school board meeting was disrupted by members of the so-called "radical" opposition. A play was staged on the platform where the board members sat; the seven people who took part in the disruption included three married women who claimed Irish background, one of whom was married to a man with a Polish name, and a married black woman. Two of the other women, both married, were white "American" and claimed no particular ethnic background. The seventh member of the theater group was Anthony Sanchez from Norman Street, whose mixed

Puerto Rican and American background was described in chapter 7. Ethnicity was thus used to attack people who actually came from similar ethnic backgrounds; they also came from similar family backgrounds, although the advertisement claimed that the opposition had no "respect . . . for marriage" and other domestic values.

I asked the Puerto Rican candidate whose name was listed on the advertisement how he felt about the neglect of his roots and the appeal of the campaign to the white ethnic residents of the area. He replied that the campaign was not in his hands. He had not seen the advertisement before it was printed, and he did not make campaign propaganda decisions. He simply allowed his name to be used in return for funding and support. Six years ago he had been a "radical" opposition candidate, supported only by the minority groups in Williamsburg. Now, as a member of the UFT slate, he no longer represented low-income interests.

The campaign for the school board was also directed against poor people. Another line in the same advertisement read: "The radicals label us racist because we're against the welfare dole." It thus brought up an issue which had little relevance to education but made clear the slate's position toward the poor.

In directing the campaign against poor people, blacks, and Puerto Ricans, board members were attacking the parents of a large proportion of the children who attended schools in the district. It was therefore not surprising that two opposition slates developed. One was made up of two blacks and two Puerto Ricans; another—a women's slate—comprised four women of different ethnic backgrounds: a black woman, an Irish-American woman, an Irish-American woman married to a man with a Polish last name (which made her appear Polish to the constituency), and Sandra Poulaski (famous from the firehouse dispute). These opposition slates cooperated to a certain extent against the UFT slate. Information was exchanged, and a few leaflets included both sets of names. Neither opposition slate raised racial issues in its campaign literature. Because of the ethnic distribution of the population, the women's slate focused on the Greenpoint area of the district, and the minority slate stayed mainly in Williamsburg.

Although both opposition slates were made up of working-class people from the area and claimed to represent parents and poor households, only one candidate, a black man, managed to win a seat on the board. The opposition candidates had support from the municipal workers in District Council 37, but none of them had sponsorship or financial aid from the UFT. Their campaign literature was directed to "parents" and against school board corruption. Only the UFT slate could afford to print advertisements in the local papers and to plaster the neighborhood with printed photographs of each candidate. The UFT also had access to major PTA meetings and church meetings, to neither of which were opposition candidates invited. Through their political connections and association with civic groups, the UFT candidates were able to build a public image without extensive effort. They were, as we have seen, also able to pay a large number of people to organize the campaign, distribute leaflets, and oversee the elections.

The UFT candidates did not have to rely on their campaign alone to defeat the opposition slates. When petitions to appear on the ballot were presented, the UFT challenged the validity of the signatures on the petitions for the women's slate. Petitions for all four candidates were thrown out two weeks before the elections. The candidates for the women's slate had to spend precious campaigning days fighting the issue in the courts. A week later two of their names were reinstated; the recount had proved that the signatures on their petitions were valid. The two remaining candidates, however, had to run as "write-ins," and thus had even less chance of winning.

The superior funding and publicity of the UFT slate, combined with citywide political connections and the support of local associations, assured victory although the UFT campaign dealt with no educational issues and attacked the minorities and poor people whose children filled the public schools. Here, as in the issue of planned shrinkage, the ability of officials to maintain positions in the face of policies directed against many of their constituents was evident. The next case will show that such apparent contradictions form at least a part of the stuff of which New York City politics are made.

Senior Citizens' Housing

Most old people in Greenpoint-Williamsburg live on income from Social Security. This is a fixed amount from which rent must be paid and groceries bought. Many people on this budget find it difficult to afford enough food to eat or decent places to live. A higher proportion of the inhabitants are aged in the longer-established white neighborhood than in the surrounding ghetto. However, when a federal loan became available to construct subsidized housing for senior citizens between an Italian and a Hispanic and black section of Williamsburg, members of a Greenpoint Democratic club mobilized against it.

One local newspaper, a Republican-run enterprise, came out vehemently against the new development. At a meeting at the local Democratic headquarters, the district leader and the editor of the paper announced that the problem would be the 176 apartments in Greenpoint-Williamsburg that would suddenly become vacant as senior citizens moved into the subsidized housing.

When an Italian woman from the community came up to the podium after the meeting, a heated argument ensued. The editor finally retorted: "You know who would take over those apartments—all those welfare mothers with hundreds of children." Although some people said the issue concerned the hiring of contractors, these remarks illustrate the tenor of the campaign and the effort to stir hostility against the new housing.

The Democratic party leader refused to endorse the plan for the senior citizens' apartments. The man who led the opposition to the center was a member of the Democratic club who also claimed to be the head of the local block association, although he lived in a different borough. Once again, key representatives of local political clubs attempted to work against community goals in order to maintain a homogeneous constituency.

Despite the opposition of the Democratic club and the Republican newspaper, members of the white population mobilized in support of the new housing. Encouraged by community organizers, working-class whites joined with black and Hispanic residents and with active senior citizens in a campaign to save the subsidized housing.

Meetings and public hearings were organized within a hostile atmosphere on the verge of violence. Residents who attended one public meeting reported they were afraid their speakers might be attacked by an audience packed with local merchants and others opposed to the homes. Such fears may have been unfounded, but they are evidence of the level of conflict generated *within* the white constituency over this issue.

This conflict shows the intensity of the struggle between the long-established and entrenched groups that have controlled the area for many years and the working-class residents of Greenpoint-Williamsburg. Because of the nondiscriminatory requirements of federal subsidies, the housing would have been rented to black and Hispanic people as well as to white senior citizens. In addition, such people might have acquired the unsubsidized apartments which would have become vacant. These possibilities were seen as an opening for more members of minority groups and poor people to come into the area. Any influx of poor people, especially blacks and Hispanics, posed a threat to the small group of politicians who controlled the electoral districts around Greenpoint-Williamsburg. Their efforts to maintain control of the area deprived constituents of opportunities for better housing and rent subsidies. The proposed housing for senior citizens was never built.

The American Legion and "the Red Invasion"

The American Legion was founded by Lt. Col. Theodore Roosevelt, President Theodore Roosevelt's son, on February 15, 1919, as an organization for veterans returning from World War I (Gellerman, 1938, p. 3). Its goals, as outlined by George S. Wheat in 1919, were to prevent the spread of communism and radical thought:

> There is a wolf at the gates of civilized Europe. If he gets inside nothing can stop him from ravishing us. . . . The wolf that I mentioned is a Mad Thought. He is Bolshevism. . . . Russia has run in a circle. From the autocracy of the classes it has arrived at the autocracy of the masses.

Why the American Legion?

Our men of the army, navy, and marine corps got a schooling in the Practical Americanism which our military establishment naturally teaches. . . . These men can and will stem the insidious guile of the wolf. . . .

Why the American Legion?

America is safe from any real danger if she can keep everybody busy. . . . The American Legion . . . program is the most important in the United States today. It means the betterment of the most stable forces in our community life, not only of today but for the next forty or fifty years. (Pp. 180–85)

The American Legion originated among officers afraid of the discontent and new ideas circulating among American soldiers returning home from Europe. One of these founding officers wrote in July 1929:

You will recall the state of things in the A.E.F. after the Armistice. Nerves the world over were on edge. Bolshevism was the bogey. Disgruntled soldiers had provided the manpower for the cataclysm in Russia, and the surface of the earth was pretty well covered with soldiers who had little to do but think of their troubles. It seems foolish to speak seriously of these things now, but in 1919 they were very real. (Gellerman, 1938, p. 4)

Thus from its inception the American Legion was intended to put down dissenters and to maintain the established political order.

Violence was also a common historical theme of the American Legion. In 1919 members led an attack on a chapter of the International Workers of the World (IWW) in Centralia, Washington, in which an IWW member was lynched (Hofstadter and Wallace, 1970, p. 354). In 1921 Legion members instigated a race riot in Tulsa, Oklahoma, in which at least eighty-eight people, including sixty blacks, were killed (ibid., p. 249). In 1949 an attack on a Communist party fund-raising concert (at which Paul Robeson and other international figures were present) in Peekskill, New York, was led by members of the American Legion (ibid., p.

365). In 1976 the American Legion was still a national organization with an expanding membership. The *American Legion Magazine* stated in January 1976:

> As of December 7, Legion national membership totaled 1,751,340 —147,537 ahead of the same date one year previous—with 47 departments registering gains. There were 138 new Legion posts chartered in 1975 up to presstime, the most new posts chartered in a year since 1957. (P. 35)

Occurrences in Greenpoint-Williamsburg in 1976 indicated that local posts were following the goals dictated by the Legion founders in 1919 and pursued since that time. The following statements were written after three members of Vietnam Veterans Against the War (VVAW) set up a table on the main commercial avenue of Greenpoint in June 1976:

> Don't look for your enemy beyond the blue horizon! He is here! Amongst you! recruited by Moscow. . . . They are waiting, very patiently, for the backbone of the country to disintegrate. They hate the American Legion because the Legion can see right through their scheming ways. As long as the American Legion is in existance [*sic*], it will be your eyes and ears to forewarn you of any dangers, to your freedom.

> An anticommunist coalition of Veterans, Fraternal, Social, Religious and Political groups is sponsoring a petition drive in Greenpoint and Williamsburg to introduce legislation to reactivate the House Un-American Activities Committee, the Senate Internal Security Subcommittee and bring back the Attorney General's subversive list. . . . Copies of this petition may be obtained by contacting this newspaper. (*Greenpoint Gazette*, June 22, 1976, p. 11)

The VVAW was organizing a demonstration in Philadelphia to coincide with President Ford's speech commemorating the Bicentennial. The demonstration was an attempt to highlight issues of unemployment and other problems of working-class Americans.

Eleven men from the local American Legion post approached the three VVAW men and, after some verbal interchange, a fight occurred. The VVAW organizers left the area, and the Legion members spray painted over the posters that they left behind. This event was reported in the local papers as a heroic action of the American Legion in pushing back "the Red invasion."

The social gatherings of the American Legion, along with politically similar associations in the area, functioned as meeting places for Democrats and Republicans. The editor of the local paper quoted was the daughter of an American Legion member and was herself a delegate to the Republican presidential convention in 1976. Her husband was nominated commander of the American Legion post in the same year. At a testimonial dinner, the couple was seated with the Democratic district leader and his co-leader alongside the New York State assemblyman from Greenpoint. The Democratic congressman from the district was also a member of the same post. The son of a previous commander was the president of the political club that supported this congressman and was employed as his aide.

Members of the American Legion were to be found on several other boards in the district. For example, school board members of Peter Dellaiacono's slate were in the American Legion, which, not surprisingly, endorsed that slate in the elections. Two influential Legion members were on the board of the YMCA.

Although not an overtly political organization, the American Legion functioned to quell dissent in the neighborhood. One of the local newspaper editorials read: "If anyone in the Greenpoint area sees these people [VVAW members] with signs or petitions, please contact an American Legion member immediately" (*Greenpoint Gazette,* June 22, 1976, p. 19). There seems little doubt that in Greenpoint-Williamsburg the American Legion saw itself, and acted, as a guard against political dissent and demonstrations.

Through organizations such as the Legion, with its influence over newspaper coverage of local events and freedom to act where elected politicians would be hesitant, local officials influenced opinion and knowledge in the area. These organizations, among them a newly formed group which included Legion members and activists from political clubs, helped to repress dissident opinions and prevent the election of critical citizens to boards and other representative offices. Attacks against dissident political organizers, whether they were local residents or not, were virulent and pervasive. The control of boards and community associations by members of political clubs and the American Legion was widespread. These avenues of local influence helped elected officials maintain their positions despite the espousal of numerous policies which were not beneficial to many of the residents.

The fate of residents of the Greenpoint-Williamsburg area has always depended on forces more influential than the local-level political boss. Such wider influences became critically visible in the New York fiscal crisis, when banks and other financial interests openly made important policy decisions for the city. While local political representatives frequently took credit for the existence of jobs and the provision of services, in fact they did little to create, maintain, or safeguard the well-being of Greenpoint-Williamsburg residents in any real sense. On the contrary, the local-level official who was obstructing federal aid in order to maintain a tighter control over his constituency was victimizing the low-income residents of the white neighborhood at the same time he enlisted them in his drive for racial exclusion.

Local politicians maintained their hold over resources through their control of the local papers, exploitation of racial divisions, high levels of financial support, wide political connections, and leadership in local associations. The poorer working-class residents of the area, including some homeowners, recognized that their interests were not being served by most officials. When white and minority groups cooperated in protest actions, political repression, both formal and informal, was directed against them.

Although local politicians sometimes supported progressive policies, they did not have the power to represent the area's interests to the city administration and the state legislature; rather, they introduced policies dictated or at least fostered by New York real estate and banking interests.

CHAPTER 12

Conclusion

Poor working-class people in Greenpoint-Williamsburg were engaged in constant conflict with the New York City administration and the state and federal agencies which affected their environment and subsistence. When protest surfaced, it was a manifestation of anger and frustration built up in relation to poor employment conditions, government agencies that caused delay and humiliation, absentee landlords, and inadequate city services. The forms protest took and the demands for city services reflected the dependent position to which the workers of Greenpoint-Williamsburg had been reduced. The racial divisions within poor people's movements were clearly related to trends in real estate precipitated by the same regional developments which had led to high levels of unemployment and a rising need for public assistance among black, white, and Hispanic workers.

The fiscal crisis in New York City in 1975 accelerated a process that had begun many years earlier: the departure of manufacturing, the creation of a superfluous labor force, and the expansion of the city as a center for management and services. Since 1975 New York City has been changing so rapidly that it is hard for many residents to absorb what they see around them. At the time of this writing, 1981, vast areas of city blocks have been razed. Row upon row of apartment buildings stand burned and empty, their residents forced to move elsewhere. Many poor communities have simply disappeared. In contrast, high-income apartment buildings, expensive stores, boutiques, restaurants, and huge office complexes are springing up in ever-widening enclaves of Manhattan, the Jersey shoreline, and the Brooklyn side of the East River. The development is concentrated in outlying areas with easy access to and a spectacular view of Manhattan. Greenpoint has become a prime target.

In the face of these trends, the working class of Greenpoint-Williamsburg is caught in a predicament in which rising rents are compounded by unemployment and lack of opportunity. Historically, people moved to Greenpoint-Williamsburg to work in a burgeoning industrial area. Workers lived in the tenements built for them and labored for bare subsistence wages. Since the nineteenth century, industrial needs have changed: methods of transportation and communication have improved, and automation has become a reality. These developments have allowed industries the flexibility to establish themselves in other parts of the country. They are no longer as dependent as they once were on New York City as a port, a market, or a corporate center. The strengthening of unions and the demands for higher wages in New York City have led factories to relocate in regions where workers are poorly organized and wages lower. This industrial shift destroyed the bargaining power of the workers left behind, for a company can respond to a union's demand for higher wages by leaving the area. The workers of Greenpoint-Williamsburg, threatened with unemployment and aware of an expanding pool of surplus labor, are in a vulnerable position.

As industry has departed, new forms of employment have not been generated for working-class people, who lack the training required to be professionals or high-level managers. Instead, masses of people have been labeled "unemployable" or "hard-core unemployed." Their unemployment and poverty have been regarded as independent phenomena, unrelated to industrial developments and regional shifts. In fact, these people have been abandoned in the decaying, poverty-stricken sections of the city. Industrial change has deprived them of their livelihoods, and they have lost the political influence they wielded as members of an indispensable work force. They are in the process of losing their homes.

As banks and major insurance companies fund the proliferation of middle-income housing and expensive office blocks, New York City is being transformed into a purely corporate center. The workers of Greenpoint-Williamsburg and other poor areas are being squeezed out of the city. In 1975 plans were being laid for waterfront housing to be built in Greenpoint. Middle-income professionals were sold brownstone houses at low prices as an inducement to bring them into the neighborhood. In 1979 one of these new residents of Greenpoint was quoted in *New York* magazine: "The new waterfront co-ops, Mrs. Lesbirel says, won't include any low-income housing, for Greenpointers would prefer 'people with more of a commitment to the neighborhood' " (Bordewich, 1979).

The people she refers to as lacking commitment are the people we have been discussing. They are the people who have struggled in a hopeless battle to survive the machinations of "urban development" and "redevelopment." They are the people who have fought to keep their neighborhood, to hold it together, despite their abandonment both by industry and the city administration. They are now disparaged by the incoming middle-class residents who have inherited their homes.

We have seen how these developments came about. It became clear during the 1975 fiscal crisis that the elected officials of New York City were implementing policies which the major banks and financial interests in the city found acceptable. The city's elected officials are faced with the difficult task of retaining votes while enacting policies against the interests of their constituencies. These officials are aware of the development plans for the city and know that their constituencies are not stable. The existence of a higher tax base gives elected officials greater room to maneuver and poses a strong incentive to politicians, elected by a poor population, to work to attract wealthier residents. Urban development funds have been redirected for commercial use, thus facilitating the process. As land values rise through commercial development and an increase in loans for middle-class home-buying and home improvement, so do potential rents. Landlords soon recognize the advantages of raising rents and evicting poorer tenants. An alternative strategy is to leave buildings to deteriorate or burn, and replace them with expensive apartments. In order to develop an area for middle-class residents and commercial use, working-class people must be displaced.

To ensure their reelection while cooperating with policies against the interests of their electorate, Greenpoint-Williamsburg politicians exploit the insecurity, fear, and racial competition endemic in the community. These attitudes are the result of on-going processes exaggerated by political and economic decisions of government officials, landlords, and banks. The insecurity and fear are a consequence of the departure of industry and the mesh of welfare regulations on which working class people are dependent. Racial divisions resulting from differential work opportunities are compounded by rigid discrimination on the part of resident landlords, neglect by absentee landlords and the city administration, and redlining by banks. These conditions have created a black ghetto on the borders of a white working-class neighborhood. Among a population of predominantly poor whites situated on the boundary of a ghetto, racism becomes an easily manipulated issue in political campaigns. In a situation of scarcity, racial competition constitutes a ready explanation for the problems of a powerless group. The fear and insecurity of the white working class has become the major target for the propaganda of the established political officials. These same officials are negotiating a redevelopment of the city which entails a catastrophic reduction of services for the poor, both black and white. In the long run, their constituents may be forced to leave their homes in search of rents they can afford.

Threatened with unemployment, caught in a net of stringent welfare regulations, harassed and humiliated by landlords and welfare officials, and betrayed by politicians, working-class residents of Greenpoint-Williamsburg have responded with continuing struggle. On the basis of links forged around domestic cooperation and child care, they have built small block associations, trying to prevent the decay and burning of their homes. Although the local police and the mayor's office have offered to affiliate with such associations, the people of Norman Street refused their control. Instead, they used the block association as a platform for collective protest. Their efforts were seldom successful but serve as a record of the struggles of working-class residents of Greenpoint-

Williamsburg against the destructive policies of the city administration.

The firehouse movement, also built on neighborhood cooperation, testifies to the persistence of this population in the face of continued frustration. After three years of organizing, the residents finally won their demands. But success was a result of cooperation between Greenpoint-Williamsburg residents, the firemen's union, and a coalition of New York State political officials opposed to the mayor's policies. Struggle is clearly evident among Greenpoint-Williamsburg's abandoned workers, but power is not. They fought in the face of frustration, but they did not have the political power of a work force necessary to the city's economy.

The political resistance of Greenpoint-Williamsburg workers, handicapped by their lack of jobs and the power to strike, was further weakened by racial hostility. Organizers tried to cooperate across racial lines, but blacks and whites seldom participated together in collective protest. Each group organized separately around the same issues. There were two separate firehouse occupations; one in a Hispanic and black neighborhood and one in a Slavic neighborhood. Only in the school board elections can one find the beginnings of cooperation across racial boundaries.

When white organizers, with little political experience, asked black groups for assistance, they received it. However, fear of violence and mutual suspicion prevented mobility between neighborhoods and effectively undercut cooperation. Although not all poor whites were hostile toward blacks, the possibility of violent repercussions was strong enough to affect many people's behavior. The distrust was clearly founded in fear that the presence of black and Hispanic people would reduce Greenpoint-Williamsburg to the condition of neighboring slums. Overlooking the significance of absentee landlords, redlining, and city policies of neglect in determining the destruction of neighborhoods, many local residents equated deterioration of living conditions with race.

Frantz Fanon has pointed out that violence among oppressed people is, first of all, directed at themselves (1963). The self-hatred and anger which oppression breeds is turned on those closest to the powerless. In this case the violence of Greenpoint-Williamsburg workers was directed both inward among themselves and toward the racial and minority groups of the same class. Homicide rates were twice as high in Greenpoint-Williamsburg as they were in the wealthier white neighborhoods of Brooklyn, and homicide rates in Bedford-Stuyvesant, the poorest section, were twice as high as those in Greenpoint-Williamsburg. Predictably, all the murders in Bedford-Stuyvesant were of black people, while most of those in Greenpoint-Williamsburg were of whites. Thus although violence against black and Hispanic people had important political implications, it is best seen in the context of the extremes of violence which misery and poverty breed.

Racial divisions among the working class both debilitated collective action in Greenpoint-Williamsburg and allowed elected officials and commercial developers a free hand in their disposal of funds. So long as racial issues kept white voters loyal, elected officials could ignore the needs of a poor white working-class constituency. If problems were blamed on the presence of black people, the solution was to develop white housing. The price of keeping Greenpoint-Williamsburg white was that the new housing would be middle income, and present working-class residents would no longer be able to afford to live there. New low-income housing, such as the senior citizen housing, would have filled a desperate need among black, white, and Hispanic people. The project was defeated by a campaign spearheaded by local Democratic officials. Their opposition was specifically aimed at keeping poor people out of Greenpoint and was probably related to development plans for a middle-income housing complex.

By supporting Greenpoint's established politicians, working-class residents deprived themselves of federal aid and other forms of benefits which might have resulted in an interracial community. As Cloward and Piven have documented for other parts of New York City, elected officials were afraid that funds channeled through federally funded poverty agencies would facilitate the building of independent power bases (Cloward and Piven, 1975). This was a further reason for their opposition to federal assistance for their working-class constituency. Because racism had obscured issues, the white working class of Greenpoint-Williamsburg was less skilled politically than their black and Hispanic neighbors. When poor white workers experienced the hardships of declining city services and unemployment, with which blacks had been familiar for a longer period, they had to learn the methods of collective action from black groups which were already mobilized.

Even when poor people capitalized on the similarities of their experiences and formed coalitions across racial and ethnic lines, established politicians could thwart them. For example, when the signed petitions of the women's slate for the school board were declared invalid two weeks before elections, candidates were obliged to put their efforts into a court case. This severely hampered their ability to campaign. Since two of the four candidates' names were never printed on the ballot, the campaign was seriously damaged. It was particularly damaging that the names which were not printed were the most well-known of the slate.

When political clout was not sufficient, poor people's movements were subject to more forceful forms of reaction. Through control of the local communications networks, and, occasionally, the application of naked force, members of the American Legion, activists in the local party clubs, and small businessmen attempted to discredit and destroy collective protest in the community. Such groups generated a sense of oppression and fear.

When protest actions in Greenpoint-Williamsburg partially succeeded, participants had confronted and surmounted major deterrents. Such actions represented political and class conflict expressed in neighborhood issues. David Harvey has argued that conflicts over the "built environment" must be seen as "mediated manifestations of the deep underlying conflict between capital and labor" (1976, p. 294). Among workers abandoned by the industry on which their political influence depended, local protest movements, centered on neighborhood preservation and the demand for resources from the state, represent a desperate last fight against heavy odds. The workers of Greenpoint-Williamsburg are holding on to the fast-disappearing resources that remain to them. They expend excessive efforts for meager results. Under such conditions protest actions and poor people's movements demonstrate political consciousness and activism among America's working class.

Class consciousness and political activism must be understood within a particular historical period and under specified conditions.

The changing economic and political requirements of capitalism may result in improved life chances among one group of workers and unemployment and poverty among those remaining behind. The temporary affluence of workers in the mainstream of industrial development at any one time has to be viewed in the context of the misery of those workers no longer needed. Strikes and effective demands for higher wages bring into play shifts of capital which leave workers without jobs around which to organize their strikes. Such changes are all part of the overall struggle between capital and labor. If only one aspect be analyzed—whether it be political apathy or class struggle—neither fluctuations in industrial development nor the political consciousness of American workers can be understood.

Bibliography

Alcaly, R., and Bodian, H. New York's fiscal crisis and the economy. In *The fiscal crisis of American cities: Essays on the political economy of urban America with special reference to New York,* ed. R. Alcaly and D. Mermelstein, pp. 30–59. New York: Random House, 1977.

Alcaly, R., and Mermelstein, D., eds. *The fiscal crisis of American cities: Essays on the political economy of urban America with special reference to New York.* New York: Random House, 1977.

American Legion Magazine, 100:35.

Anderson, C. *The political economy of social class.* Englewood Cliffs, N.J.: Prentice-Hall, 1974.

Arensberg, C., and Kimball, S. *Culture and community.* New York: Harcourt, Brace & World, 1965.

Aronwitz, S. *False promises: The shaping of the American working class.* New York: McGraw-Hill, 1974.

Ash, R. *Social movements in America.* Chicago: Markham, 1972.

Ashton, P. The political economy of suburban development. In *Marxism and the metropolis,* ed. W. Tabb and L. Sawers. New York: Oxford University Press, 1978, pp. 64–89.

Beetham, D. *Transport and turbans.* London: Oxford University Press, 1970.

Bell, D. Labor in the post-industrial society. In *The world of the blue collar worker,* ed. I. Howe, pp. 159–98. New York: Quadrangle, 1972.

Bellush, J., and David, S., eds. *Race and politics in New York City: Five studies in policy-making.* New York: Praeger, 1971.

Belmonte, T. *The broken fountain*. New York: Columbia University Press, 1979.

Benson, H. Apathy and other axioms. In *The world of the blue collar worker*, ed. I. Howe, pp. 209–27. New York: Quadrangle, 1972.

Berger, B. *Working-class suburb*. Berkeley: University of California Press, 1980.

Bianco, B. *The petty supporters of a stratified order: The economic entrepreneurs of Matriz, São Paolo, Brazil, 1877–1974*. Ph.D. diss., Columbia University, 1981.

Binzen, P. *Whitetown, U.S.A.* New York: Random House, 1970.

Blauner, R. *Alienation and freedom*. Chicago: University of Chicago Press, 1966.

———. Internal colonialism and ghetto revolt. In *Racial conflict: Tension and change in American society*, ed. G. Marx, pp. 52–61. Boston: Little, Brown, 1979.

Bonacich, E. A theory of ethnic antagonism: The split labor market. *American Sociological Review* 37 (1972): 547–59.

Bookchin, M. Economics as a form of social control. *Liberation* 19 (1975): 6–8.

Bordewich, F. The future of New York: A tale of two cities. *New York*, July 23, 1979, pp. 32–40.

Bott, E. *Family and social networks*. London: Tavistock, 1957.

Brecher, J. *Strike*. San Francisco: Straight Arrow, 1974.

Brecher, J., and Costello, T. Wage labor in the U.S. today. *Radical America* 10 (1976): 2–7.

Brody, D. *Steelworkers in America: The non-union era*. New York: Russell, 1970.

Brokensha, D. Maximum feasible participation. *U.S.A., Community Development Journal* 9 (1974): 17–27.

Burawoy, M. *Manufacturing consent*. Chicago: University of Chicago Press, 1979.

Caplovitz, D. *The poor pay more: Consumer practices of low-income families*. New York: Free Press, 1963.

Caro, R. *The power broker*. New York: Knopf, 1974.

Castells, M. The wild city. *Kapitalstate*, 4–5 (1976): 2–31.

———. *The urban question*. London: Arnold, 1977.

Chinoy, E. *Automobile workers and the American dream*. Boston: Beacon, 1965.

Cloward, R., and Piven, F. *The politics of turmoil: Poverty, race and the urban crisis*. New York: Vintage, 1975.

Cohn, N. *The pursuit of the millennium.* New York: Oxford University Press, 1970.

Cordasco, F., and Bucchioni, E. *The Italians: Social backgrounds of an American group.* Clifton, N.J.: Kelley, 1974.

Costikyan, E., and Lehman, M. *Restructuring the government of New York City: Report of the Scott Commission Task Force on jurisdiction and structure.* New York: Praeger, 1972.

Crotty, J., and Boddy, R. Class conflict and macro-policy: The political business cycle. *Review of Radical Political Economics* 7 (1975): 1–19.

Culp, D. *The American Legion: A study in pressure politics.* Ph.D. diss., University of Chicago, 1939.

Dahl, R. *Who governs?* New Haven: Yale University Press, 1961.

———. Equality and power in American society. In *Urban politics and public policy: The city in crisis,* ed. S. Davis and P. Peterson, pp. 55–65. New York: Praeger, 1973.

Dahya, B. Pakistan ethnicity in industrial cities in Britain. In *Urban ethnicity,* ed. A. Cohen, pp. 77–118. London: Tavistock, 1974.

Darnton, J. Banks rescued the city in 1933. In *The fiscal crisis of American cities: Essays on the political economy of urban America with special reference to New York,* ed. R. Alcaly and D. Mermelstein, pp. 225–27. New York: Random House, 1977.

Davies, J. Toward a theory of revolution. *American Sociological Review* 27 (1962): 5–19.

Davis, M. Why the U.S. working class is different. *New Left Review* 123 (1980): 3–46.

———. The barren marriage of American labour and the Democratic party. *New Left Review* 124 (1980): 43–84.

Dorman, M. *The making of a slum.* New York: Delacorte, 1972.

Drake, S., and Cayton, H. *Black metropolis.* New York: Harcourt, Brace, 1945.

Duffield, M. *King legion.* New Jersey: Cape & Smith, 1931.

Edwards, R. *Contested terrain.* New York: Basic Books, 1979.

Eidheim, H. The Lappish movement: An innovative political process. In *Local level politics,* ed. M. Swartz, pp. 205–16. Chicago: Aldine, 1968.

Epstein, A. *Politics in an urban African community.* Manchester: Manchester University Press, 1958.

Epstein, J. The last days of New York. In *The fiscal crisis of American cities: Essays on the political economy of urban America with special reference to New York,* ed. R. Alcaly and D. Mermelstein, pp. 59–78. New York: Random House, 1977.

Fainstein, N., and Fainstein, S. *Urban political movements.* Englewood Cliffs, N.J.: Prentice-Hall, 1974.

Fanon, F. *The wretched of the earth.* New York: Grove, 1963.

Fitch, I., and Walsh, A., eds. *Agenda for a city: Issues confronting New York.* Beverly Hills: Sage, 1970.

Fox, K. Cities and city governments. In *U.S. Capitalism in Crisis,* ed. Crisis Reader Editorial Collective, pp. 174–82. New York: Economics Education Project of Union for Radical Political Economics, 1978.

Frazier, E. *The Negro family in the United States.* Chicago: University of Chicago Press, 1939.

————. Theoretical structure of sociology and sociological research. In *E. Franklin Frazier on race relations,* ed. G. Franklin Edwards, pp. 3–42. Chicago: University of Chicago Press, 1968.

Friedland, R. Class power and social control: The war on poverty. *Politics and Society* 6 (1976): 458–64.

Furer, H. *New York: A documentary history, 1524–1970.* Dobbs Ferry, N.Y.: Oceana, 1974.

Gans, H. *The urban villagers.* New York: Free Press, 1962.

Garden Spot News, Brooklyn, N.Y. Various issues from 1975 to 1978.

Gelb, J., and Sardell, A. Strategies for the powerless: The welfare rights movement in New York City. *American Behavioral Scientist* 17 (1974): 507–30.

Gellerman, W. *The American Legion as educator.* New York: Columbia University Press, 1938.

Georgakas, D., and Surkin, M. *Detroit: I do mind dying.* New York: St. Martin's, 1975.

Giddens, A. *The class structure of advanced societies.* London: Hutchinson, 1973.

Ginzberg, E. *New York City is very much alive: A manpower view.* New York: McGraw-Hill, 1973.

Gitlin, T., and Hollander, N. *Uptown: Poor whites in Chicago.* New York: Harper and Row, 1970.

Glick, N. *The formation of a Haitian ethnic group.* Ph.D. diss., Columbia University, 1972.

Gluckman, M. Analysis of a social situation in modern Zululand. *Bantu Studies* 14 (1940): 1–30, 147–74.

Goldthorpe, J.; Lockwood, D.; Bechhofer, F.; and Platt, J. *The affluent worker in the class structure.* Cambridge: Cambridge University Press, 1969.

Gordon, D. *Theories of poverty and underemployment.* Lexington, Mass.: Lexington, 1972.

————. Capitalist development and the history of American cities. In *Marxism and the metropolis,* ed. W. Tabb and L. Sawers, pp. 25–63. New York: New York University Press, 1978.

Gordon, D. R. *City limits: Barriers to change in urban government.* New York: Charterhouse, 1973.

Gouldner, A. *Patterns of industrial bureaucracy.* New York: Free Press, 1964.

Greenberg, S. *Politics and poverty.* New York: Wiley Interscience, 1974.

Greenpoint Gazette, Brooklyn, N.Y. Various issues from 1975 to 1978.

Greer, S. *Big steel: Black politics and corporate power in Gary, Indiana.* New York: Monthly Review Press, 1979.

Griffin, J. *Industrial location in the New York area.* New York: City College Press, 1956.

Gurr, T. *Why men rebel.* Princeton: Princeton University Press, 1970.

Gusfield, J., ed. *Protest, reform and revolt: A reader in social movements.* New York: Wiley, 1970.

Gutman, H. *Work, culture and society in industrializing America.* New York: Vintage, 1976.

Hallman, H. *Emergency employment.* University, Alabama: University of Alabama Press, 1977.

Hamill, D. A Brooklyn neighborhood battles City Hall. *Village Voice.* December 6, 1976, pp. 30–31.

Hannerz, U. *Soulside: Inquiries into ghetto culture and community.* New York: Columbia University Press, 1969.

————. Ethnicity and opportunity in urban America. In *Urban ethnicity,* ed. A. Cohen, pp. 37–76. London: Tavistock, 1974.

————. *Exploring the city.* New York: Columbia University Press, 1980.

Harrison, B. Public employment and the theory of the dual economy. In *The political economy of public service employment,* ed. H. Sheppard et al., pp. 41–75. Lexington, Mass.: Lexington, 1972.

Harvey, D. *Social justice and the city.* Baltimore: Johns Hopkins Press, 1973.

————. Labor, capital and class struggle around the built environment in advanced capitalist societies. *Politics and Society* 6 (1976): 265–94.

Hershkowitz, L. *Tweed's New York: Another look.* New York: Anchor, 1978.

Higham, M. *"Big Brother" joins the Fire Department: An essay on the effects of computer-dictated fire department policy on life and property in the city of New York.* Unpublished paper, New York, 1976.

Hill, R. Fiscal crisis and political struggle in the decaying central city. *Kapitalstate* 4–5 (1976): 31–50.

Hobsbawm, E. *Primitive rebels.* New York: Norton, 1955.

————. *Laboring men.* Garden City: Anchor, 1964.

Hobsbawm, E., and Rudé, G. *Captain Swing: A social history of the great English agricultural uprising of 1830.* London: Lawrence and Wishart, 1964.

Hofstadter, R., and Wallace, M., eds., *American violence.* New York: Vintage, 1970.

Hollingshead, A. *Elmstown's youth and Elmstown revisited.* 1945. Reprint. New York: Wiley, 1975.

Howe, I., ed. *The world of the blue collar worker.* New York: Quadrangle, 1972.

Howe, L., ed. *The white majority: Between poverty and affluence.* New York: Vintage, 1970.

Howell, J. *Hard living on Clay Street: Portraits of blue collar families.* New York: Anchor, 1973.

Hugh, H. *Modern social politics in Britain and Sweden: From relief to income maintenance.* New Haven: Yale University Press, 1974.

Humphries, J. Women: Scapegoats and safety valves in the Great Depression. *Review of Radical Political Economics* 8 (1976): 98–122.

Hunter, F. *Community power structure.* Chapel Hill: University of North Carolina Press, 1953.

James, D., ed. *Analyzing poverty policy.* Lexington, Mass.: Lexington, 1975.

Javits, E. *SOS New York; a city in distress and what can be done about it.* New York: Dial, 1961.

Katznelson, I. Community, capitalist development, and the emergence of class. In *Politics and society* 9 (1979), 203–37.

Jewell, J. *Historic Williamsburg: An account of the settlement and development of Williamsburg and its environs, from Dutch colonial days to the present.* Brooklyn: Privately printed for the Williamsburg Savings Bank, 1926.

Katrowitz, N. *Ethnic and racial segregation in the New York metropolis: Residential patterns among white ethnic groups, blacks and Puerto Ricans.* New York: Praeger, 1973.

Kimball, P. *The disconnected.* New York: Columbia University Press, 1972.

Komarovsky, M. *Blue-collar marriage.* New York: Random House, 1964.

Kornblum, W. *Blue-collar community.* Chicago: University of Chicago Press, 1974.

Kotler, M. *Neighborhood government: The local foundations of political life.* New York: Bobbs-Merrill, 1969.

Kranzler, G. *Williamsburg, a Jewish community in transition: A study of factors and patterns of change in the organization and structure of a community in transition.* New York: Feldheim, 1961.

Lamphere, L. Strategies, cooperation and conflict among women in domestic groups. In *Woman, culture and society,* ed. M. Rosaldo and L. Lamphere, pp. 97–128. Stanford: Stanford University Press, 1974.

Laslett, J., and Lipset, S., eds. *Failure of a dream? Essays in the history of American socialism.* New York: Anchor, 1974.

Lawrence, W., and Leeds, S. *An inventory of federal income and transfer programs, fiscal year, 1977.* White Plains, N.Y.: Institute for Socioeconomic Studies, 1978.

Leacock, E., ed. *The culture of poverty: A critique.* New York: Simon & Schuster, 1971.

Leggett, J. *Class, race and labor: Working-class consciousness in Detroit.* New York: Oxford University Press, 1968.

Lewinson, E. *Black politics in New York City.* New York: Twayne, 1974.

Liebow, E. *Tally's corner.* Boston: Little, Brown, 1967.

Lipsky, M. *Protest in city politics.* Chicago: Rand McNally, 1970.

Lipsky, M., and Olson, D. The processing of racial crisis in America. *Politics and Society* 6 (1976): 79.

Lynd, R., and Lynd, H. *Middletown.* New York: Harcourt, Brace, 1929.

McCourt, K. *Working Class Women and Grass Roots Politics.* Bloomington: Indiana University Press, 1977.

Manoni, M. *Bedford-Stuyvesant: The anatomy of a central city community.* New York: Quadrangle, 1973.

Marcuse, H. *One-dimensional man: Studies in the ideology of advanced industrial society.* Boston: Beacon, 1968.

Markusen, A. Class and urban social expenditures: A local theory of the state. *Kapitalstate* 4–5 (1976): 50–66.

Marx, K. *The German ideology.* New York: International, 1970.

Mayer, A. The significance of quasi-groups in the study of complex societies. In *The social anthropology of complex societies,* ed. M. Banton, pp. 97–122. New York: Praeger, 1966.

Melman, S. The federal rip-off of New York's money. In *The fiscal crisis of cities: Essays on the political economy of urban America with special reference to New York,* ed. R. Alcaly and D. Mermelstein, pp. 181–89. New York: Random House, 1977.

Merchant's Association of New York, Industrial Bureau. *The Newton Creek industrial district of New York City.* New York, 1921.

Milkman, R. Women's work and economic crisis: Some lessons of the Great Depression. *Review of Radical Political Economics* 8:73–98.

Mollenkopf, J. The post-war politics of urban development. *Politics and Society* 5 (1975): 247–95.

Moscow, W. *The last of the big-time bosses: The life and times of Carmine de Sapio and the rise and fall of Tammany Hall.* New York: Stein & Day, 1971.

Mullings, L. Ethnicity and stratification in the urban United States. In *Annals of the New York Academy of Sciences* 318 (December 29, 1978): 10–22.

Mumford, L. *The culture of cities.* New York: Harcourt, Brace, Jovanovich, 1970.

Newfield, J., and DuBrul, P. *The abuse of power: The permanent government and the fall of New York.* New York: Viking, 1978.

New York City Bureau of Health Statistics and Analysis. *Summary of vital statistics, 1961, the city of New York.* New York: Department of Health, 1961.

––––––. *The Puerto Rican population of New York City, 1950–1960.* New York: Department of Health, 1962.

––––––. *Summary of vital statistics, 1971, the city of New York.* New York: Department of Health, 1971.

––––––. *Health district report: 1970.* New York: Department of Health, 1972.

––––––. *Vital statistics by health areas and health center districts.* New York: Department of Health, 1973.

––––––. *Vital statistics by health areas and health center districts.* New York: Department of Health, 1974.

New York City Department of Labor Market Information. Personal communication, 1978.

New York City Department of Research and Program Planning Information. *Characteristics of the population of New York City health areas: 1970.* New York: Community Council of Greater New York, 1974.

New York City Fire Department Monthly Report. January 1976.

New York City Mayor's Task Force on Fire Protection. Fact-finding presentation. September 30, 1976.

New York Planning Commission. *Plan for New York City: A proposal,* part 3. Brooklyn, N.Y. 1969.

————. *Greenpoint: Striking a balance between industry and housing.* New York, 1974.

New York Daily News. Eight fire companies to get axed: O'Hagan sees peril to life. November 21, 1975, p. 29.

————. Leone seeks activation of Engine 212. August 1976.

————. Restart Engine 212, residents demand. December 6, 1976, p. B-1.

————. Reopen our firehouse or "lid will blow off." January 14, 1977, p. KL-7.

————. Fire sirens proclaim a victory of the people. March 20, 1977, p. 3.

New York Post. An arsonist hunted in fatal fire. January 27, 1976, p. 11.

————. Out of the ashes grows a revitalized community. November 1, 1976, p. 84.

————. Two arson teams tracking the killer of Brooklyn tot. March 17, 1978, p. 14.

New York State Department of Social Services. *Medicaid.* New York, 1977.

————. *Income maintenance: Sourcebook for regulations.* New York: Division of Income Maintenance, in conjunction with the Office of Manpower Management and Development, n.d.

New York State Senate Finance Subcommittee to Investigate Fire and Police Protection in the city of New York. *Na false alarm: Police and fire protection are in trouble.* Albany: New York State Finance Subcommittee, May 1976.

New York Times. Stay of eviction at Northside is denied. September 12, 1973, p. 51.

————. Tenants evicted in Brooklyn as demolition begins. September 13, 1973, pp. 1, 93.

————. Northside zoning to allow housing: Homes for families evicted for factory gains in estimate board. September 14, 1973, p. 43.

————. Beame cuts ribbon at Brooklyn S&S plant as bitterness fades. January 17, 1975, p. 37.

————. City shuts down four firehouses. November 23, 1975, p. 57.

O'Connor, J. *The fiscal crisis of the state.* New York: St. Martin's, 1973.

Oppenheimer, V. *The female labor force in the United States.* Berkeley: University of California Press, 1970.

Orgel, C. *Structuring social conflict: The politics of space in a Long Island town.* Ph.D. diss., Columbia University, 1981.

Parker, R. *The myth of the middle class.* New York: Liveright, 1972.

Pelling, H. *American Labor.* Chicago: University of Chicago Press, 1960.

Perlman, S. *A theory of the labor movement.* New York: MacMillan, 1928.

Pilcher, W. *The Portland longshoreman.* New York: Holt, Rinehart & Winston, 1972.

Piven, F. Who gets what: Cutting up the pie. *New Republic,* February 5, 1972, pp. 17–22.

Piven, F., and Cloward, R. *Regulating the poor.* New York: Pantheon, 1971.

————. *Poor people's movements: Why they succeed, how they fail.* New York: Pantheon, 1977.

————. The urban crisis as an arena for class mobilization. *Radical America* 11 (1977): 9–19.

Poll, S. *The Hasidic community of Williamsburg: A study in the sociology of religion.* New York: Schocken, 1969.

Pratt, E. *Industrial causes of congestion of population in New York City.* 1911. Reprint New York: AMS, 1968.

Rainwater, L.; Coleman, R.; and Handel, G. *Workingman's wife.* New York: Oceana, 1959.

Rex, S., and Moore R. *Race, community and conflict.* London: Oxford University Press, 1968.

Rogers, D. *The management of big cities: Interest groups and social change strategies.* Beverly Hills: Sage, 1971.

Rosenberg, I. *Residence, employment and mobility of Puerto Ricans in New York City.* Department of Geography Research Paper No. 151. Chicago: University of Chicago, 1974.

Rosenzweig, R. Organizing the unemployed: The early years of the Great Depression, 1929–33. *Radical America* 10 (1976): 27–37.

Rowbotham, S. *Woman, resistance and revolution.* New York: Vintage, 1975.

Rubin, C. *Worlds of pain: Life in the working-class family.* New York: Basic Books, 1976.

Rudé, G. *The Crowd in History; a study of popular disturbances in France and England 1730–1848.* New York: Wiley, 1964.

Rydell, L., and Rydell, C. Poverty: Waning or waxing. *Social Praxis* 1 (1973): 389–97.

Sale, K. Six pillars of the southern rim. In *The fiscal crisis of cities: Essays on the political economy of urban America with special reference to New York,* ed. R. Alcaly and D. Mermelstein, pp. 165–81. New York: Random House, 1977.

Schaffer, R. *Income flows in poverty areas: A comparison of community income accounts of Bedford-Stuyvesant and Borough Park.* Lexington, Mass.: Lexington, 1973.

Schlozman, K. Coping with the American dream: Maintaining self-respect in an achieving society. *Politics and Society,* 6 (1976): 241–63.

Schneider, D., and Smith, R. *Class difference and sex roles in American kinship and family structure.* Englewood Cliffs, N.J.: Prentice-Hall, 1973.

Schorr, A., and Lekachman, R. *Public policy and income distribution.* New York Center for Studies of Income Maintenance Policy, New York University, 1974.

Scott, J. *Glassworkers of Carmaux.* Cambridge: Harvard University Press, 1974.

Sennett, R., and Cobb, J. *The hidden injuries of class.* New York: Vintage, 1973.

Sexton, P., and Sexton, B. *Blue collars and hard hats.* New York: Vintage, 1971.

Sheehan, B. *The Boston school integration dispute: Social change and legal maneuver.* Ph.D. diss., Columbia University, 1981.

Sheehan, S. *A welfare mother.* New York: Mentor, 1975.

Shostak, A. *Blue-collar life.* New York: Random House, 1969.

Skolnick, J. *The politics of protest: A neighborhood study.* Brooklyn: Brooklyn Council for Social Planning, 1940.

Southside United Housing Development Fund Corporation. *Housing recommendations: The Los Sures moderate rehabilitation report.*

New York: Southside United Housing Development Fund Corporation, 1975.

Spear, A. *Black Chicago: The making of a Negro ghetto: 1890–1920.* Chicago: University of Chicago Press, 1967.

Stack, C. *All our kin: Strategies for survival in a black community.* New York: Harper and Row, 1974.

Starr, R. Making New York smaller. *New York Times Magazine,* November 14, 1976, p. 32.

Steffens, L. *The shame of the cities.* 1904. Reprint New York: Sagamore, 1957.

Sternlieb, G., and Hughes, J. Metropolitan decline and inter-regional job shifts. In *The fiscal crisis of cities: Essays on the political economy of urban America with special reference to New York,* ed. R. Alcaly and D. Mermelstein, pp. 145–65. New York: Random House, 1977.

Stone, M. Housing and class struggle. *Antipode* 7 (1975): 2.

Susser, I. Review of *Blue collar community. American Journal of Sociology* 83 (1977): 235–38.

—————. *Poverty and politics in a New York City neighborhood.* Ph.D. diss., Columbia University, 1980.

Suttles, G. *The social order of the slum: Ethnicity and territory in the inner city.* Chicago: University of Chicago Press, 1968.

Tabb, W. The New York City fiscal crisis. In *Marxism and the Metropolis,* ed. W. Tabb and L. Sawers, pp. 241–46. New York: Oxford University Press, 1978.

Thernstrom, S. *Poverty and progress.* New York: Atheneum, 1964.

Thompson, E. P. *The making of the English working class.* New York: Vintage, 1966.

Tilly, C.; Tilly, L.; and Tilly, R. *The rebellious century.* Cambridge: Harvard University Press, 1975.

Turner, V. *Schism and continuity in an African society.* Manchester: Manchester University Press, 1957.

U.S. Bureau of the Census. *Census of population 1960: General social and economic characteristics.* Washington, D.C.: U.S. Government Printing Office, 1962.

—————. *Census of population 1970: General social and economic characteristics.* Washington, D.C.: U.S. Government Printing Office, 1972.

—————. *Census of manufactures 1972.* Vol. III, Area statistics, part 2. Washington, D.C.: U.S. Government Printing Office, 1976.

————. Unpublished preliminary returns for 1980.

U.S. Congressional Budget Office. New York City's fiscal problem. In *The fiscal crisis of American cities: Essays on the political economy of urban America with special reference to New York,* ed. R. Alcaly and D. Mermelstein, pp. 285–96. New York: Random House, 1977.

U.S. Department of Commerce. *Congressional district data book.* Washington, D.C.: Social and Economic Statistics Administration, U.S. Bureau of the Census, 1973.

Valentine, B. *Hustling and other hard work.* New York: Free Press, 1978.

Vance, J. Housing the worker: The employment linkage as a force in urban structure. *Economic Geography* 42:294–325.

Van Til, J. Becoming participants: Dynamics of access among the welfare poor. *Social Science Quarterly* 54 (1973): 345–58.

Van Velsen, J. The extended-case method and situational analysis. In *The craft of social anthropology,* ed. A. Epstein, pp. 129–49. London: Social Science Paperbacks, 1969.

Vincent, J. The structuring of ethnicity. *Human Organization* 33 (1974).

————. The political economy of ethnicity. Paper delivered at Annual Conference of American Anthropology Association, Cincinnati, Ohio, December 1979.

Wallace, D., and Benway, A. *Fire company elimination and permanent relocation in New York City: Its technical basis and impact on citizens.* A New York Scientists and Engineers for Social and Political Action preprint. Unpublished paper, New York, 1975.

Warner, W. *Yankee city.* New Haven: Yale University Press, 1963.

Welischar, E. *Si, No Hay Bombaros (Yes, we have no firemen).* Unpublished paper, New York, 1975.

Wertheimer, B., and Nelson, A. *Trade union women: A study of their participation in New York City locals.* New York: Praeger, 1975.

Wheat, G. *The story of the American Legion: The birth of the legion.* New York: Putnam, 1919.

Whelton, C. The landlords who happen to have fires. *Village Voice.* November 7, 1977, pp. 1, 15.

Whyte, W. *Street corner society.* 1943. Reprint Chicago: University of Chicago Press, 1966.

Willmott, P., and Young, M. *The symmetrical family.* New York: Pantheon, 1974.

Wilson, J., ed. *City politics and public policy.* New York: Wiley, 1968.

Wilson, W. *The declining significance of race.* Chicago: University of Chicago Press, 1980.

Wolf, E. *Peasant wars of the 20th century.* New York: Harper and Row, 1969.

Wong, B. Elites and ethnic boundary maintenance: A study of the roles of elites in Chinatown, New York City. *Urban Anthropology* 6 (1977): 1.

Worsley, P. *The trumpet shall sound.* New York: Schocken, 1968.

Index

Index of
Pseudonyms